Strategic Marketing

Cases and Concepts from the Indian Business

C Bhaktavatsala Rao

LeaderCrest Academy

Logo

ISBN 979-8-89026-978-2

Contents

List of Figures

Other Books by the Author

From Start-up to Ramp up: Indian Context and Global Insights

Technology and Competitive Strategy: Strategies for Innovators, Differentiators and Followers

Competitive Strategy: A Contemporary Retake

Leadership for India Inc.: An Experiential Treatise

India as Global Start-up Hub: Mission with Passion

India's Economic Resurgence: A Modified Paradigm for a Welfare State

Work-Life Balance: Essays in Individual and Organisational Behaviour

Product Strategy and Corporate Success: Cases and Concepts from the Indian Automobile Industry

Strategic Management: Practice and Philosophy for India Inc.

STEM: Strategy. Technology. Entrepreneurship. Management

Legendary Leaders: Insights and Lessons

Dharmic Management: Lessons from the Indian Social Ecosystem

Foreword

Strategic marketing is the extended domain of marketing that deploys a mix of marketing and strategic approaches for the firm to achieve sustainable competitive advantage. Marketing aims at creating conditions for effective sales, distribution, and brand development within the ambit of the business strategy of a firm. Strategic marketing goes a step further and seeks to identify positions of sustainable future growth for the company.

Strategic marketing provides the landscape for the company's leadership to look at the environment and market opportunities from a strategic perspective. While marketing and sales are closely allied in planning and execution for the development of brands and sales, strategic marketing and business strategy are closely allied in terms of developing a vision and strategy for the future. Strategic marketing is the bridge between the business strategy for the future and the sales and marketing strategy for the current.

This book titled "Strategic Marketing: Cases and Concepts from the Indian Business" is a practical exposition of the domain of strategic marketing with practical case studies from the Indian business over the last few decades. The book provides a fusion of academic frameworks and practical constructs, and sketches out multiple principles of strategic management that can be deployed in different industries.

The book comprising, thirty chapters, is divided into four sections. Section 1 on Automobile has eight chapters pertaining to the Indian automobile industry that bring out the interrelationships of business strategy, product strategy, and strategic marketing. Section 2 on FMCG and Retail has six chapters that are focused on the vast landscape of these segments that is enabled by the Indian demographic profile. These chapters bring out the indigenous nature of strategic marketing opportunities and challenges in these domains. Section 3 has nine chapters dedicated to marketing as the core discipline, discussing cases and constructs related to demand management and brand development, among others. Section 4 on Strategy has seven chapters discussing various aspects of competition and business strategy, from the perspective of strategic marketing.

With its comprehensive and in-depth coverage, this book should be of interest to students, academicians, and professionals interested in strategy, marketing, and business growth.

C Bhaktavatsala Rao

Chennai

August 15, 2023

Section 1
Automobile

Chapter 1

Tata's Nano: A Missed Opportunity

The development by Tata Motors of the Nano car, packed with creative features and priced amazingly at Rs one-lakh, was a true 'Innovate and Make in India' phenomenon. By conceptualizing and commercializing the Nano car, Mr Ratan Tata unveiled a new industrial paradigm for India. The manufacture of the car had to be shifted to a new site postponing, due to extraneous reasons, an effective mass launch by over a year. In this context, the significance of the Nano and strategies to avoid this kind of impediments need discussion. For records, Tata Nano as a concept was announced in 2005 and commercially launched in 2009. The company halted its production in 2018 due to tepid sales.

Strategic Significance

The significance of Tata Nano lies in the fact that it is not merely a cheap car or low-cost car. If it were just that, it would not have received the global attention the way it did. To view the Nano in perspective, there have indeed been several low-cost products in India in the past. For example, cellular phones have been designed for, and introduced, at say 10 per cent of the price of a high-end mobile phone while televisions have been marketed at 50 percent of the price of a brand-leader's television.

However, these were essentially low-cost developments with stripped-down features or with procurement economics and were also dependent on overseas technologies.

On the other hand, Tata Nano represented a breakthrough indigenous technology, which harnessed innovative efforts and intensive investments to not merely breach a price floor but more importantly offer a whole new user paradigm. That Indian talent could design and manufacture superior products with high technology and low prices to create vast new markets is the quintessence of what Tata Nano meant for the Indian industry, economy and society.

Technologically, Tata Nano represented the utilization of thought-leading concepts for a mini car design such as a four-seater, four-door form factor, a rear-mounted 623 cc all-aluminium engine, full 4-speed transmission, rear wheel drive, tubeless tyres, high-roof monocoque body and high visibility glass, all of which were integrated for contemporary safety and emission standards. By conceptualizing and commercializing this novel car, Tata Motors offered an alternative and safer transportation medium to the millions of small families in India. These could be young couples with dependent elders or evolving families with young kids. The usage need not be confined only to city landscape either. Nano car was designed to trigger a total transportation revolution across India covering urban, semi-urban and rural areas. Figure 1.1 illustrates the diverse features of Tata Nano.

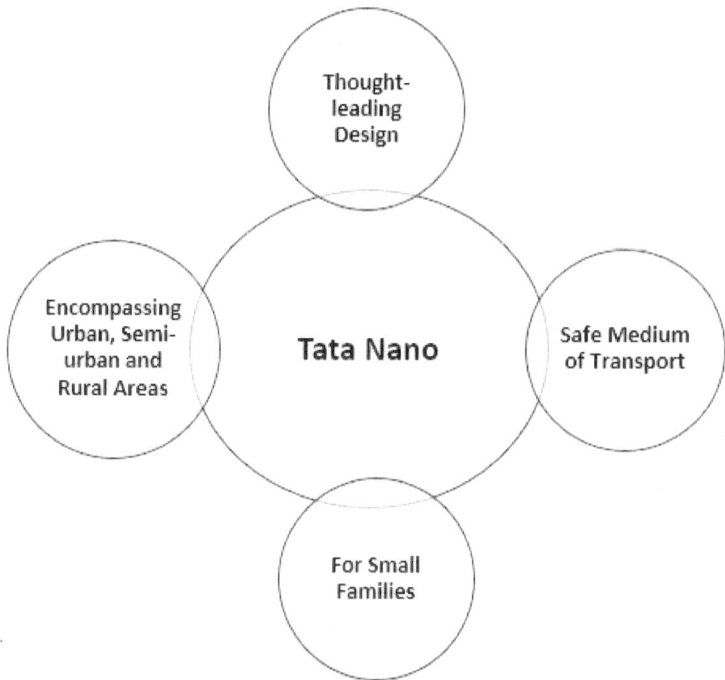

Figure 1.1: Diverse Features of Tata Nano

While Nano had its critics, in terms of the perceived impact on the roads of mass market car, the criticism is not well-placed. Environmentally conscious people could car-pool even on a Nano. Similarly, disciplined Nanos would make for a better and safer utilization of road space compared to swarms of speeding two-wheelers. Moreover, the same visionary leadership and the same innovative company DNA that brought out a Nano could continue to innovate in terms of incremental innovations such as more economic fuels, exotic materials and multi-terrain transmission as well as electrification.

The success of Tata Nano would have had an overwhelmingly positive industrial and economic implications for India, encouraging the Indian frugal engineering concepts to be leveraged across various industrial verticals and along multiple value chains.

Design Drives Development

The noted management expert, Dr CK Prahalad brought out in his book, The Fortune at the Bottom of the Pyramid, as to how an innovative design, whether of a product or a service, can discover new fortune at the bottom of an economic or social pyramid.

Tata Nano had the profile to not merely substitute a two-wheeler but also cater to new users and create new markets. The demand would likely have been far greater than the annual 150,000 Nanos envisaged initially. Had Tata Motors and State Governments aligned their development strategies, Nano factories could have sprung across several States with a central facility serving as the mother plant for key systems and assemblies. The economic transformation it would have brought across material, component, and vehicle sectors on one hand, and the sales, service, and spare parts sectors on the other hand, on a pan-Indian basis, would have been stupendous. Fortune was sure to be discovered at the bottom of the Indian social and economic pyramid.

Tata's Nano also illustrated how a breakthrough concept needs a shared vision, inspired collaboration and cost-focused development across industries, spread across years. In view of such intrinsic features, projects such as Nano would have multiplier effects beyond the end-product industry and its markets. A successful Nano, for example, would have helped all industrial sectors connected with the project to achieve product miniaturization coupled with value maximization, whether it was an engine component or a filter element.

It would also have led to new material compositions and novel metal processing technologies.

All these developments would have provided new export opportunities not only for Nano but all associated component and materials manufacturers. Regardless of the muted commercial outcome, the young engineering team of 500 plus at Tata Motors that developed Nano symbolized the capabilities and potential of the Indian scientific and technical base to achieve globally competitive product offerings. Nano type of initiatives could, therefore, accelerate India's drive towards becoming a global hub for design and manufacturing of mini and small cars to start with, eventually qualifying as a global development centre for all types of automobiles.

Nano has product and market implications beyond the automotive sector. The concept of developing designs that shift up the user paradigms to higher points of value chain while pushing downwards established price parameters has relevance across industries. Post-Nano, it seems feasible that well-conceptualized engineering can optimize any product to add several features at lower costs and create new markets. A reliance on product and process design as a strategy will uncover and eliminate industrial waste on one hand and develop new upgraded products at attractive price points. This will not only improve economic efficiency but also expand economic spectrum through broad-based consumer demand. India can then become a distinctively competitive global industrial base, taking a lead over China which is much vaunted majorly for its low-cost manufacturing options. The impetus for competitive and innovative design provided by Tata Nano should be leveraged to position India as a global design and manufacturing powerhouse. Figure 1.2 summarises the implications of Tata Nano design.

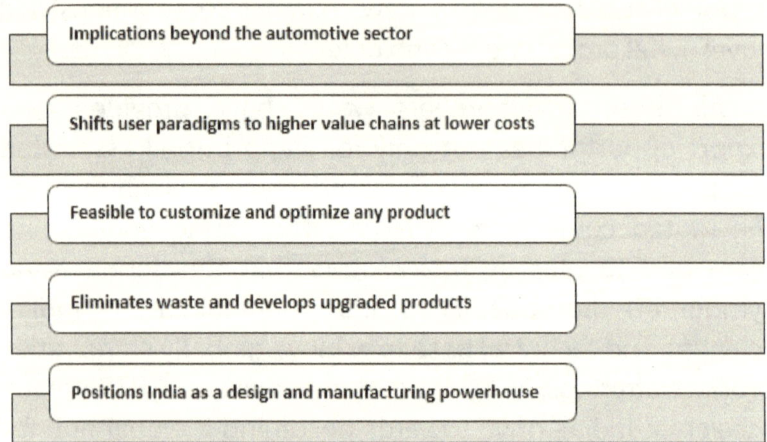

Figure 1.2: Implications of Tata Nano Design

Global Appetite for Innovation

Globally, there is an unprecedented appetite for innovation. New waves of innovation aim to bring tantalizing features at attractive price points to consumers, creating new markets and expanding existing markets. Apple's iconic iPod, iPhone and iPad symbolize the global aspiration for competitive innovation. Integrating several applications within a single device, with heightened performance and reduced price, Apple has redefined the global consumer electronics game. Tata's Nano has sought to do that in the Indian automotive sector.

India's Nano was iconic in its own right, albeit in a different field. Global leaders from General Motors to Nissan-Renault acknowledged the quantum jump that Nano represented for the Indian industry. Without getting dismayed by the eventual stoppage of Nano, the enterprising Indian designers and project engineers and leaders across various industries must innovate and develop their own 'Nanos' to bring India to the centre-stage of global innovation. No device, equipment or service needs to be beyond the challenge and opportunity of India's Nano-like transformation through innovation.

Chapter 2

Technological Innovation: The Need for Marketing Muscle

Ratan Tata set out, in 2005, on a mission to have Tata Motors design and manufacture the world's smallest four door micro car with a capacity to seat comfortably a family of five adults at a price of Rs. 100,000 (USD 2,000 approximately) which was less than half of the then prevailing price of India's ruling small car, Maruti Suzuki 800. It was a dramatic and pathbreaking vision. The disbelief gave way to applause when Nano was finally unveiled in the 2008 AutoExpo. When it could not be manufactured in the originally envisaged green-field plant at Singur there was disappointment all round that one of the best indigenous industrial marvels of India was being stymied. Well-wishers followed Nano's manufacturing journey from Singur in West Bengal to Sanand in Gujarat and appreciated Ratan Tata's commitment and gumption to commercialize Nano despite the multitude of challenges.

Post its launch, however, Nano car did not exactly set the Indian car market afire. It received a rather muted response, and neither did the initial glitches help the car in its image. Given that the pricing was attractive and the car was cute and spacious, the inability of Nano to translate the consumer and corporate expectations into robust market demand and sales was intriguing. Nano's maximum monthly sales did not exceed 10,000 units while the sales languished below the 1,000 units per month for most months since its commercial launch in 2009. This compared with the market-leading sales of Maruti Suzuki's Alto sub-compact car at over 35,000 units per month. In fact, there would be no comparison of a new product that had, or probably would have, its performance-price equation so favourable for the consumer. It is, therefore, important to analyse Tata Nano from a management perspective. This chapter fills a vital gap in this respect, also throwing some useful pointers that could have made Nano a mega success, a feat that the car, Tata Motors and Ratan Tata richly deserved.

'Design to Demand' Variance

The primary reason for Nano's failure relative to its potential can be traced to the huge variance between the concept that triggered its design genesis and the platform on which it was eventually positioned in the marketplace. The genesis of Nano was in Tata's desire to offer an affordable and safe car for the typical Indian small family comprising husband, wife, and two children; the family otherwise travels riskily on a two-seater two-wheeler. Given that a high-end two-wheeler would cost Rs. 70,000 (at that time), Nano as a five-seater, four-door car at Rs. 100,000, with all its features, had an unbeatable value proposition. Given that India absorbed then each year 20,000,000 two-wheelers, the demand potential for Nano, even based on conversion of only 10 percent of two-wheeler buyers into Nano buyers, would have been huge. Nano would have easily become the largest selling car in the Indian car market had events gone right for the car, several of the events being in the management's own control.

This potential has not been realized mainly because the company fought shy of converting its design inspiration into a marketing value proposition. Either because of the

Tatas' corporate ethic of not directly attacking competitors or because of a casual hope that Nano would have its own natural demand pull, the company never had an aggressive marketing campaign that directly appealed to the Indian small family, especially the young family, on a platform of safety, security, and comfort, relative to two-wheeler and three-wheeler travel. The dilemma for the Tatas would have been whether such a campaign would imply that its co-industrialists market two-wheelers as unsafe family transportation vehicles or that the Indian traffic system turns a blind eye to the overloaded Indian two-wheelers on the road. Independent of such conundrums, the important lesson for corporations from the Nano experience is that the original design genesis and the ultimate marketing platform must have a clear nexus and alignment. The other lesson is that marketing must rise above the paradoxes to deliver a clear product proposition to the consumer, without fear or favour, and without prejudice or bias. Figure 2.1 illustrates the lessons for corporations from the Nano experience.

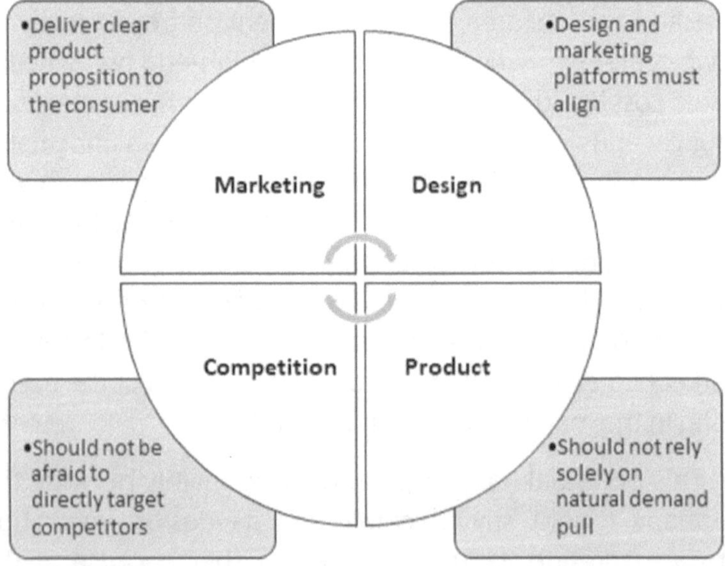

Figure 2.1: Lessons for Corporations from the Tata Nano Experience

Gross and Subtle, Mind and Heart

Whenever the design inspiration for a new product is extraordinary and out-of-the-box, even if it is seemingly explicit, the challenge for the marketer increases manifold. Successful companies focus time, effort and cost to market and institutionalize new concepts in the consumer mind. A classic example is that of Samsung launching a massive campaign for its large smart phone Galaxy Note as a phone cum tablet, 'phablet', with the unique proposition of a stylus to write and sketch. The company did not think that it was distorting its own smart phone and tablet markets that were growing exceedingly well under the Galaxy umbrella brand, nor did it think that it was cannibalizing its own smart phones or tablets. The Company has repeated this with its foldable phone range. The power of unique technological concepts needs to be demonstrated to the marketplace, also positioned in the minds of the consumers, and instilled in a gross manner. In respect of Nano, the technological innovation of the product should have been demonstrated with unceasing and high-force campaigns rather than sporadic and low-profile advertisements. Mindspace can be secured only through powerful, explicit, and rational delineation in respect of technological factors.

Gross campaigns need to be reinforced with subtle messaging too, particularly when the product really needs to change the segment proportion within the overall market, and wrest the overall market share in competition with a different group of products made by competition. Nano was indeed faced with the dilemma of challenging the two-wheeler segment with a superior value proposition of safety of a micro four-wheeler. Gross messaging would have not served the purpose, apart from possibly being a strict no-no for the Tatas corporate competitive behavioural philosophy. Emotional subtlety that appeals to the heart is the key to such messaging. Here again, we have the example of Cadbury positioning its milk chocolates as a 'sweet' for homely and auspicious occasions in competition with traditional Indian sweets. For the Indian small family, the concept of caring for the life partner and protecting the kids through the small car as opposed to leaving them to the vagaries of environment and turbulence of road traffic in a two-wheeler would have been highly effective, for example. Equally, in a society where owning a car is a symbol of having arrived to a noticeable stage in life, owning a Nano car at the very early start of the career, independent of the relative affluence, would have been an impressive value proposition. Subtlety, which is simple and direct, impacts heart positively, which in turns influences the mind share of the buyer.

Value Qualifiers

Marketing literature talks about value for the consumer being a function of price and features of a product. In respect of Nano, technology spoke for itself in terms of compact exterior and spacious interior on one hand as well as the power and fuel economy on the other. Any additional value drivers must appeal to both the mind and heart, if the above gross and subtle messaging is accepted. Electronic braking system and front and side air bags would reinforce the safety tag. Experimental evidence of crash test safety would reinforce the safety image even further. An ability to upgrade Nano to a Manza sedan as the family evolves in life, through Tata exchange and finance schemes, could be another value driver. It was important for the company to first develop a list of various additional features that could add value as a comprehensive list of value qualifiers, and then select value drivers which are appropriate to different groups of customers. For example, a 2 DIN music system would be a stronger value-add for a couple while a safety kit as outlined above will probably be a more welcome value-add for a couple with babies or kids.

The fundamental value creation, however, starts at the dealer point. The low price of Nano meant that the turnover on Nano sales and service would be the lowest for the typical dealership in the Tata family of vehicles. This problem was further compounded by the initial strategy of having a combined dealership covering all Tata vehicles, from cars and utility vehicles to trucks and buses. The implication for Tata Motors as also to all other automobile manufacturers in India, from such generic approach which did not work, was that dealership could no longer be considered just a point of sale. The infrastructure and organization for automobile dealership would need to extend vertically along the product value chain as a continuum of design, development, manufacture, distribution, sales and service. Ideally, Tata Motors needed to have completely different dealerships for cars and utility vehicles on one hand and commercial vehicles (light, medium and heavy trucks, and buses) on the other (now implemented). In each case, the product should receive the same level of care; for example, an affordable micro car should receive the same attention as a luxury crossover and a low-cost mini-truck the same attention as a high-end premium truck. Value qualification by dealership should have been an important component of Nano resurgence strategy. Figure 2.2 summarises how Tata Nano failed at the dealership point. The remedies that were required are obvious from this.

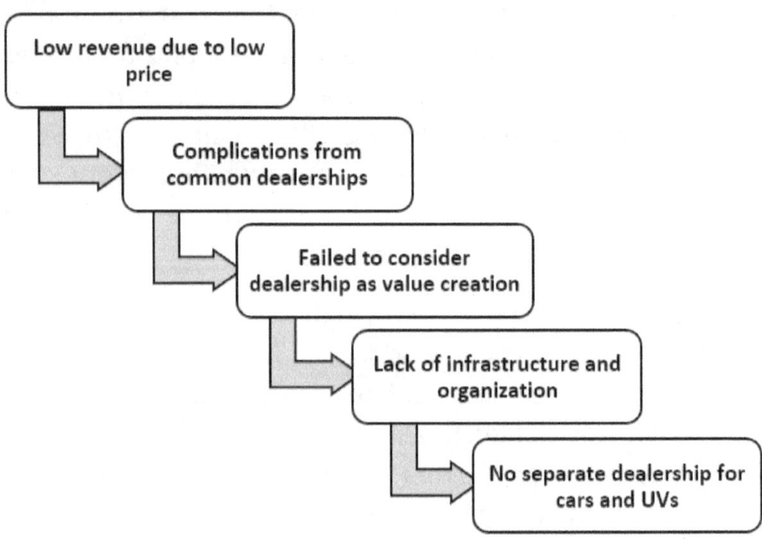

Figure 2.2: How Tata Nano Failed at the Dealership Point

From Breakeven to Breakthrough

Tata Motors which received acclaim for being the pioneer in indigenous development of passenger cars and utility vehicles had been losing ground in that segment from 2010, until the launch of Nexon in 2017. This was admitted by Ratan Tata himself in the annual shareholders meeting of Tata Motors. Tata Nano should have been a beneficiary of the highest attention for reinvention, given that Tata Nano car initiative quickly came to crossroads. Even with the monthly high of 10,000 Nano cars, the production level was below the breakeven point of 150,000 Nanos per annum. To utilize the capacity of 250,000 Nanos per annum and the potential capacity of 400,000 Nanos at the 75-acre site which also had an adjunct component park, Tata Motors required breakthrough strategies, which were not taken up.

Tata Nano, even today, is more than just one another passenger car model. It represents the passion and creativity of the Indian business and the innovation and skill of the Indian engineers to develop and manufacture a passenger car with a feature and cost profile that no other automobile company, global or Indian could ever conceive of and commercialize. More than the success of Nano as a car model of the Tatas, far more was, and continues to be, at stake for the Tata Group as well as the Indian industry. Tata Motors should persevere and make an enduring success of Tata Nano based on an effective strategic format. An integrated techno-marketing strategy, customized to the marketplace, was required to reposition Nano car for accelerated growth in India and also position it for successful entry into advanced countries. This playbook will be essential for all new innovative product offerings.

Chapter 3

Bajaj Quadricycle RE 60 and Tata Nano: Technology-Business Issues

Bajaj Auto Limited (Bajaj), India's largest two-wheeler manufacturer, secured limited Government approvals in 2013 for its quadricycle, code named RE 60. The four-wheeler RE 60 vehicle is powered by a water-cooled, 216-cc, single-cylinder engine which can develop 20 HP. This is about 40 percent more than the power generated by a 175 cc powered three-wheeler and about the same in power as a 200 cc powered three-wheeler, historically manufactured by Bajaj in India for domestic and export markets. RE 60 sports a metal-polymer monocoque body and weighs 400 kg, has a turning radius of 3.5 meter and can reach a top speed of 70 kmph. It can seat the driver and three passengers and run 35 kilometres on a litre of petrol. RE 60 should not be misunderstood as a mini-car like Tata Nano – it is just half as powered as Nano. Tata Nano is powered by an air-cooled two-cylinder engine which produces 37 HP. It has an all-metal body and weighs 635 Kg (all data and inferences as could be drawn during the initial phases of the two vehicles).

Bajaj positioned RE 60 quadricycle as an alternative to its three-wheeler. RE 60 has four wheels instead of three wheels that Bajaj's all-pervasive three-wheeler of India has. RE 60 was intended by Bajaj to eat into Bajaj's own market for three-wheelers, of which Bajaj is, undoubtedly, the world's largest manufacturer. The company sells approximately 225,000 three-wheelers per annum and records growth rate of around 11 to 12 percent on a compounded basis, according to the statistics of Society of Indian Automobile Manufacturers (SIAM). Analysts expected Bajaj's quadricycle to be priced anywhere between Rs 1.5 lakh (USD 2500) and Rs 2 lakh (USD 3300) while a Bajaj three-wheeler auto rickshaw's ex-showroom price in Delhi was Rs 1.35 lakh (USD 2250) – the exchange conversions being at USD 1 equals Rs 60. Having invested Rs 550 crore (USD 92 million) in developing the platform and creating the capacity to produce 5,000 of the vehicles every month, the price became nearly that of India's cheapest and proper mini-car, Nano at Rs 2 lakhs (USD 3300).

Industry Response

The Indian car and other two-wheeler manufacturers took up cudgels against RE 60 quadricycle on the grounds that it was unsafe compared to a passenger car. They wanted the Indian government to lay down norms as stringent as those applicable to cars. Bajaj, on the other hand, maintained that the RE 60 was not a car and would not compete in the car market. Bajaj had been seeking less stringent safety standards for the vehicle on the basis that the quadricycle with doors and seat belts, et al, was, in any case, a safer and more stable alternative to the three-wheeler. It has a seating capacity of four passengers, with owner-chauffeur possibility as opposed to three-wheeler carrying capacity of only three passengers (that too tightly packed) with sole chauffeur mode. RE 60 has also a better ground clearance compared to the three-wheeler. It is noteworthy that RE 60 has low carbon emissions, better than a three-wheeler or a

Nano. Figure 3.1 summarises the characteristics of Bajaj's RE 60 Quadricycle.

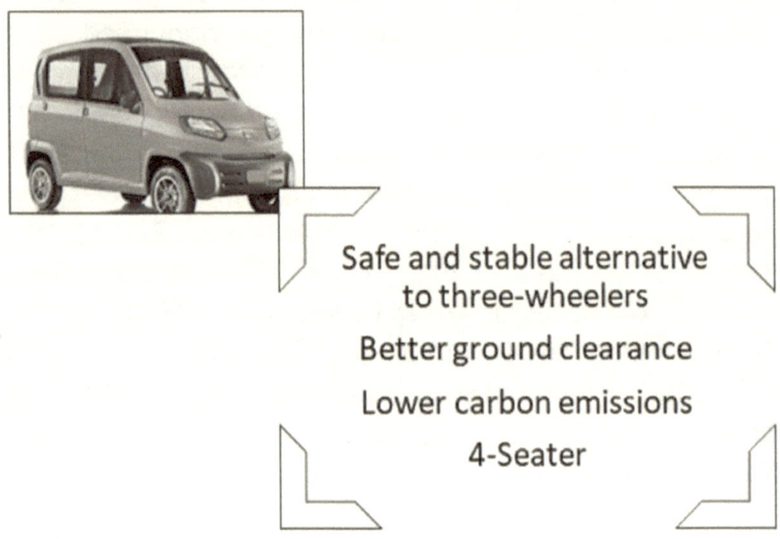

Figure 3.1: Characteristics of Bajaj's RE 60 Quadricycle

To be sure, the concept of a quadricycle was not new at the time of Bajaj RE introduction. Though the quadricycle existed as an approved legal product in the European Union, it was being sold only in small numbers; for example, only 23,800 quadricycles were sold in Europe in 2011. The three main traditional markets for quadricycles, France, Italy, and Spain, had seen their sales fall from a high of 29,000 in 2007 to just 18,000 in 2011. As a concept, the vehicles are still used either by the elderly or those not old enough to qualify for regular driving licenses. They are also used as golf carts and recreation vehicles. That said, such use which may be well suited to the European road conditions, regulated traffic intensity, and driving discipline may not be appropriate in India given that those factors are much worse in India. Just because quadricycle is a convenient mode for select applications in Europe, it need not be so in India.

France was the first country to define technical standards and traffic rules for quadricycles. The French ministerial decree of May 29, 1986 legally defined the quadricycle as a vehicle included in the moped category, equipped with four wheels and a body. In 1992, the European Union published Directive 92/61/EEC which considered that quadricycles fell into the same category as mopeds. Framework Directive 2002/24/EC then refined this definition by distinguishing between light and heavy quadricycles (L6e and L7e categories). The European Commission was set to revise this 2002/24EC directive in order to simplify legislation, to improve road safety and to set new standards for gaseous emissions. Furthermore, Directive 2006/126 (3rd Driving Licence Directive) establishes a common framework for light quadricycles driving licences. It imposes the same requirements for light quadricycles as for mopeds, including the driving age, for which it recommends 16 years as a minimum. The transposition deadline of the directive was 19 January 2011. The recent EU directive 2020/239 requires that quadricycles meet Euro 5 and Euro 5+ emission standards.

Unlearning Nano?

As we consider Bajaj Auto's initiative to indigenously design, develop, manufacture and commercialize its RE 60 quadricycle, several issues of strategic technical and business considerations arise. The first and foremost is whether the lessons of Nano had been learnt by Bajaj. As we know, Nano was a socially relevant innovative design initiative by Ratan Tata to replace the risky family travel on two-wheelers by a relatively safer, elegant, and affordable full-family travel through a small car. Unfortunately, the technical sensation and social initiative that Nano represented did not translate itself into enthusiastic acceptance by the target customer-families. One important reason, probably, has been that the typical two-wheeler user nurtured a dream, and even esteem value, in terms of catapulting to a full-fledged "middle class" car than graduating to a specially designed low-end transport solution that Nano represented.

Bajaj should have kept in mind that the auto-rickshaw owner/driver of India could similarly consider catapulting into a full-fledged taxi through a proper hatchback or sedan (or even a Nano) as his dream and of greater esteem value than just graduating into the quadricycle of a boxy design that could be as costly as a Nano but not as safe and powerful as a passenger car. This perception-risk was indeed real, given that the Indian market was flooded, even in the 2010s, by several attractive models of entry and mid-level small cars, hatchbacks, and sedans. The design concept of RE 60, which probably originated seven to eight years ago, became far less relevant in the rapidly maturing Indian automobile market and rapidly upgrading social stratification by the time RE got introduced in 2014. This example points to the need for business strategists to continuously validate, as times progress, what originally start out as innovative design concepts in terms of market relevance in rapidly changing environments.

Enduring Design Innovation

One way to insulate a company's efforts from environmental volatility is by developing designs that are enduringly innovative. In the context of contemporary designs that were prevalent and were on the anvil in the Indian automobile industry, RE 60 was spookily designed, to say the least. A three-wheeler loyalist could find the well-tested three-wheeler design more elegant compared to RE 60. One could compare RE 60 design effort with the new Nissan Datsun entry level car, also designed and developed in India, and conclude that the latter was miles ahead in terms of true car-like design elegance and integrity. Design innovation must be durable and sustainable, capable of successfully piloting through at least the full design-manufacturing-commercialization cycle of say 5 years, besides offering the basic platform for launching successive generational improvements.

The other approach of design innovation involves an integrated value proposition rather than a hotchpotch of incremental benefits in different performance components. Seat belts and doors, addition of a wheel, marginal improvements in torque and horse power, and increased ground clearance need not necessarily add up to becoming a radically new value proposition for the Indian automobile user, as a Maruti 800 car or a Toyota Innova multi-utility vehicle represented at their respective times of entry into the market. Bajaj must really reevaluate whether RE 60 offers such a value upgrade. Even as a low-cost and safe mini-public transport solution, other options such as Tata Ace and Magic passenger variants were, and continue to be, available for the three-wheeler operators and users alike.

Strategy-technology Nexus

There are several strategic pointers that could arise from the RE 60 strategies of Bajaj, when fully executed (based on the author's analysis of possible future outcomes as well). Fundamentally, technological innovation and business inventiveness must go hand in hand for strategic success. Secondly, it would be impossible to create new markets without a deft combination of product innovation and market positioning. Thirdly, incremental product enhancement may help in lifecycle management but certainly not enable new product entry and market growth. Fourthly, product innovations should be sufficiently innovative to form the market and create a product family base. Fifthly, strategic plans of business must integrate technology plans that enable sustainable and durable product innovation. Sixthly, new product introductions must aim at creating a total value proposition of distinctive functionality. Seventhly, any product introductions that are based on tenuous regulatory options could face the risks of policy vagaries and industry collectivism. Figure 3.2 summarises the strategic pointers that arise from the RE 60 strategy of Bajaj.

Figure 3.2: Strategic Pointers that Arise from RE 60 Strategy of Bajaj

Business strategists would do well to keep the above perspectives in mind as they develop business plans that are dependent on product enhancements and new product introductions. Product functionality and market segmentation would carry a nexus that would be difficult to perceive at the time of product conceptualization but could become patent as products and markets evolve. Repositioning of products could even be an option to consider as a retrospective strategy relevant for a new product-market equation. For example, Tata Nano mini-car could well turn out to be a better upgrade option vis-à-vis a three-wheeler, compared to RE 60 as a quadricycle. Had the marketing of Nano been done effectively, it would have emerged as an effective, flexible and safe family transport solution, leaving no room for a quadricycle to be thought of even as a concept. Commercial failure of Nano, however, does little to overcome the inherent design limitations of a quadricycle!

Chapter 4

Reviving Nano: An Electric Option

Ratan Tata, the legendary leader and the Chairman Emeritus of India's Tata Group said in an interview (The Times of India, November 29, 2013) that it was a mistake to have described and positioned the innovative Tata Nano small car as the world's cheapest car. He even went to the extent of stating that the Nano should be launched in a new country like Indonesia in a new Avatar and brought back to India with a new image. Ratan Tata also stated that the car was developed as a safe alternative for the Indian small family of husband and wife and their children who travel unsafely on a two-wheeler and implied that Nano car failed to take its place due to the stigma of a cheap car. He also felt that it could be launched as a changed product in Europe where it could evoke a lot of interest. For all those who believed in Tata Nano as a hallmark of Indian innovation, Ratan Tata's views on Nano must have come as a surprise.

By any yardstick, Nano was a technically brilliant package. It is a 4-door bubble design car, with a 2-cylinder rear mounted gasoline engine and a 4-speed gearbox, capable of comfortably seating 5 persons of a small family (couple and the kids). With a wheel base of 2.2 meters and an overall length of 3.1 meter and a width and height of 1.5 and 1.6 meters respectively, the car beat the Volkswagen Beetle small car in external compactness and internal spaciousness. With a power and torque output of 38 PS and 51 NM respectively, and a kerb weight of 600 Kg and a turning radius of only 4 meters, Nano was also an ideal city car. The no-frills car had a launch price of Rs 100,000 (then USD 2,000), becoming the world's cheapest car to be designed, manufactured, and commercialized ever in the world. This level of techno-commercial brilliance is undoubtedly a matter of significant pride for India, a country that was till the 2010s dependent on imported dated technologies of overseas automotive majors for Indigenization. Figure 4.1 illustrates the technical brilliance of Tata Nano car.

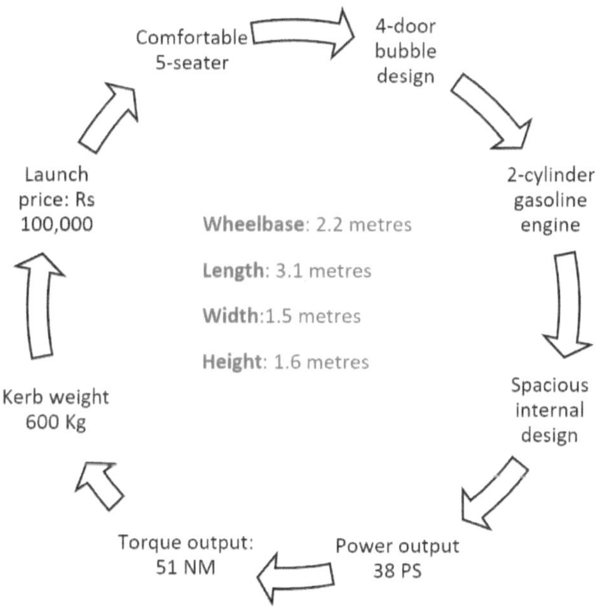

Figure 4.1: Technical Brilliance of Tata Nano Car

Cheap Price, the Only Factor?

Ratan Tata's articulation that the cheap price and the associated stigma had been the main causes of Nano's failure was probably an oversimplification of the issue.

It was as much oversimplification as assuming that the lowest price that would not be achieved by any other car manufacturer would automatically set the market on fire for Nano. A 2008 forecast by a reputed agency, CRISIL, for example, estimated that Nano would singlehandedly expand the car market by as much as 65 percent, that is creating an annual additional demand in lakhs of Nano cars. In actual practice, the Nano car could only be sold in thousands. The car underwhelmed rather than overwhelmed the fast-growing Indian car market. The revised hypothesis by Ratan Tata that the low price acted as a deterrent does overturn the entire theorem of strategy about market being weighed down by high entry deterrent prices. Clearly, there is more to Nano, or any other product, than mere price.

The corollary hypothesis that an unbelievably low price carries a stigma is also questionable. Nor is it sustainable that low price products would need to target only consumers of lower economic strata, in this case such strata not being the appropriate users of a Nano-type car. There exist several examples in both overseas and Indian environments that invalidate these two hypotheses of stigma. Akihabara, the electronics shopping city of Tokyo and Shinjuku, the up-market shopping district of Tokyo are dotted by luxury shops as well as discount shops, the latter patronized by even the more affluent clientele. If Nano were truly positioned effectively for the two-wheeler bound small families as intended by the design envelope, both as a conceptual and practical proposition, Nano would have been a symbol of prestige rather than a sign of stigma. Nano has certain broader leadership lessons to offer in this context to students and practitioners of management and strategy, five of which (as illustrated in Figure 4.2) are discussed below.

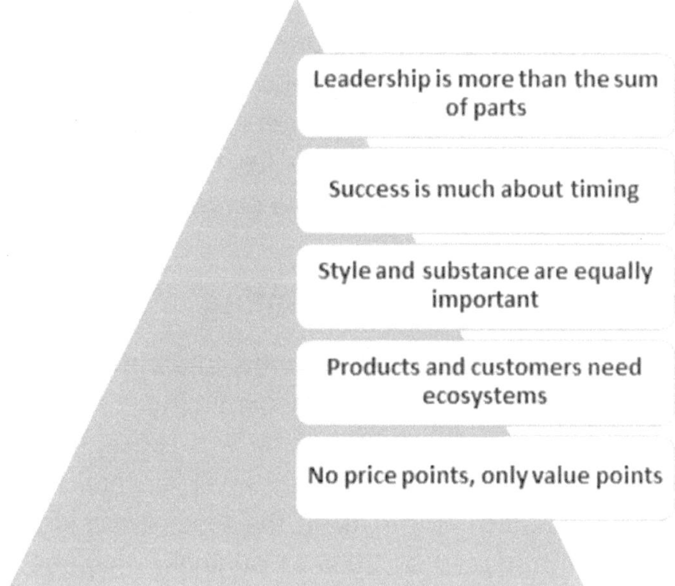

Figure 4.2: Leadership Lessons from Tata Nano Car

Leadership is more than the Sum of Parts

A brilliant and focused leader can pull off unparalleled accomplishments by his or her personal charisma, commitment, and competence, aligning and moving broad teams with him or her. That is what Nano had been – without Ratan Tata's leadership there could not have been a Nano car at all. However, for a product to become a phenomenon, it requires brilliance in strategy and excellence in execution in all functions that directly enable or indirectly support the design, manufacture, and marketing of the product. Certain functional performances whether relating to the location decision of the plant or the marketing of the car were probably not on the dot as certain other functional performances relating to design, project engineering, supply chain and manufacture had been, in respect of Nano. Business leadership at the apex level cannot substitute functional leadership; in other words, brilliant business leadership leads to sustainable brilliant results only when all the functions display equal brilliance. While it is very much necessary to have inspiring leadership at the helm, the minimal foundational imperative for sustainable business leadership is a synergy of leadership in functions as well.

Success is much about Timing

Time and tide, it is said, wait for none. In a business setting, competition never stays still. Strategic timing is the essence of business success. When Tata Nano was conceptualized in the early 2000s, India was a hugely small car market with a dated Maruti 800 small car ruling the roads like a king. Had Nano been introduced by 2004 as originally envisaged, the car would have caught the peoples' fancy. As the events moved, Maruti introduced a more modern small car, Alto, while Hyundai introduced i10, both of which influenced an important upward shift in consumer expectations. The prolonged political standoff on the Singur land in the State of West Bengal (where the Nano facility was to originally come up) and the consequent shift of all the facilities and equipment to a new site, Sanand, in the state of Gujarat which pushed the launch to 2009 did not also help matters. Breakthrough initiatives, which include market shaping product development and launch, often require a near perfect timing. If Tata Motors would seek to reengineer and reposition Nano, the timing would be as important as strategy.

Style and Substance are Equally Important

Products in the contemporary market space are preferred as much for experience as for functionality. A product-specific ecosystem helps in merging the twin requirements.

Styling determines not merely a look-feel but also leads to upgraded design and manufacture. To the extent that Nano was brought in as a no-frills car in an environment which was getting used to more up-market features, the consumers might have felt that style lacked substance in the Nano. Some of the cost-cutting measures like lack of external access to rear trunk, lack of airbags, lack of power windows and lack of air-conditioning probably compromised the stylistic and substantive aspects. An approach that enabled customers choose their preferred combinations of style and substance would have resulted in better customer engagement and superior management of customer expectations. Even though Tata Motors decided to launch an updated Nano, the features were kept under wraps. It would have been helpful for Tata Motors to release the new features in advance and calibrate the design and manufacture to take care of customer responses.

Products and Customers need Ecosystems

Products shine in ecosystems that add demonstrative value to their hardware and software. The Apple stores showcase Apple phones while iTunes provides the applications boutique. Customers had plenty of accessories to choose from to add value to their iPhones and iPads in offices and homes. In contrast, Nano despite being a prestigious product was put in as a poor sibling of the mighty trucks in the dealer network of Tata Motors. More distressingly, the target customers probably had parking spaces for their two-wheelers but no parking spaces for their new Nano cars! A complete lifecycle analysis would have provided the product and marketing architects of Nano with valuable inputs on the availability and non-availability of supportive ecosystems for the car.

Nano would have got reengineered and repositioned with greater confidence had the importance of an appropriate ecosystem been appreciated.

No Price Points, Only Value Points

Any discourse on price being excessive or attractive (that is, entry deterrent or entry supportive) would not be of relevance without considering certain basic principles. To recapture, firstly, any product or service initiative must be a well-made holistic offering of all the functions of a corporation. Secondly, the product or service must be timed well to be ahead of competition and capture the imagination of the users. Thirdly, the style and substance of a product or a service must complement each other, in terms of specifications, performance, functionality and experience. Fourthly, there must be supportive and well-tuned ecosystems that enable a home for the product or service, both at the company delivery end and at the customer usage end. The levels at which these four principles are established, in conjunction with the pricing levels, determine value points, constituting the essential fifth principle. If and when Nano embarks on a new journey, the discourse on price points would need to be rechannelled into an appreciation of the value points.

India, a Qualifying Path in Itself

The author believes that there was never a need to reposition Nano in Indonesia or a European country and then import the concept into India. No doubt, some of the important products of Japanese car majors have been first launched in Indonesia and brought to India subsequently. No such product, however, rode on the Indonesian success story as a qualifier for entry and ramp-up in India. There are opportunities and challenges in 'direct to India' as well as 'to India through Indonesia' options, however. Indonesia (or, for that matter Malaysia) being a small homogenous country provides steady feedback to perfect a product. India, which is heterogeneous in states and preferences, on the other hand, challenges designers and manufacturers with varied demands and requirements.

Gritty designers and manufacturers believe that if they succeed in India, they can succeed anywhere else in the world. There has been no better example of succeeding in India than the Tata group itself with its constituent firms, not in the least Tata Motors as its corporate crown jewel. And, notwithstanding the faltered experience of Nano, there was no reason why Tata Motors should explore other emerging markets as a path to a win in India. Well into the 2020s, Tata Motors did demonstrate its competencies on a wide range of automotive products. The five principles of this chapter should be a solid foundation for Nano to conquer the world, in a new electric avatar, with India as its hub. All believers in Indian innovation would look forward to multi-functional excellence at Tata Motors, not in the least technological innovation and marketing brilliance matching up to, and synergizing with, each other!

Chapter 5

Customer Value Chain: Prompting A Solutions Mindset

Every time one travels in the crowded traffic on the Indian roads one cannot but notice the sight of small families (husband and wife with their two children) navigating dangerously. As discussed in the previous chapters, Ratan Tata's vision of providing such families a safe, comfortable, and economical transportation mode in terms of Tata Nano car unfortunately got stymied in commercialization. The failure of Tata Nano to fulfil the dream was seen by the company as a technical and marketing issue. As a result, there had been sincere and consistent efforts to upgrade the car and reposition it as a vehicle for the young Generation Next. These moves had also not set the sales graph soaring. The changes made indeed were significant given the fact that Nano with its micro-compact form factor was already an engineering marvel.

The new 2015 Nano GenX car came with an expanded product line up, covering three manual and two automated transmission variants. Apart from cosmetic changes like improved bumpers and smoked headlamps, the range came with two key enhancements: automated manual transmission (with enhanced fuel economy) and hatchback opening for accessible boot space. At a higher ex-showroom price of Rs 215,000 to Rs 300,000, Nano car was positioned as a car for the well-to-do young people, a major departure from the original positioning as the world's lowest priced small car (at Rs 100,000) for the needy. Clearly, the repositioning of Nano as a peppy car for the college going students and young executives was underway. That left the fans of Nano's original concept as a unique affordable car for the bottom of the income pyramid in India quite disappointed.

Space-constrained

Indian transportation scenario is woefully space-constrained. India's population density per kilometre of metalled road is one of the highest in the world even as the per capita vehicle ownership is one of the lowest in the world (Over 210 million registered motor vehicles, 6.37 million-kilometre roads, and 1.4 billion population). To compound the stress, annually 31 million vehicles are manufactured (based on 2018-19 annual peak) for use on Indian roads, aggravating the problem beyond imagination. Most metropolitan and upcoming cities suffer from hours of traffic gridlocks. Habitats are built with inadequate parking space. Even modern-day offices have poor parking space. A study of office development shows that for every 100 employees in an office only around 10 car parking slots and around 40 two-wheeler parking slots are likely to be available. The situation in shopping districts is no better; a 100-store shopping mall (with a multiplex additionally thrown in) or a hi-street of retail and pavement shopping, each of which sees 5,000 shoppers daily has no more than 300 car parking slots and strangely just the same number of two-wheeler parking slots!

The fact that approximately 77 percent of the output of 22 million units of automobiles in India is contributed by two-wheelers indicates the tremendous need for mobility and the attractive potential for a switch to passenger car mode (right now, 13 percent of the total output, at 4 million units is in the passenger car segment), and of course, more importantly, to the public transport mode as well. The Indian automobile industry is the third largest in the world selling more than 31 million vehicles. The relentless march of automobile congestion on Indian roads is likely to only intensify in future. While part of this may be mitigated by greater expansion in rural markets (where practically no metalled roads exist), the inevitability of an overall space-constrained transportation scenario in a growth-oriented India is easy to imagine. The challenge for Tata Motors is whether this represents an opportunity but only with reference to other larger cars and countless two-wheelers on the roads. No extent of technical upgradation or market repositioning would have helped Nano achieve its full potential for one important reason. Although it was optimally developed for the purpose, the optionality of Nano in customer mind was related to the parking space and not to the specifications of the car. Figure 5.1 illustrates the limitations of upgradation and repositioning of Tata Nano.

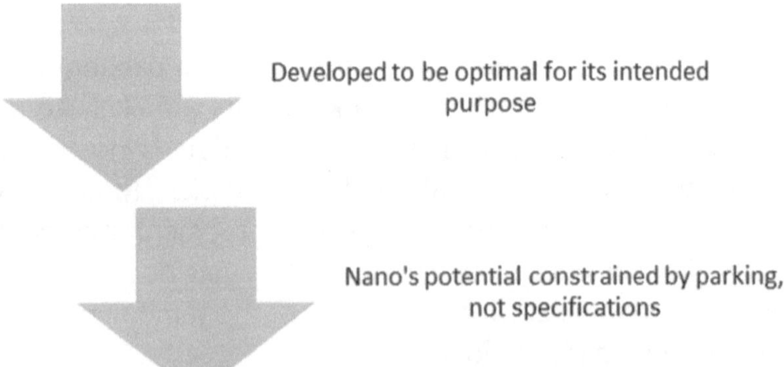

Figure 5.1: Limitations of Upgradation and Repositioning of Tata Nano

Logistics Challenge

As mentioned in the earlier chapters, Nano has been innovatively designed vis-à-vis contemporary small cars and appropriately positioned in the huge potential market space. The challenge in driving up Nano sales to its full potential is neither a product nor a market challenge, therefore. It is simply a logistics challenge that is two-fold: (a) identifying target users who have adequate parking space but need to be weaned to Nano concept and (b) reaching out to natural Nano customers and finding a parking space for them. This strategy must be city and habitat specific. If Tata Motors was serious about realizing the full potential of Nano nothing short of a user-parking census was required to be implemented. Depending on the resources the company was willing to commit, the project should have been taken up as a regional project or a national project. Figure 5.2 explains overcoming the logistics challenge of Tata Nano to harness the car's full potential.

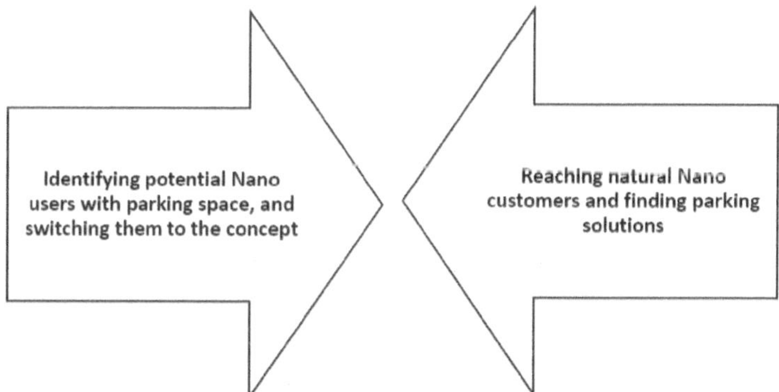

Figure 5.2: Overcoming the Logistics Challenge of Tata Nano's Potential

In this Nano paradigm, Tata Motors should have found collaborative stakeholders who would have seemed unlikely collaborators at the first go. Real estate developers are the first stakeholder group, for such an initiative. Tata Motors as an entity, and Tata Group as a whole, may carry out some introspection in this regard. Tata is a major player in the real estate sector covering both luxury and affordable home sectors (the latter with Tata Value Homes). There is no evidence at all that Tata Motors had any coordinated strategy to link up with Tata Value Homes whose customers were also likely to be Nano customers. Similarly, coordination with high-rise developers and gated community developers as well as urban planners in each city would have developed pathways to identify customer groups who would have usage overlaps. It was necessary for Tata Motors to deploy such logistics analytics to map out the workable market.

Value Propositions

Once the seriously inclined target customer pools were identified, the next challenge would have been to develop value propositions that would make them the buyers of Nano cars. While the high fuel economy of 26 kmpl was a major value proposition, more relevant and customised value propositions were needed. Tata Motors should have tied up with Tata Value Homes to offer Nano cars instead of cash discounts on its houses. With other developers, more arm's length promotional deals could have been considered. There could be other options like reducing lifecycle ownership through subsidized sales, mobile dealer and servicing units especially near target communities, bundled offers with other cars, and assured buybacks. Nano could also have been positioned as a call-taxi, specially customized for lady drivers and lady customers with GPS tracking and other safety features.

Tata Nano has been one of the most complex consummate product-market configurations that was ever attempted. An elegant design and expansive market ought to have laid the path for perpetual value. However, the product and market failed to discover even the basic value. Nano's issue and the discussion in this chapter on rediscovering the potential point to an immutable but underexploited law of marketing that some products are not just products but are fundamental ecosystem concepts. Xerox copying, Kodak film and Sony Walkman of yesteryears and Apple iPad and iPhone and Apple Watch of current times are such concepts. Nano car, in retrospect, was also nothing less than that. It is unfortunate that its routine introduction as any other car erased the value of the fundamentally differentiated concept of what Nano would have been. It is not too late, however.

Electric Mobility

Nano's future does not merely lie in rediscovering its potential as discussed herein. It would lie in taking it to the next logical technological horizon, which is its transformation into an electric car. Nano, in terms of its lightweight and cute-looking design is an ideal platform for conversion into an electric car. Nano Electric would be an ideal concept in terms of environmental sensitivity and lifestyle complementarity. The stakeholders discussed in this chapter would be more than delighted to tie up with Tata Motors to provide exclusive charging points and parking spaces to Tata Nano. Even the urban planners and city space developers would be happy to provide exclusive and preferential parking lots in public spaces for Nano Electric.

Tata Motors should forthwith perch Nano motors as an electric car first, and as an electric self-driving car in this quest for newer technological horizons. Tata should forge a multi-entity collaboration with firms committed to clean transportation such as Google and Tesla to take Nano to the next higher level, even globally. Philosophically, some products need not be products of individual firms adding numbers to their annual income statements. They have an amazing potential to evolve as global heritage products, transforming the way certain conventional activities are performed. Tata Motors should continue to treat Nano as a unique product in its large portfolio and re-develop and re-release it for a futuristic global evolution. Nano could be a perfect example of a product concept innovated in India, designed, developed, and manufactured in India and scaled up and transformed for a meaningful global impact, in a futuristic era of clean mobility!

Chapter 6

Tata Aria, India's First Crossover: Lessons from the Market Response

Tata Motors unveiled in AutoExpo 2010 India's first crossover vehicle, Tata Aria, combining the features of a Sports Utility Vehicle (SUV), a Multi Utility Vehicle (MUV) and a sedan car. The objective was to provide to the Indian automobile users a vehicle that meets every conceivable requirement, from weekday serious business transport to weekend holiday travels, and from highway cruising to off-road adventure. The vehicle was offered in four variants, Pure, Pleasure, Pride and Prestige, with the last two models being the high-end models with all-wheel drive (4x4) capability. The vehicles had a host of electronics and safety features not offered in the Indian automobiles at that point of time, with a great combination of style and performance as well as comfort and safety. In fact, one of the campaigns of the company claimed at least thirty-six features that were first-in-class for indigenous automobiles.

Tata Aria also benefitted from the design inputs provided by Tata Motors' JLR team, which is reflected in the quality of trim and the various bells and whistles for driving and passenger comfort. Clearly, the emphasis was on providing an international class vehicle to the Indian consumer. The prices ranged from Rs 15 lakhs (USD 30,000) to Rs 20 lakhs (USD 40,000) ex-showroom. The introduction was accompanied by a marketing campaign that emphasized the capability to seat seven passengers and conquer off-highway applications without any compromise to the feel of a premium car. Due emphasis was also placed on the several sophisticated features of the car. Despite so much going for the car, Aria failed to take off. The sales trickled to hundreds and showrooms started collecting unsold Arias. In a sense, Aria represented for Tata Motors a failure larger than that of Nano. An analysis of Aria saga teaches several lessons in competitive strategy and strategic marketing.

Positioning, the Core

The genre of utility vehicles (UVs) in India comprised, apart from Aria, Tata Motors' Sumo, Grande Dicor and Safari, Mahindra & Mahindra's Scorpio, Bolero and XUV 500 and Xylo, Maruti-Suzuki's Grand Vitara and Ertiga, Force Motors' One, Premier Rio, and Toyota's Innova in the largely indigenously manufactured category, and Renault's Duster and Koleos, Nissan's X-Trail and Evalia, Skoda Yeti, Toyota's Innova, Fortuner, Land Cruiser and Prado, Mitsubishi's Outlander and Pajero Sport, Honda's CRV 4, Hyundai Santa Fe, Mercedes G, GL , M and ML Audi's Q3, Q5 and Q7, BMW's X3, X5 and X7, Volvo XC90, and finally, Land Rover and Range Rover in the largely imported category. Clearly, for a few thousand vehicles that were being produced and sold in the 2010s, the utility vehicle model variety was mind boggling. Amongst these, Tata Aria could lay claim to be different from all the SUVs with its car like profile and performance. This had, however, failed to translate into a positioning proposition.

At one level, Aria had to take share away from Innova which had, for long, been the acknowledged king of MUVs in India. With a length of 4780 mm which is longer by 200 mm and a width of 1895 mm which is larger by 125 mm compared to Innova but with the same seven-seater profile, Aria began to be positioned in the marketplace by the buyers against the tried and tested Innova rather than against any of the other SUVs, despite the off-road capability, imposing looks (with 17″ wheels), and the several sophisticated features it possessed. Yet, the sophistication and awesomeness of Aria was not a match for the simplicity and friendliness of Innova for the Indian market. This was borne out by the fact that Aria's hundreds were, in fact, better sales than those of any of the imported vehicles but were just a fraction of the numbers notched up by the indigenous simpletons like Innova, Scorpio and Bolero. M&M's newer SUVs, Xylo and XUV with greater sophistry also did substantially better. Probably, had Aria been positioned as just a superior Innova, the marketing game would have been set differently.

Entry Deterrent Price

As Michael Porter theorized, entry deterrent price is a vital concept in the success of new products. The price of a product is closely linked to the positioning of a product. Tata Motors might have calculated that Aria is substantially cheaper than the imported comparable SUVs by 25 to 75 percent. On the other hand, given that it was positioned vis-à-vis Innova, it was perceived to be 25 percent costlier than Innova. Although Aria was made available in several variants with increasing sophistication, the premium of 30 percent for the high-end model relative to the base model was also seen by the market to be unattractive. Relative to the positioning, therefore, Aria suffered from the classic burden of entry deterrent pricing. The subsequent introduction of Pure LX as a new base model at Rs 10 lakhs, at a dramatic 50 percent discount in price to the earlier base model queered the pitch even more. While the new pricing was certainly entry stimulating, clearly the problem of entry deterrent pricing for other models continued.

Aria's inflexibility with positioning and experimentations with pricing illustrate that a successful product entry requires both these factors to be properly benchmarked ab initio, failing which they are to be at least dynamically aligned as the market evolves. Had the vehicle been promoted with a clear crossover niche vis-a-vis imported vehicles, the positioning-pricing equation would have been more positive. Just as the new Camry of Toyota was successfully positioned for corporate leaders, Aria should have been positioned for business leaders with long commutes and who could at times be required to have colleagues to travel with them too. Figure 6.1 sums up the reasons for Aria's failure. Organizationally, positioning and pricing decisions need to be taken by a group of conceptually astute senior leaders well supported by market analytics on the product positioning and price elasticity of demand. Internal and external test marketing of positioning and pricing concepts helps companies identify hidden dangers of imperfect decisions.

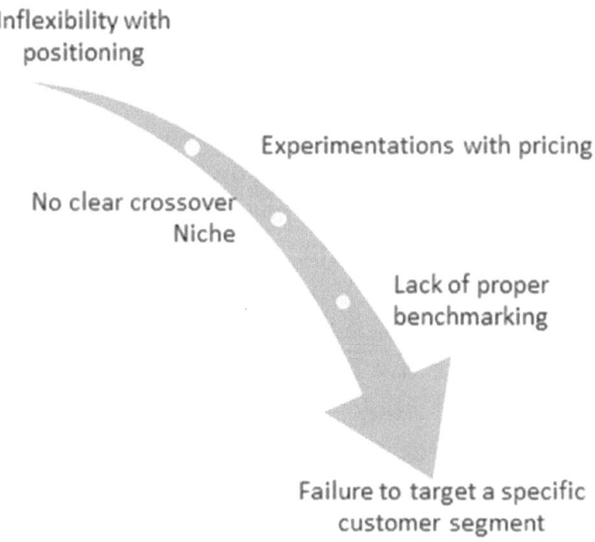

Figure 6.1: Reasons for Aria's Failure

Service - Makes or Mars

If positioning and pricing are the strategic enablers of product success in the automobile industry, after-sales service is the tactical assurance of product sustainability and customer delight in the marketplace. Ideally, a well designed and manufactured automobile should require minimal servicing. Unfortunately, in the case of Aria the incorporation of new generation of electronics caused considerable service issues. The lack of preparedness of the service infrastructure to handle a new generation automobile in the vehicle family was a concern. This could have been obviated through extensive road testing on one hand and intensive training of service engineers in the new generation electronics on the other. Many of the observations made in the previous chapter on Tata Nano in terms of exclusive dealerships for passenger cars apply equally well to Aria. The typical sedan customer expects to have his or her high-cost automobiles to be sold and serviced with exclusivity and timeliness.

The post-design and post-manufacturing value chain comprising distribution, sales, and service chain (DSS chain) is a significant tactical enabler of successful new product introduction. Pre-certification of this vital DSS chain and the infrastructure is rarely done by companies to the same scale it is done in respect of design and manufacture. Pre-certification of the DSS chain helps a company make important tactical choices in respect of regional versus national launch, pilot marketing versus full-scale marketing, and flexible positioning versus harmonized positioning. The service part of the value chain is also an important component which lets the company know how several of the add-on features that are offered in the new model are effective in practice and how they are perceived by the customers. Even a limited period regional launch provides a great opportunity for a subsequent national launch with greater assurance. Aria would have certainly benefitted from such an approach.

Options Unexplored

Tata Aria crossover vehicle was yet another testimony that Tata Motors and its team of dedicated and innovative engineers could develop, manufacture, and commercialize pioneering automobile concepts. In an effort to straddle all the segments, Aria probably was stuck in the middle as a people carrier, pitted in the process against the most popular vehicle in that class, Innova. Innova by then became a utilitarian combination of form, performance, price, reliability, and service providing the best value for money. Innova was perceived as an excellent traffic manager as its form profile of a sedan helped navigate city traffic more effortlessly compared to the larger Aria. Aria's off-road and highway superiority probably did not overcome the disadvantages of city traffic negotiation. An option Tata Motors could have explored with considerable probability of success was a shorter and less awesome 5-seater variant for the city traffic and the larger 7-seater variant for the long-distance cruise. With most aggregates and components as well as trim remaining common, the economies of scope on a larger volume base would have been significant.

The other option would have been to connect each variant of Aria as launched to different customer segments with appropriate add-on features, in a pick and choose manner. A whole new consumer experience could have been provided to build and order a crossover of one's preferences. That would have been a great way to align the features and users, given the vehicle's unique profile of multiple features and multiple usages. The third option could have been to accept all the criticisms, refresh the models to new standards and launch a new Aria series with a suitably upgraded DSS system. To facilitate this, all Arias on stock should have been liquidated with aggressive discounts rather than allowed to linger on. In Aria, Tata Motors, as it had in respect of Nano, a technology winner that was not completely tested to perfection and supported in the field with commitment. It becomes incumbent on the part of the company to convert every technology promise into a positioning success in the marketplace with the right performance, price, and service. Figure 6.2 summarises the potential options that Tata Motors could have considered to improve Aria's success.

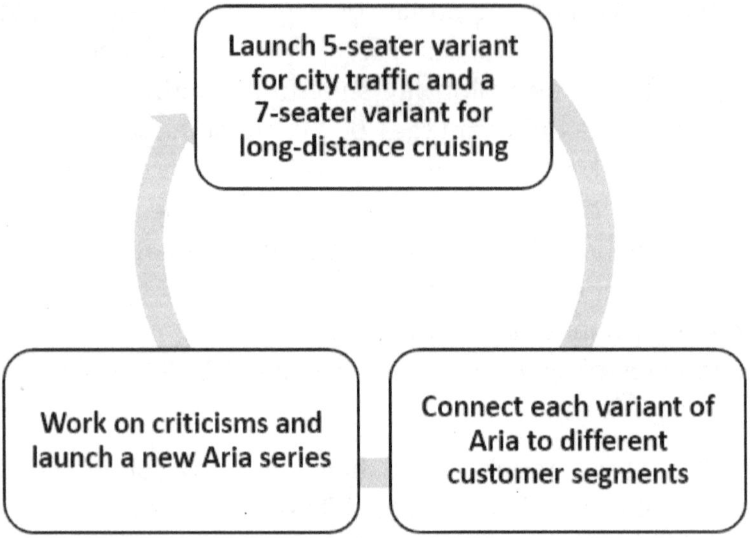

Launch 5-seater variant for city traffic and a 7-seater variant for long-distance cruising

Connect each variant of Aria to different customer segments

Work on criticisms and launch a new Aria series

Figure 6.2: Potential Options for Tata Motors to Improve Aria's Success

The lessons of Aria were eventually assimilated and acted upon by Tata Motors, leading to the successful introduction of Nexon, Harrier and Safari utility vehicles, each with unique design language and strong performance profile. With appropriate positioning and pricing of these vehicles, Tata Motors had winners on hand in the rapidly growing utility vehicle market.

Chapter 7

Market and Market Share Growth: Five Principles of Marketing

India, from just 30,000 passenger cars and utility vehicles in the early 1970s, five decades later absorbs over 4 million passenger cars, utility vehicles and vans; a number set to increase steadily, say, around 10 percent. According to the data released by the Society of Indian Automobile Manufacturers (SIAM), a total of 3,792,356 passenger vehicles were sold in India against 3,082,421 passenger vehicles sold in the year 2021. The sales of passenger vehicles reached a record high of 3.8 million units, exceeding the previous peak in 2018 by approximately 400,000 units. Passenger vehicles grew by 23%, compared to the previous year. The utility vehicle segment has become diversified with multi utility vehicles (MUVs), sports utility vehicles (SUVs) and crossover vehicles (COVs). With certain excise duty concessions for utility vehicles less than 4-metre length, a new breed of compact SUVs has also emerged. Typically, MUVs are 7 to 8 seaters while compact SUVs are 5 seaters. UVs are offered in both petrol and diesel versions; with diesel being the preferred mode in this segment in the past. With the emission concerns becoming critical in the recent years, diesel has lost sheen as the preferred option in this segment.

In the utility vehicle segment, Toyota with its Innova MUV remains a segment choice (against other MUVs such as Mahindra Scorpio and Bolero, Ford Endeavour, and Tata

Safari) although several other car manufacturers such as Renault, Nissan, Hyundai, Honda and Maruti have succeeded in building new franchises around their more compact SUVs. Renault Duster and Nissan Terrano helped popularize this segment a few years ago but Hyundai Creta and Maruti S Cross and Vitara Brezza represented the follow-on challengers. Over time, Maruti established itself as a leader in the UV segment with its Ertiga. Toyota upgraded its Innova to Crysta as a new generation of MUV, while Tata Motors, Hyundai and Kia came up with brand new models. With a continuous slew of introductions from manufacturers, the utility vehicle segment will keep growing strong. The Indian utility vehicle segment offers five interesting and relevant principles to drive market growth and market share growth, as discussed below.

New Products Make New Markets

The first ever (and the only) utility vehicle ever known to the Indian market was Mahindra Jeep which was sold in low volumes from the 1940s. Bajaj Tempo (now, Force Motors) introduced a desi version of Jeep, Tempo Trax, in 1998 which was not a great success. The first spark in the utility vehicles market came when Tata Motors introduced the well-designed (by the 1990s standards) Tata Safari in 1998. Thereafter, Mahindra introduced its own designs such as Bolero (2000) and Scorpio (2002). The real impetus to the Indian vehicle market came when Toyota introduced Innova, in 2004, as its successor to its first entry in 1998, a boxy Qualis. The next revolution took place when Renault introduced its sporty Duster in 2012 which caught people's fancy as an urban SUV, an image fortified by Nissan Terrano further. Thereafter, other manufacturers jumped into the fray with sleek-looking urban SUVs, including a steadfastly small car and sedan oriented Maruti doing so (with Ertiga in

2012, S-Cross in 2015 and Vitara Brezza in 2016). Today, the utility vehicle, whether MUV or SUV, has become not merely the preferred family car or second car option but, more strikingly, the dominant first option. Figure 7.1 illustrates the timeline of utility vehicle first launches.

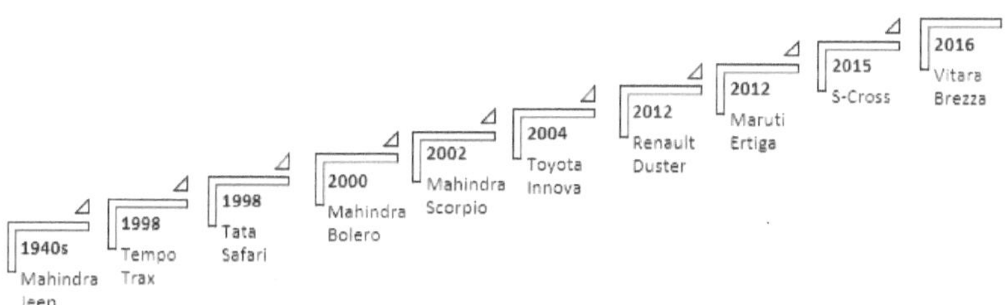

Figure 7.1: Timeline of Utility Vehicle First Launches

During 2022, Indian buyers showed a strong preference for SUVs, particularly crossovers and sub-compact SUVs. To establish a significant presence in this segment, several car manufacturers have begun to introduce new SUVs in their line-up in 2023. SUV introductions in 2023 include Jeep Avenger which will compete with compete with Brezza, Magnite, Sonet, Nexon and more, Maruti Fronx and Jimny, Tata Harrier/Safari facelifts, Nissan X-Trail, Honda Elevate, MG Hector facelift, Volkswagen Tiguan Allspace, Mahindra Bolero Neo Plus and Toyota Fortuner Next-Gen, to name a few.

The Indian utility vehicle market which has grown from 2 percent of the passenger vehicle market to 51 percent of the market is another endorsement of the business truth that it is only new products that make new markets. The initial trepidation that existing players have when a competitor launches a new product with a new positioning is misplaced. They must follow up the competitor launches with their own similar or new products; new market segments will thus be created and expanded. This is true of utility vehicles as proven above, and would be true for any other segment or business too. In fact, the more aggressive such new product entry is, the better it would be for market growth and consumer choice. Patanjali's aggressive Ayurvedic product foray in India, long considered the home of Ayurveda but traditionally dependent on the Western personal hygiene products, created a totally new market of AFMCG industry (Ayurvedic Fast Moving Consumer Goods Industry). The Indian automobile industry should logically look forward to utility vehicles more than doubling in sales every five years, and this product class may overtake the sedan class in sales.

New Themes Make New Products

Newly introduced products will be perceived as new products only when they have novelty. Thematic novelty is one of the big drivers of new product acceptance. In a utility vehicle scenario monopolized by the World War vintage Jeep designs, Tata Safari offered a fresh thematic breeze. In a utility vehicle design space that was characterized by large exteriors and cramped interiors with low regard to finish, Innova brought car-like comfort and quality to the space. In a segment which catered to large families, Duster brought urbanism with easy navigation of crowded urban drive as a new theme. Ford Ecosport (2013), Hyundai Creta (2015), Maruti S Cross (2015) and Vitara Brezza (2016) and Mahindra TUV (2015), KUV (2016), Nuvo Sport (2016), Tata Nexon (2016) and Tata Harrier (2019) brought youthfulness and sharpness to the utility space, integrating more carlike features. At each turn of design philosophy, thematic novelty helps establish new designs as new products.

There is never an end of the road for novelty. Just as the customers would think that the choice is between a 5-seater urban SUV and a 7-seater family MUV (if spaciousness is desired in both options), Kia, through its launch of Carens, brought in the concept of a relatively spacious 7-seater urban SUV at a highly affordable price point. Through Innova Crysta, Toyota provided higher power and torque as well as advanced features and finishes with additional safety to family users. The challenge is to combine improvements in such a manner that they stand out together for thematic novelty. The next level of challenge is to bring in such novelty that would make an SUV, the first personal vehicle rather than the second one. As another example, cars that have inbuilt arrangements for child safety, including child car seats could be the next evolution to cater to urban couples with small families. At another level, Tata revolutionised the electric vehicle space with its pioneering Nexon EV. This electric transformation will continue across the automobile industry.

Global Style with Local Substance

Indian automobile industry is unique because of the strong presence of both Indian and foreign players. Companies such as Tata Motors and Mahindra & Mahindra have gone global with JLR and Ssangyong acquisitions (2008 and 2011, respectively). Tata-JLR has been a great success while Mahindra had to pull out of Ssangyong venture. Both Tata and Mahindra have also continued their indigenous development efforts. Companies such as Maruti, Hyundai, Ford, Honda, and Toyota have been essentially global companies with Indian presence; however, having seen the potential of the Indian market, they have started designing products for India with Indian engineers. Despite having formidable global automotive engineering capability through JLR, Tata Motors went through a completely 'lost decade' (from 2005 to 2015) by not accessing modern global design thinking from its JLR engineering centres and persisting with dated approaches from its Indian development centres. Despite having strong global executive controls, Maruti, Hyundai and Honda have been able to engineer India-specific but globally stylish designs that have found quick resonance with Indian customers. On the other hand, some of the world's largest automotive makers present in India such as GM and VW failed to make the grade in the Indian market due to their reluctance to customize.

Indian requirements are stringent as acknowledged by global automotive leaders. In terms of durability, expectations are of lifetime trouble-free usage. In terms of style, expectations are contemporary. The real differentiators for India are the requirements for high ground clearance and low turning circle, coupled with spaciousness to meet Indian body configurations, and luggage requirements. India also places considerable emphasis on fuel economy and low lifecycle costs. What adds competitiveness is localization. An Indian made car could cost a fraction of a similar imported car. Going forward, those manufacturers who can combine global contemporary styling with Indian cost-competitiveness by working with Indian engineering teams would have a significant competitive advantage. It is indeed gratifying that Renault Kwid, Maruti Brezza, Hyundai Creta and Honda BRV have been products of Indian engineering, albeit with global guidance. After a decade long hiatus, it appears that Tata Motors is also finding the right fusion of global and Indian engineering as demonstrated by Zest, Tiago, Nexon, Harrier and the new Safari vehicles.

Segmentation Drives Share

The traditional theory of market segmentation continues to hold relevance in market share play. The more a company can segment its markets perceptively, the more dominant it can become in the overall market. From a time when utility vehicle category itself was seen as an extended segment of the passenger car market, today the utility vehicle category itself is seen as a discrete market with a few sub-segments of its own. As a result, there has been a complete rejig of the market share pecking order. In the early days of the utility vehicle product expansion, Tata led the duopoly with Mahindra. Later it was Toyota with Innova that led the market share charts. In 2022, the top five players have been as follows (with market share percentages in the brackets): Maruti Suzuki (41.63), Hyundai (13.87), Tata (13.15), Mahindra (8.58) and Kia (7.04). These five manufacturers have captured an overwhelming 84 percent of the utility vehicle market, elbowing out the once market leader, Toyota and pushing down the subsequent leaders Renault and Honda.

The statistics also illustrate how the compact UVs of Tata Motors, M&M, Hyundai and Maruti captured close to 56 percent of the total UV market. More importantly, market segmentation and product engineering geared to segmentation has propelled Maruti Suzuki and Hyundai, both predominantly small car players, as the top two players in the utility vehicles market. Segmentation and product introductions have helped a traditional player like M&M retain its market presence. By the same token, it is also evident how Toyota lost the game to an extent by refusing to play in the SUV segment despite the existence of a sprightly RAV4 in its global product range and several others in the associated Daihatsu range. Interestingly, in the total UV space, M&M have 6 major products, Tata Motors 3, Maruti Suzuki 3, Toyota 5, Hyundai 4, and Kia 3 (overall, there are more than 100 SUV models, past and present!). Clearly, with others such as Honda noticing the importance of thematic segmentation, there is still huge potential for market share growth for late-stage entrants.

It is Never too Late

The Indian utility vehicle market provides a few important insights for leadership which has the responsibility for corporate strategy, marketing, and product decisions of a company, usually the CXOs, CEO and boards of companies. Some insights are evident from the above discussion and are not repeated. A few additional insights are as follows. Several companies that were covered in this chapter would have triggered better market expansion and achieved better market share for themselves had they made proactive and region-specific decisions in a timely manner. Only two companies, M&M (in the utility vehicle segment) and Hyundai (in the sedan segment) have demonstrated such decision-making capability. Secondly, customisation to local needs is not a concept that can be taken back to global boards and executed in overseas design centres. Rather, it is a concept that needs local decision making, and local execution with local engineers and with local validation. Figure 7.2 illustrates the insights for product launch leadership.

Figure 7.2: Insights for Product Launch Leadership

While timeliness makes a significant difference, it is never too late to make an entry and score success and sustainability. While Toyota would have been so high in the pecking order had it entered India along with Maruti such delayed entry has not prevented the company from creating a niche for itself years later. Similarly, Maruti would have had a great presence in the utility vehicles segment had it entered in the segment along with Toyota but the delay has not stopped it becoming the largest player in the utility vehicles segment even after a highly belated entry with the acclaimed Ertiga, S Cross and Brezza. The same has been true of Hyundai Creta, and is likely to be true with other models. Delayed market entry can be offset by innovative product engineering. It is never too late to dominate markets with creative positioning of high-quality products with thematic novelty.

Chapter 8

The Beetle-Ambassador Paradox: The Essence of Product Perpetuity

Beetle subcompact car produced and sold by Volkswagen of Germany worldwide is an iconic product that came to be timeless in its acceptability with the young and old alike across generations. First designed and produced by Porsche in 1934 as a family car, Volkswagen sold over 20 million Beetle cars until the mid-1980s. It was probably the first car with an air-cooled rear engine. Its peak production was 1.3 million units a year but dipped to 30,000 units a year, prior to its production halt. It also became a car that signified multi-country production and was 'reverse exported' from an emerging country to the country of origin, Germany. Beetle had been coming back in the game, from time to time, evolving for the last several years as an urban car from Volkswagen for a fun-loving modern generation of the 21st Century.

Ambassador compact car produced and sold by Hindustan Motors (HM) of India is, in its own humble way, an iconic product in India that became synonymous as much with the inception and growth of the Indian automobile industry in the 1950s as with the frustration of technological obsolescence in India. First made by Morris Motors Limited as Morris Oxford II model in 1956 in the United Kingdom, it began to be manufactured by HM in

1958 under a technical collaboration at its Uttarpara plant in India. From a dominant market share in a diminutive automotive market of India (30,000 cars per annum or so in the 1970s), Ambassador collapsed in output to just 2,500 cars per year in a super-grown contemporary automotive market in India (3.8 million cars per year presently).

Comparisons and Contrasts

Beetle, doubtless, represents a product concept and a product profile that has been timeless. Despite the plethora of manufacturers and car segmentations and designs that overwhelmed the world automobile scene from the 1960s, Beetle retained a niche. The car looked the same but continued to integrate internal changes. All said and done, the Ambassador also stayed on as a car produced in India for the longest number of years on the same assembly line, without any notable change – a staid feat unique in the automotive world. No other car made in the world has surpassed this record of non-development. In fact, as opposed to Beetle, there was never a long-term break in the production of Ambassador, until it ceased production completely due to obsolescence. Interestingly, Beetle and Ambassador share the rounded, curvy retro looks. The comparisons probably stop here.

Beetle got evolved over the years, and reinvented in recent years, as a very modern design that integrated high-end electronics with hi-precision mechanicals. In contrast, Ambassador continued to remain the same old car with minimal design changes, except the engines getting updated to basic improvements in emission norms progressively. Volkswagen, the producer of Beetle has been marching on to become one of the world's largest car manufacturers, with sales of 4.56 million vehicles in 2022, covering 10 global brands and 200 models, produced in nearly 120 factories and a global workforce of 662,600. HM, the producer of Ambassador, even by Indian benchmarks shrunk perilously down, with an output of only a few thousand vehicles of all types, and mounting losses. Ambassador's deep decline happened notwithstanding the feeble revival attempts based on further foreign collaboration arrangements. Figure 8.1 illustrates a comparison between Beetle and Ambassador.

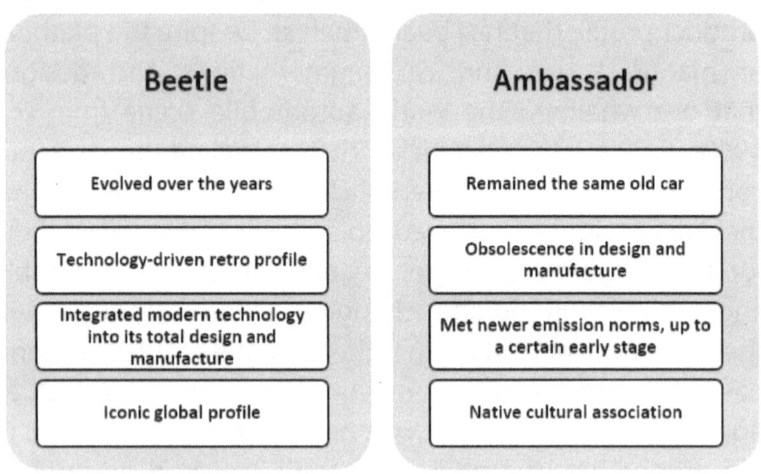

Figure 8.1: Comparison Between Beetle and Ambassador

The formula for product perpetuity can be gleaned from the positive profile of Beetle and Volkswagen as well as the negative profile of Ambassador and Hindustan Motors. The history of both Beetle and Ambassador indicates that certain products can have a lasting presence, if the manufacturers set their heart on their retention, allied to or independent of product-specific viability. It also teaches us that if mandatorily linked to technological evolution, product lines can stay onto near perpetuity. Three critical aspects are discussed below.

Tradition with Technology

Product functionalities may change or new ones may emerge but usage traditions remain. As far as automobiles are considered, while the basic functionality of movement or transportation does not change, several others have got added over the years. However, the tradition of a family vehicle, an urban vehicle or a semi-urban vehicle remains. How an old basic design is updated to modernity retaining the tradition is the key to product perpetuity. While retaining the original "The Beetle," new models such as GSR for sporty applications and Cabriolet in the '50s, '60s and '70s, with branding for lifestyle applications, were added. Power and safety options were offered at the level of a large sedan even though Beetle was a small car. As if it were an ultramodern car, both hard top and soft top variants were offered. Sophisticated electronics and high-class trim were offered. Even if the shell was of vintage design, elegant lines and accessories were added to provide a pleasingly modern but traditionally retro look to Beetle. Ambassador which got stuck with the design of the 1950s did nothing of that sort, and the negative results became obvious from the 1970s.

The concept of novel product development combining tradition with technology has wider applicability. The latest to emerge is the smart watch which redefines the traditional concept of wearing a wrist watch with cellular connectivity and communication. The traditional concept of handwriting has been restored with tablets and phablets that can accept writing and drawing while that of physical book reading has been revolutionized with electronic book reading, a few years ago. Many traditional practices like wrist bands and spiritual bands are modernized with healthful metals, elements, sensors, and other digital electronics, and made contemporary with designs. The concept of retrospective products with futuristic technologies has revolutionized food processing and lifestyle industries. There could be virtually no limits to this trend. Products and functionalities can remain in perpetuity so long as technology updates them to modern functionalities.

Innovation with Investment

Innovation cannot happen without investments – in people, assets, and supportive infrastructure. However, investments need viability which, in turn, comes from a successful product portfolio. Volkswagen did not stop only with Beetle; it continued with aggressive additional product development for multiple segments in global markets. In contrast, HM did not, and could not, go beyond Ambassador for India. Though the company entered, from time to time, into collaborations with world-class Japanese automotive giants such as Isuzu (for trucks) and Mitsubishi (for cars and SUVs), the company could not provide the requisite investments. Strategically, the company needed to support product diversity, scale and scope economics so that the new products, in turn, could support updating of an aged but popular niche product such as Ambassador. However, HM was in no position to do so. As a product that was entrenched for decades in a sub-scale automotive market of India which was no more than 30,000 cars per annum for the three manufacturers combined, Ambassador lost the game of innovation from the start.

Innovation and investments, however, require a business sense. What Ambassador could not achieve in India, Maruti-Suzuki could achieve in the same Indian market with aggressive investments, innovative products, and intensive marketing. Maruti 800 car was a path-breaker. Though it was discontinued a few years ago, the concept staged a comeback with small cars having more contemporary technological flourishes. Hyundai which blazed new trails, years later, with i10 car set to keep up the product perpetuity with i10 Grand car, and i20 as well as others. The ability to make timely investments and support product innovation is the essence of enabling product perpetuity. The task becomes complex as well as easy when a product has several outsourced components. There are several marquee products and brands in India which can be brought to contemporary standards (Leyland Comet truck, Tata Indica car, Bajaj Scooter, for example) while investing in new products. What Bajaj did not do for the perpetuity of its highly popular scooter (in fact, it stopped the manufacture of the scooter product), its originator Vespa continued to do.

Brands with Brain and Brawn

Products with potential for perpetuity typically enjoy significant brand power, initially and for several years of growth. Ambassador had brand power in India as much as Beetle had in its global markets. Even when products go out of perpetuity, the brand pull remains. Nissan's strategy of reinventing a new low-cost car model, "Go", for India and other emerging markets through the revival of Datsun brand is a classic example. Reliance brought out its clothing brand Vimal after several years of retirement. It goes without saying that if investments on popular products on the lines considered in the earlier sections are accompanied by commensurate investments on brands, product perpetuity can be ensured. It implies that even when erstwhile popular products face temporary setbacks, it would be a futuristic move to keep the brands in public recall in gross or subtle ways.

For product perpetuity, brand building must happen with both brain and brawn. The potentially perpetual brands get identified with native traditions in an intuitive yet refined way, oftentimes with emotionally identifiable icons. Air India's Maharaja and Amul's little girl are outstanding examples, as illustrated in figure 8.2. However, for product perpetuity to occur there must be a one-to-one association between the product and the brand. When companies attempt to leverage popular brands across a product range it becomes difficult to support perpetuity of a product. The ideal conditions are that the product must have a distinctive, even if vintage, design, and the brand must have a specific user association. Jeep, Land Rover, Innova and Sumo (all utility vehicles), Comet and Viking (truck and bus), and Lambretta and Vespa (two-wheelers) are a few examples. Unfortunately, companies seem to be losing their interest and penchant to build products and brands correlated for perpetuity.

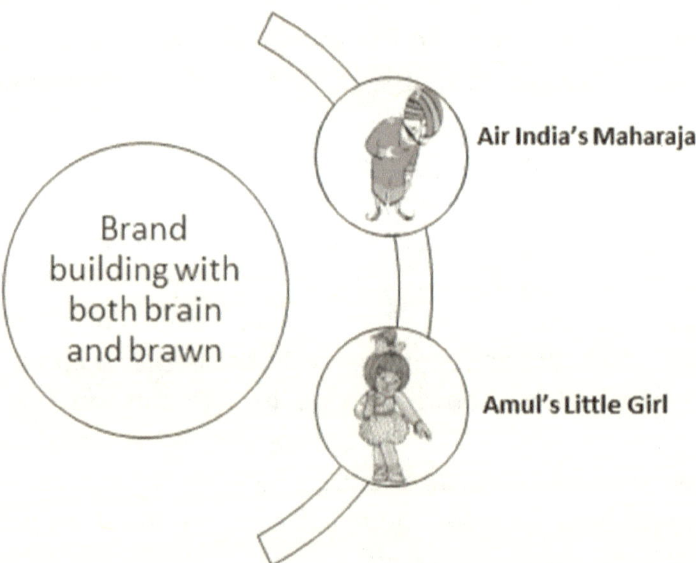

Figure 8.2: Examples of Brand Building with Emotionally Identifiable Icons

Product perpetuity would present an attractive fallback option for companies in a never-ceasing rush for product diversity in highly fragmented and intensely competitive markets. Products of vintage standing can be akin to family silver that could be worth a fortune when chips are down; such products need to be tended with technology, investments and branding in a manner exclusive to them, however. There is nothing to be bugged about dated models if they are cared for enough not to be outdated, as the classic example of Volkswagen Beetle (or "Bug" as it is also popularly called) demonstrates!

Section 2
FMCG and Retail

Chapter 9

Super-Fast Moving Consumer Goods Industry: The Cradle of New Management

Established management thought and practice owe much to two major industries: the automobile industry and the fast moving consumer industry. These two industries, more than any other industry, demonstrated how firms could achieve stability and efficiency in design, manufacturing and marketing of products. Management principles rooted in these two industrial sectors epitomized effective ways of conducting businesses. In today's knowledge economy driven by new modes of technological convergence, a new industrial sector of Super Fast Moving Consumer Goods is taking shape, rewriting the principles of management.

Automobile and FMCG Industries

Automobile industry was the cradle of management ever since the design, manufacturing and marketing of automobiles became the leading component of the industrial revolution. The automobile industry contributed several path-breaking concepts in functional management, geographic management and strategic business unit (SBU) management, with a special focus on operations management, supply chain management and technology management. Specific national and company systems with origins in Japan such as by 5S, Toyota Production System, Kaizen, and Just-in-Time System became industry standards and management role models globally. The automobile industry was also the leader in globally networked design and manufacture, heralding in the 1970s an era of globalization. In the 1990s, the automobile industry took new strides in integrating electronics and digital technologies. Today, it is striving to transform itself into an era of clean mobility.

The automobile industry was, and continues to be, driven by technology to achieve better fuel economy, safety and user satisfaction for the singular, unchanged objective of road transportation. That said, automobile technology has been characterized by incremental improvements, and yearly model changes. The industry became a prototype of a standardized template of management that withstood vicissitudes of time as well as cyclicality of demand, often linked to economic factors. In one sense, the automobile industry by the 2000s could contribute all that it could to the development of management theory and practice. The author's pioneering work in the application of Porter's theory of Competitive Strategy to the Indian automobile industry validated several of the breakthroughs in management theory and practice in the automobile industry.

In parallel, a new industry was developing globally and contributing to new managerial paradigms. Organized retail, combined with what are euphemistically called Fast Moving Consumer Goods (FMCG), set the stage for new paradigms for global supply chain management, cost and profit management, production outsourcing, market segmentation and shaping consumer behaviour. If the automobile industry shaped its management paradigms out of research laboratories and manufacturing complexes, the FMCG industry shaped its management paradigms out of turning around product manufacture and consumption at a rapid pace. The fact that the FMCG goods represent daily necessities lent a new dimension to management of cost economics and consumer perceptions. Leading-edge technology was less relevant compared to management of hundreds, if not thousands of, store keeping units (SKUs), related distribution logistics and advertising to perk up demand. As with the automobile industry, the FMCG industry came to be typecast in terms of management ethos of outsourcing economics and perception management, with 'freshness management' becoming the key driver of managerial success. Figure 9.1 illustrates the new paradigms in the FMCG industry.

Figure 9.1: New Paradigms in the FMCG Industry

Super FMCG

The late 2000s, however, saw the emergence of a totally new breed of consumer products which are driven by rapid strides in technology on one hand, and challenges of global supply chain management on the other. These consumer products, such as cellular phones, portable audio and video devices, gaming devices and other consumer electronic products combine leading edge design and manufacturing technologies with rapid-fire management of supply chain. These products, which may be called Super FMCG products, have clearly raised the bar on technology and management. To illustrate, unlike an automobile or a tooth paste, a cellular phone is designed and launched with the objective of making itself obsolete in 3 to 6 months of launch. Unlike an automobile which is segmented on clearly defined user needs (be it carrying capacity, fuel economy, or driving sophistication) or an FMCG item which is segmented on abstractly defined user perceptions (be it savings, esteem, or functionality), the Super FMCG creates new markets based on new technologies at an amazing speed. Super FMCG is as tangible as an automobile is in technology and as intangible as an FMCG product is in freshness.

The SFMCG product typically has multiple technological dimensions, which is best illustrated by the example of a cellular phone. In the 2010s, a cellular phone used to be based on one of the three operating systems (Symbion, Android or Windows, each of which was getting updated at least twice a year), RAMs and processor speeds (from 128 MB and 1 GHz to successive higher levels), internal and external memory (up to 64 GB), input technology (hard Querty, touch Querty, handwriting recognition, regular cell input), imaging technology (from 1.3 to 12 MP cameras, with or without flash, and with or without video conferencing and camcorder capabilities), communication technologies (2G, 3G or 4G), panel technologies (LCD, Super LCD, retina display, or AMLOED), screen size (from 2 to 5 inches), documentation technologies (office document editing), application technologies and a plethora of other options (like radio, music player, organizer and so on). Every manufacturer used to have scores of models of combining these variations, with challenges of forced technological obsolescence almost every three months.

Moving over to 2020s, one can see dramatic leaps in convergence of technologies, multiplicity of manufacturers and a quantum jump in specification limits for various functionalities. In some cases, the jump has been even 100X or 200X. It is easy to realize therefore that SFMCG products pose managerial challenges like no other product. The basic principles of management such as economies of scale and scope, product lifecycle, learning curve, globalization, cross-industry integration are challenged by the technological factors that drive innovation in SFMCG. As SFMCG firms break new ground in managing the aforesaid complexities they not only stay ahead of the efficiency curve in their own industries but also offer new managerial insights for the other less complex industries just as the Japanese automobile industry revolutionized the management thought and practice for the industrial sector as a whole.

SFMCG Management

There are a few special features of Super Fast Moving Consumer Goods management (called from now on, SFMCGM for simplicity) that are clearly contrarian to the established management thought. Fundamentally, SFMCGM continuously accelerates innovation in multiple yet inter-linked facets as a combined trigger for market expansion. Secondly, SFMCGM embraces technological discontinuities to create new markets, accepting product obsolescence as a welcome need. Thirdly, it relies on unconventional marketing to maximize sales and achieve quickest possible paybacks. Fourthly, it relies on globally networked design, manufacturing, and supply chain processes with a high mix of outsourcing to optimize investments and push down breakeven points. Fifthly, it creates a sustainable brand loyalty based on customized functionalities and harmonized user experiences. These features can be set out as the five essential principles of SFMCG Management as illustrated in Figure 9.2.

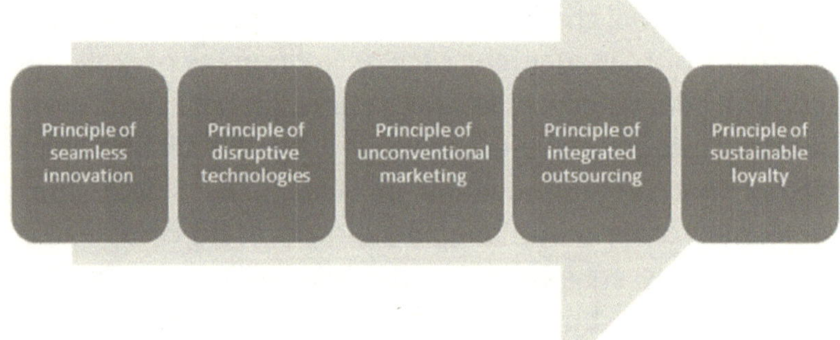

Figure 9.2: Five Essential Principles of SFMCG Management

Principle of Seamless Innovation

Innovation is not new to industrial development. SFMCGM differs from the experience of innovation in the other contemporary sectors in terms of its continuous and comprehensive nature, often backed by creation of intellectual property by SFMCGM firms. As a result, multiple product generations are under parallel processing in an

SFMCG firm. SFMCG firms have an ability to innovate on multiple platforms, oftentimes combining multiple products under a single umbrella design platform. This is driven by a clear conceptual clarity on how successive generations of products will be conceptualized within the firm and delivered for the marketplace. SFMCG firms typically do not see innovation in the typical risk-reward lens. On the other hand, they utilize innovation as a survival tool. They believe that if they do not innovate, some other firms would, to the detriment of the incumbents.

SFMCG firms oftentimes adopt a scaled approach in the functionality of individual components to develop several permutations and combinations of end-products. In this endeavour, SFMCG firms generate enormous flexibility for components to work for a range of performance parameters. To revert to the basic example of cellular phone, it would be possible to fit a low-end or a high-end chip in a common configuration. One cannot, however, imagine a light axle to be fitted on a large truck. In other words, SFMCG firms design internal components in a manner that they can function independent of external form factors. From the lowest common multiple (LCM) oriented basic approach to the highest common multiple (HCM) oriented premium approach, SFMCG firms revel in innovating to varied functionalities and user experiences, thus providing another facet of seamless innovation.

Innovation in SFMCG firms typically tries to expand market base through user experience. By making product usage multi-functional yet highly intuitive, SFMCG innovation brings knowledge to the consumer. SFMCG products, in one sense, are highly educative products which stimulate intellectual curiosity in the users and expands market base. The popularity of telecommunication and gaming products in relatively less literate or less affluent sections of emerging markets is attributable to innovative simplicity. This simplicity automatically provides the leverage to raise the bar for high-end products. A product such as Kinect which provides for the simplest of movements thus leading to as universal appeal as possible also retains a sophisticated gaming capability to cater to the well-initiated. SFMCG firms thus typically break the ceiling as well as crash the floor to create a seamless expanse of user base.

Principle of Disruptive Technologies

Unlike traditional industries such as the automobile industry or watch industry which were unwilling to proactively embrace substitute or even complementary technologies until it became inevitable, SFMCG firms tend to readily integrate disruptive technologies to create new products and advance product obsolescence. Apple proactively leveraged touch screen technology to virtually reinvent cellular phone. Samsung stole a march over Sony by pioneering a new generation of televisions based on flat panels. Nintendo pioneered Wii by integrating motion recognition technology in its gaming devices. Amazon simplified digital technology to enable avid readers access books anytime, anywhere. Google saw Cloud as a new way of disrupting the established model of physical infrastructure-based computing. And the examples would only abound in future, with the onset of Artificial Intelligence.

From incremental innovation in products and processes to disruptive leapfrogging in technological development, SFMCG firms could use either of the two or both the approaches. An SFMCG firm which bases itself on the foundation of disruptive technology and seeks incremental innovation is, however, likely to be more successful than firms which are based on a foundation of continuous innovation with only an occasional disruptive development. The benefit (sales turnover) to cost (R&D expenditure) ratio of product development at Apple is several times over that of Samsung or Sony, for example. A continuously innovative Samsung, however, fared far better than other giants less inclined towards seamless innovation. Clearly firms are advantageously placed when they pursue original as well as incremental innovation.

To be successful in the disruptive technological model, firms must be prepared to take bets on such sunrise technologies with "perfection at first attempt" objective. Firms which dabble in disruptive technologies without aiming for maturity are likely to fail rather than succeed. The first generation of tablet computers introduced in the early 2000s failed because of the imperfect nature of handwriting recognition technology. Disruptive technologies need to be carefully cultivated and imbibed based on observation of technological maturity of internal as well as external technology sources. Many times, an industry needs to bet on disruptive technologies to be pioneering. For the automobiles, global positioning systems (GPS) was one such disruptive technology of the recent past while automated (driverless) driving would be the disruptive technology of the future.

Principle of Unconventional Marketing

Firms in several industries rely on keeping their products under wraps until they are able to launch their products. Automobile industry is a classic example, with several other FMCG and white goods firms following a similar philosophy of secrecy until product launch was imminent, or at best closely preceded, by open advertisement. Possibly, this reflects a philosophy of avoiding signals to competition. On the other hand, SMFCG firms follow an entirely different and largely unconventional marketing model. SFMCG firms follow a model based on three approaches of (i) expectation marketing, (ii) technology marketing, and (iii) saturation marketing, which together present a wholly new and challenging marketing model.

SFMCG firms typically indicate the profiles of their futuristic products almost at the same time as that of their current new product launches. Consumer expectations are built up as the products go through their development phases, are offered in their beta versions, and are finally showcased in industry conferences and exhibitions. In a sense, expectation marketing of SFMCG firms is akin to the marketing of a celluloid movie, expectations on which are built up right from the launch date of the movie through several phases of casting, information release on shoots, music launch and finally screening of trailers. SFMCG firms believe that current products will continue to be purchased because of compulsive needs even as expectations of futuristic products will lead to future compulsive buying. Experience indicates that expectation marketing helps SFMCG firms retain and broaden their customer base.

Technology marketing is unique to SFMCG firms. While other industries such as white goods industries also seek to market products based on their novel technological platforms (for example, filtration efficiency or cooling efficacy by air conditioners), SFMCG firms take technological marketing to an entirely new level. Additionally, the technological impact of each component of the SFMCG product is felt more tangibly than in the case of a white goods product which makes technological marketing a veritable tool for SFMCG. The flip side to technological marketing is the need for the design to live up to the value propositions. Whether it is signal response or screen clarity, technology must speak with performance. The positive side to technological marketing is the build-up of a virtuous opinion base linked to technological performance.

The third component of SFMCG marketing is based on saturation marketing. The SFMCG marketing model does not follow the conventional product lifecycle marketing model which prescribes almost equal phases of introduction, growth, plateau and decline. On the other hand, SFMCG marketing considers an urgent and rapid growth phase, immediately upon launch with little concern for plateau or decline phases both of which are treated as bonuses, if at all. This helps SFMCG firms recover their investments with saturation sales before the new expected competing products reduce the impact. This model requires SFMCG firms to adopt an aggressive multi-chain and multi-store format with maximal exploitation of all trade channels, including online options. Online marketing including access to critical review portals helps in saturation marketing in a big way.

Principle of Integrated Outsourcing

SFMCG firms share with their FMCG counterparts a reliance on global networking and outsourcing to enhance their manufacturing efficiencies and achieve cost and price competitiveness. Several mainline vendors (such as Acer) played a useful role in multi-brand computer development. HTC supported manufacture of many leading mobile phone products, despite having its own line-up. Global-scale factories like Foxconn play a pivotal role to deliver millions of products to multiple end-product makers (OEMs). These examples are reflective of the approach to optimize global manufacturing for maximal supply efficiency.

SFMCG firms, however, differ from FMCG firms in that they consider manufacturing advantage as a source of firm-level competitive advantage which must be preserved internally. This is reflected in the efforts by the OEMs to internalize some of the advantage by establishing manufacturing bases in countries providing such efficiencies. The bases established in China by global electronics firms and in India by global auto makers are clear examples. They have helped such global firms to align demand and supply points for certain least-cost factor supply and product distribution solutions. They have, more importantly, enabled global firms overcome the vicissitudes of exchange rate variations and other macroeconomic factors.

SFMCG firms, however, are more unique in their internalization of key technologies (as is practiced by technology-driven mainstream established firms) in contrast with the philosophies of FMCG firms which could totally outsource both design and manufacture. The efforts made by SLR camera makers to develop in-house their image processing engines, the notebook computer makers to develop solid state devices, and the cellular phone makers to develop capacitive or super bright screen technologies are indicative of the need for SFMCG firms to retain core competencies within their in-house industrial systems.

Principle of Sustainable Loyalty

SFMCG firms need a constant and ever increasing customer base to give effect to, and derive benefit, from the SFMCG business model discussed above. Brand switching as a concept accepted in other industrial sectors acts to the detriment of SFMCG firms. The principles of loyalty in SFMCG sector are more challenging than in other sectors where a generic strategy such as cost position (e.g., Wal-Mart for budget products) or product differentiation (e.g., Mercedes for esteem and quality) build long-lasting brand loyalty. The user of SFMCG products evaluates at least three facets before developing loyalty – technology markers, usage versatility and esteem value. Typically, therefore, SFMCG firms build lifelong loyalty around one or more of the above three factors.

A user of automobile is less likely to be impressed with the use of fuel injection system than with the fuel economy or acceleration that it provides. On the other hand, the user of an SFMCG product would tend to be fascinated by specific technology markers such as the operating system, screen technology, camera competence, or application repository. Technology has thus a standalone appeal for users which provides a feel of customized preference. The power of choice that is embedded in a typical SFMCG product is an extremely important lever to play for the SFMCG firms.

Unlike several other products which are mono-functional delivering one usage functionality (a detergent just cleans, an automobile just drives and a microwave oven just cooks, for example), SFMCG products tend to be convergence products delivering multiple functionalities, and at least provide multiple options within a single functionality. As a result, the versatility of functions provides the second most important lever to build loyalty with SFMCG products.

SFMCG products, however, share with other products the lever of esteem as a driver of customer loyalty. A premium automobile user would any day love to drive a car with Mercedes Tristar, BMW logo or Toyota brand. An electronics equipment user would always consider a Sony or a Bose to represent higher senses of listening pleasure. In a similar manner, SFMCG firms can convert their products into products of esteem. When technology of design, manufacture and usage provides a unique experience and feel, SFMCG products tend to assume a cult phenomenon. Apple has emerged as the most skilful company in leveraging esteem as a driver of sustainable customer loyalty.

Others: Quo Vadis?

The above discussion has led to an interesting profile of what defines an SFMCG product and the five essential principles that shape the evolution and sustainability of an SFMCG product. Yet, it would be facile to assume that the other sectors and products would, for ever, be moulded in conventional laws of development, manufacture and marketing. The rate of technological change would, in the coming years, be even more intense and comprehensive. The new laws of SFMCG would need to be studied and adapted by all firms which believe in product reinvention and competitive rejuvenation as strategies to dominate future industrial evolution.

Chapter 10

Patanjali Phenomenon in Indian FMCG: Industry Level Competitive Strategy

The rapid growth of Patanjali Ayurved Ltd (PAL), with its range of natural or ayurvedic products, has shaken up the Indian Fast Moving Consumer Goods (FMCG) industry. Established in 1996, and with humble origins as a small pharmacy in Haridwar in 1997, PAL has had a tepid growth during the first five years but moved on to an exceptional growth track thereafter, increasing the revenue to Rs 40,000 crore by 2022-23. The company is aiming to achieve further rapid growth to Rs 1,00,000 crore by 2027-28. The company became a large developer, manufacturer, and seller of diversified ayurvedic or natural FMCG products. India has not been new to natural products; Himalaya has a ninety-year legacy of ayurvedic drugs and nutraceuticals while several companies such as Zandu, Dabur, Emami, Vicco and Jyothi have notable natural product portfolios. Some of the companies, in the past, gave significant competition to the MNCs operating in India with their potential; however, no company could jolt the established MNC and Indian players as PAL did.

The case of PAL is an interesting study in competitive strategy. It has valuable lessons on overcoming entry barriers and scaling up. It helps one understand industry definition and industry segmentation from multiple angles. It also offers insights on generic competitive strategies that a firm could pursue, and how aspirant firms could establish their unique selling propositions (USPs). It also helps one appreciate the importance of value chain management in the development of competitive strategy. It also rewrites some principles of organizational management. PAL's success would offer relevant lessons for a new breed of native companies seeking to nibble away shares from established players, more so from the Indian subsidiaries of multi-national companies (MNCs). It also indicates the challenges PAL would face, and the strategies it could adopt, to remain on the growth path. Finally, it also makes a powerful case of management theory and practice needing to be unique to the Indian context.

Uniqueness

A new entrant needs certain unique propositions to make an entry into the industry (beyond generic competitive strategies). The fundamental uniqueness of PAL stems from the fact that it has been set up by a highly popular Yoga guru, Baba Ramdev, who struck a chord with vast sections of Indian population as a highly committed Yoga practitioner cum teacher. The Yoga guru setting up a natural Ayurvedic products company has significant conceptual synergy and emotional appeal. This is quite akin to a reputed doctor setting up a hospital, and thus bringing in an additional level of confidence to patients, medical fraternity, and investors. That the establishment and growth of PAL coincided with a world-wide revival of interest in Yoga and natural products as a safe and efficacious alternative to western practices was probably more than a coincidence. The market for natural wellness products was not small by any standard; it has been growing at a fast clip. Given that India, and other Asian countries have an unorganized natural supplements practice, setting up a dedicated venture by a committed Yoga practitioner was certainly a coup of sorts.

There are other unique points as well. The second uniqueness lies in the aggressive promotion of the natural Ayurvedic concept in two different formats. Unlike Himalaya and Dabur that sought to market their products as therapeutic medicines, PAL positioned its products as wellness products capable of enhancing strength and immunity. It also sought to aggressively promote the wellness characteristics, rather than be cautious and circumspect about it. The third uniqueness lies in the claims of backward integration. PAL claims to be the only company that produces its own rare herbal plants; it has extended the concept to claim its "herbo-minerals" as unique ingredients. As a delayed response to PAL's integration proposition, Dabur began to say that it has its own "nursery" for rare plants, required for natural preparations. The fourth unique proposition was, of course, what sells in India – more affordable price. Virtually every Patanjali product is priced lower, typically 20 to 50 percent cheaper than a comparable competitor product. This compares with HUL Ayush products that are sold 2 to 2.5 times higher! Figure 10.1 illustrates the uniqueness of Patanjali.

Figure 10.1: Uniqueness of Patanjali

Generic Home Strategy

Michael Porter proposed cost leadership, differentiation, and niche as the three principal generic competitive strategies. PAL strategy involves all the three strategies. With practically no advertisement and promotion expenses, compared to competitors, and with lower organization and retail costs, PAL built cost leadership into its supply chain from the beginning. The differentiation strategy was built around the authentic Ayurvedic link through the founder Baba Ramdev. While HUL tied up with Arya Vaidya Sala for its Ayush products, the tie-up was not promoted as a strong proposition nor was it adequately reflected in product claims. The mass-niche strategy of PAL relates to the focus on health-conscious middle-class customers across mini-metros and major towns. PAL found its niche in the spiritual and yogic wellbeing that Baba Ramdev brings and the natural, Ayurvedic wellness facet that the products provide.

At the same time, PAL chose a strategy that sought to rebel against Porter's discipline on business definition. Rather than define its business around only Ayurvedic wellness and personal care products, the company decided to branch off into groceries such as atta, home care products such as detergent powders and washing bars, and breakfast products such as cereals and noodles. The emphasis was on the good old marketing approach of brand extensions utilizing the umbrella brand goodwill of Patanjali. Rather than generic product or business strategies, PAL was focussed on developing its own 'generic home strategy', seeking to convert its consumer homes into Patanjali homes! While in one perspective such a broad strategy would help in scaling up rapidly and achieve the goal of giving tough competition to MNCs on their turf, the strategy had its challenges.

Patanjali Group also acquired Ruchi Soya, a prominent player in the edible oil industry, through an insolvency process in 2019. Ruchi Soya has since acquired Patanjali Ayurved's food business. This strategic move accelerated Ruchi Soya's foray into the fast-moving consumer goods (FMCG) segment, thus expanding its product portfolio. In line with the acquisition, the company effected a name change from Ruchi Soya Industries Ltd to Patanjali Foods Ltd. The food business comprised 21 distinct products, such as ghee, honey, spices, juices, and flour, which will be integrated into Patanjali offerings. In 2022-23, out of Rs 45,000 crore yearly revenue, nearly Rs 31,500 crore (70 percent) came from Patanjali Foods.

Enablers to Sustainable Scale-up

What Patanjali achieved so far is indeed remarkable. The ambitious goals are even more formidable. Continued success would depend on three key enablers: quality, distribution, and digitization as illustrated in Figure 10.2.

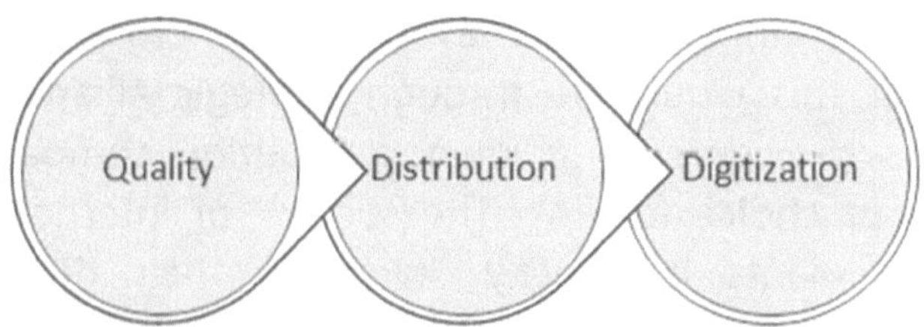

Figure 10.2: Three Key Enablers for Continued Success of Patanjali

Quality

While a great entry and rapid growth profile have been achieved by PAL, further ambitious scale-up of the order indicated would require a demonstrated quality platform.

Customers would be greatly reassured if the company sets up top-class analytical laboratories, and takes assiduous care in establishing the product specifications including purity profiles, shelf life, labelling and product claims. Given the multiplicity of testing laboratories in India due to central and State level FDA regulations, each product development and product release must conform to the best of laboratory and manufacturing practices. Quality Assurance and Quality Control as well as Regulatory Affairs and Compliance functions must be established as strong departments.

Distribution

PAL has chosen to sell its products through the franchisee model of Patanjali stores and direct online marketing. It has also tied up with Future retail group for national marketing, but to no avail as the Future Group went into insolvency. Successful FMCG retailing depends on efficient national supply chain and distribution systems. This is the greatest strength the established MNCs have. PAL must have a distribution system that would reach every store throughout India directly as the MNC products reach. Whether this would be through strategic alliances with logistics providers or its own distribution company is a matter of choice for PAL. The success of Internet online delivery giants is directly linked to their distribution efficiency. Serving India's 1.4 billion population, across all the urban and rural habitats, would require even more extraordinary distribution reach.

Digitization

The success of Patanjali organization is attributed to a very hardworking managing director, Acharya Balkrishna and a compact board (besides Baba Ramdev's organizational messaging). Exponential scaling up of the business with a portfolio of thousands of SKUs would require an organizational depth not envisaged so far by the company. There could be newer avenues open to PAL to develop a hybrid swadeshi organization structure. Digitization would be a very important organizational tool to ensure repetitive purchases and brand extensions. The current online store needs a major transformation linked to an enterprise resource planning system. PAL should have a digitization strategy and infrastructure at the earliest.

Mindfulness

Yoga is all about mindfulness and decluttering. The current business model of PAL is, however, cluttered with every product that may be conceived of for home consumption. One would feel that demonstrating volume and revenue superiority over the MNCs, rather than serving customers the way really required, became the motto for PAL. Wisdom could lie in focusing on fewer product categories that are directly linked to the principles of Ayurveda and natural organic attributes and play in such domains well. If PAL could back its foray into other products based on organic farming, sourcing and development principles, it would emerge as a strong indigenous option for the consumers. The cost leadership that currently exists would, doubtless, be eroded as the organization expands and overheads build up. Whether hyper-rapid growth or sustainable growth should be the primary driver is a matter for deliberation for PAL management.

While most analysts feel that the success of Patanjali Ayurved has been due to Baba Ramdev and his dedicated team, the truth is also that Indian customers are eager to use natural products without harmful chemicals and utilizing the science of Ayurveda. The company now needs to demonstrate the scientific aspects even more vigorously if it aims for a sustainable lead. Modern technology as well as structured management processes would help Patanjali fulfil its mission. It would be a great contribution to society if the company deploys science to identify the key therapeutic ingredients in natural products and carries out clinical studies to study and establish the correlation between the various Ayurvedic ingredients and development of immunity and wellness in the users. If Patanjali Ayurved has benefitted from the use of Ayurveda as its signature claim, it should be gracious and progressive to use its prosperity to further develop and demonstrate Ayurveda as a pristine science, and as India's gift to humanity.

Chapter 11

Nilgiris in Biyani Shelf: An M&A Gone Wrong

For those living in South India, Nilgiris has been a highly visible and iconic brand that brought style and substance to purchases of day-to-day food product, grocery and general merchandise needs of the population. The retail format popularized by Nilgiris over the last several decades ensured convenient availability of high-quality products, both third party branded and self-branded, in neighbourhood communities. As a result, the store founded as Nilgiri's in 1905, has become a household name in the South, with stores in all the five states. The company sells a wide range of products, including an assortment of dairy and bakery products churned out by its manufacturing facilities in Bangalore. No wonder then that the large customer base of Nilgiris was saddened that the heritage brand of Nilgiris was acquired by Kishore Biyani's Future Group on November 20, 2014. Future Group informed the BSE that it bought a 97.97 per cent in the retail chain. According to press reports, the deal was worth around ₹300 crore. Future Group was said to have acquired a 65 per cent stake in Nilgiris from PE firm Actis Capital and the balance from the company's promoters, the Mudaliar family. The Nilgiri Dairy Farm, the retailer's operating company, became a subsidiary of Future Consumer Enterprise, the acquiring company of the Future Group. In retrospect, it was not a great decision as Future Group went into insolvency in 2022-23.

The first attempt by Nilgiris to significantly scale up its retail presence came in November 2006 when it accepted an investment (of USD 65 million, then worth about INR 300 crore, for a 65 per cent stake) by Actis. At that point of time, Nilgiris had just about 30 stores, built over 80 odd years. The Actis investment helped the chain to grow nearly five-fold to 150 stores as of date (adding nearly 120 stores in just 8 years), besides strengthening Nilgiris' dairy, bakery, and food manufacturing operations. The exit by Actis was reported to be related to the differences between the promoter family and Actis on several issues including a move to get into large-format stores. For Biyani, the acquisition could be synergistic helping the Group expand its footprint in Kerala, Karnataka, Andhra Pradesh, Telangana, and Tamil Nadu, where it lacks a broad presence, and also through franchises. Typically, Biyani's group believed in centralized large format, multi-line stores such as Big Bazaar, and the convenience chain retail format of Nilgiris could, therefore, be quite complementary. In addition, it provides a foothold in food processing by virtue of Nilgiris manufacturing operations. In an era where even globally iconic brands such as Nokia are acquired (and eventually phased out), the acquisition of Nilgiris may not seem surprising. However, like all heritage stories Nilgiris has its lessons which the Future group should have been cognizant of, if it was keen on ensuring a new future for Nilgiris, and for itself.

Humble Beginnings

Nilgiris had a humble but focused start nearly 128 years ago! In 1905, Muthuswami Mudaliar, a mail runner, used to carry butter and dairy products from Mettupalayam at the foothills of the Nilgiris to the English living in the picturesque hill stations of Ooty and Coonoor. Later, after acquiring a butter business from an Englishman, Mudaliar moved to Ooty in 1922 and then to Brigade Road in Bangalore (now, Bengaluru) in 1936, where the Nilgiris supermarkets story really began. In many ways, Nilgiris was a forerunner of the organised retail chains one sees today. This had much to do with the visit of Mudaliar's son, Chenniappan, to the US where he saw the supermarket model at work. In 1945, Nilgiris revamped its Brigade Road store to set up a milk and ice cream parlour and added grocery and general merchandise to its portfolio in addition to the bakery and confectionery it was selling. Perhaps it was the first 'modern' retail store which also had its own private label with its dairy products. Its dairy offerings were further enhanced with the setting up of a dairy at Erode in Tamil Nadu in 1962. In 1971, its stores moved to the self-service format. At present, Nilgiris produces, procures and processes 50,000 litres of milk a day, a bulk for its own dairy products, and sells milk in some markets.

In 2006, the family owning Nilgiris sold a majority of its stake to private equity fund Actis. Actis owned 65 per cent, while a section of the family retained the rest of the stake. Actis brought in professional CEOs to run the business and the Nilgiris chain saw rapid expansion. With a franchise network comprising of more than 200 stores, Nilgiris became a prominent brand in South India that specializes in dairy and bakery by as well as other consumer staples of multiple brands. The chain followed a franchisee model of expansion where franchisees pay royalty for use of the Nilgiris brand and stock their stores through a central purchasing model. Nilgiris registered a peak annual consolidated revenue of Rs. 700 crore in the pre-Covid years. As The Hindu Business Line observed, Mudaliar could never have imagined that his small butter business would, one day, be a pioneer in modern retail; however, that is how heritage stories are made of! Like another iconic heritage brand, MTR which also got acquired with its business by an overseas entity, Nilgiris stands out as an example of how tradition and modernity can be blended on a platform of quality and convenience to keep growing, albeit at a scale just possible. Figure 11.1 illustrates the timeline of Nilgiris.

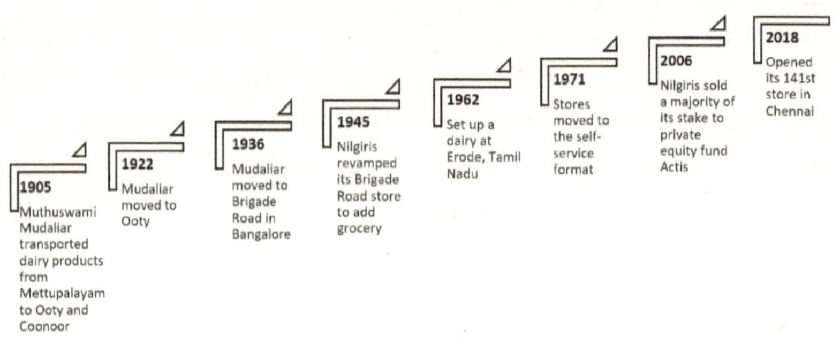

Figure 11.1: Timeline of Nilgiris

Principles of Success

Although an annual turnover of Rs. 765 crore and a deal value of Rs. 300 crore may not appear awesome in relation to the potential of the food processing sector in India, Nilgiris deserves praise for not only being a pioneer but holding on its own over a century, despite the entry of large business houses and corporate firms into convenience retailing. Reliance and Birlas as well as Heritage (besides Biyani himself) brought scale to convenience retailing but could not displace the brand equity of Nilgiris. Part of the reason, if not the whole, is that unlike these competitive ventures, the Mudaliar family knew the food processing business thoroughly through its experience. In a period when logistics were poor and the concept of cold chain was less heard of, Nilgiris brought fresh processed produce and products to the customers over long distances overnight. The decision to strategically locate the manufacturing operations with geographically contiguous expansion of the retail stores helped the chain preserve its uniqueness all through the years. Unlike other chains which have had poor reception to self-labels, Nilgiris could leverage its industrial knowledge to develop its own brands of dairy products, processed foods, and groceries, competing with other well-known brands. For Nilgiris, if the milk and butter business was its bread, its grocery and processed foods business became its butter!

The marketing approach of Nilgiris had been simple. Figure 11.2 summarises the marketing approach of Nilgiris. It facilitated self-selection by consumers with a little locational help by the store's personnel. Each store had, typically, a manager who would volunteer to find the products a consumer wants even if there would be stores personnel to do the job, lending huge customer-centricity. Nilgiris understood that the success of retail marketing would come about only when the visits to the store become a part of the consumer's regular life. By offering additional and independent selections like vegetables and bouquets within the premises, Nilgiris became a one-stop shop in one's life. Nilgiris provided support to novel concepts such as pre-cooked chapathis for lunches and dinners, and ready-to-convert batters for breakfast needs like idlis and dosas, developing local supply sources in each case. Nilgiris also appreciated that to be a retail icon one needs to be a locational landmark. The company took particular care to choose highly visible and easy to access locations for its stores. It was always keen to venture into newer suburbs, with gated communities and suburbs quoting the location of Nilgiris in the vicinity as an added plus for their real estate projects. Despite a principled approach of product quality and customer care, and despite pioneering in India several principles of retail success, Nilgiris had to accept an acquisition which points to certain other influencers on indigenous business development.

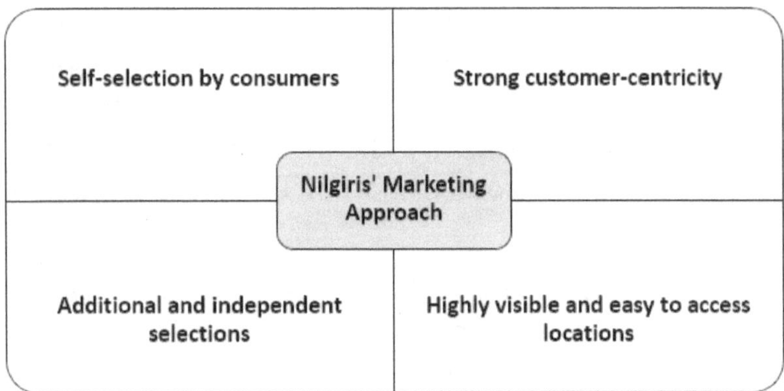

Figure 11.2: Marketing Approach of Nilgiris

Founders' Dilemma

The Nilgiris episode brings to the fore the dilemma of the founders of a successful indigenous business with high growth potential but with low financial resources to grow. This is particularly true in emerging markets such as India which provide niche footholds for initial success but encounter multiple barriers for logical scale-up. When, how and to what extent to dilute the founders' control in the equity of the firm constitutes the founders' dilemma. For Nilgiris themselves, whether the sale of a huge chunk of 66 percent in the first stage itself to a private equity firm was the right option is debatable. This one-shot approach contrasts with the Western start-up approach of diluting less (usually even cumulatively to a level less than the threshold of majority control) with increasingly higher valuations in multiple rounds of fundraising as the value gets built up. Quite possibly, even an initial public offering would have laid a more value building pathway. That Nilgiris has not been able to do that could relate another aspect of the classic founders' dilemma. The dilemma also encompasses when and how to induct as well as how to utilize professional talent to resolve the 'founders' dilemma' and build greater value in the business.

Admittedly, in founder-led businesses with thin margins it is difficult to get professional leaders who have the passion to take forward the founder's dream, balancing the founder's values and aspirations with the business potentialities and needs. Having such professional leaders, however, can be of great help in identifying multiple strategic choices and selecting the optimal ones. They could also be of significant help in developing the right financing and dilution strategies for the firm, enabling the founders to stay on longer and build greater institutional value. Many promoter-led Indian pharmaceutical companies took a calibrated approach by deploying professionals or getting the family members trained in technology and business management. There are many other successful niche businesses in the indigenous business sector in India, especially in the food processing, food product marketing, restaurant and multi-brand retail space which could benefit from resolving the founders' dilemma in a win-win manner. Hopefully, the higher management institutes such as the Indian Institutes of Management (IIMs), Indian School of Business (ISB) and SP Jain Institute which have custom courses for family businesses would not only develop solutions but also encourage the graduates of mainstream programs to enter the indigenous family businesses to upscale them.

The Failed Direction

Nilgiris could have continued its growth phase with the acquisition by the Future Group, had Future Group set its own house in order. The Future Group was by itself not too financially strong, having built up huge debts on multiple initiatives and having been forced to divest a few non-core businesses to pare down debt to some extent. It also had multiple store formats, which it was struggling to develop or consolidate. The value proposition was that the multiple retail formats would cross-sell each other's products which would also be sold through the Future Group's retail outlets such as Big Bazaar, Central and Foodhall. Even before Biyani could figure out the best way to harmonize all the retail businesses and leverage the brand equity as well as the manufacturing and marketing capabilities of Nilgiris, the Future Group itself became a non-performing asset (NPA) for the banks. There is no evidence whether the Future Group's management tried to overwhelm, if not belittle, the native wisdom of Nilgiris that had seen generations of success. Scaling up the Nilgiris plants, distribution network and retail network and adding new product development capabilities with the requisite investments in a positive frame of mind should have merited high priority.

Equally, learning from MTR and Nilgiris cases, Biyani must have put in place a virtuous cycle of incremental value creation and reinvestment in the Nilgiris business so that its organic growth impulses are preserved. Whether the Nilgiris brand was acquired by the Future Group for perpetuity or for only a limited period, the due respect and attention from the Future Group to the Nilgiris brand could have helped the Future Group to an extent. Had the acquisition been integrated harmoniously and scaled up resourcefully it could have helped the Future Group scale new azure heights (Nilgiris, as freely translated in Sanskrit) and the acquired Nilgiris business could move into a new future of sky-high potential! The stakes for Biyani and the Future Group were high. However, there is no evidence that the Future Group handled the acquisition to the advantage of both the parties. As a result, the retail business of Future Group came to crossroads sooner than expected. The lesson is that in any acquisition, the acquirer should be financially strong and managerially wise.

Chapter 12

Retailing Format and Culture: The Three Drivers for an Indian Retail Revolution

India has today several glitzy malls with shops dedicated for homegrown brands as well as multinational brands. The retail channels are a combination of single brand retail or multi-brand retail shops. Also coexisting in the normal shopping districts are standalone shops and the ubiquitous kirana shops (mom and pop stores). Quite obviously, the investments in the mall-based retailing are significantly higher than those in the more traditional ones. Frequenting the variety of shopping options, one would certainly find a step function increase in product choices but an inexplicable lag in terms of salesmanship and customer service. Even the traditional retailers seem to be less concerned about attracting customers and retaining customer loyalty. As India would continue to witness an explosive retail growth, in terms of infrastructure mainly, long term viability would depend on full utilization of such infrastructure.

The new Indian retail revolution seems to be based on mall and shop infrastructure on one hand and product portfolio on the other. Communication is largely through media advertisements and text messaging. New product launches, discount periods and festival seasons are leveraged to inform customers of product availability. The expectation of the retailers, however, largely is for customers to reach out and choose for themselves the products they need. The importance of customer service to connect the customer with the products on one hand and the retailer on the other seems to be less recognized. There is, of course, a hypothesis that the customer of today is well-informed and he or she need not be burdened with excessive verbiage on the products. Such hypothesis misses the point that customer service has a more holistic meaning to it.

Physical and Virtual

Customers are aware that there are now several options to source anything through the Internet, often at lower prices, and based on considered evaluation of alternate product characteristics. Yet, the physical format, despite its price premium, offers one unique advantage of person to person contact and a conversation to help the customer. The physical malls and shops of today seem to miss on this element all together. Even where product displays are provided, the emphasis is more on the customer-product contact than on customer-sales person contact. In rare cases where customer-sales person contact is enabled, the emphasis is more on meeting the sales target rather than on understanding and fulfilling the customer need. The two key influencers are the ratio of sales persons to customers and the marketing personality of the sales person.

It is important to note that while the virtual format cannot replicate any of the unique features of the physical format, the physical format can combine the best of both the formats. At an intense level, it could be providing a suite of computers and tablets for customers to first develop their short list of choices through virtual retailing and then taking them on to more focused physical marketing. At a subtle level, it could be in terms of electronic displays that stream live the high points of the shop and its products. While the virtual format can rise to the physical challenge by promising the earliest possible delivery (for example, the promise by amazon.in of a 24-hour delivery), the physical format can extend itself by promising wider access beyond what is on the shelves through in-store Internet kiosks. The key to the success of the physical-virtual combination lies in making 'browsing while shopping' feasible and pleasurable.

Retailing Format

Apart from multi brand and mono brand retailing options, category retailing options also exist. For example, Reliance has chosen to develop specific retailing channels and store formats for product categories such as home needs (including FMCG), footwear, apparel, accessories, jewellery, and electronics. Future Group also followed a similar approach, though on a lower scale, with Big Bazar and Pantaloons. Tata Group has Westside and Croma for apparel & accessories, and electronics respectively. The logic is that such segmented retailing enables focused customer groups which can be served with better product choices in each category. The results have, however, been mixed. Given the relatively high work pressures in India, it is a moot point if consumers would like to visit dedicated shops or would prefer one location for all their needs. The success of malls is perhaps attributable to the need to have one-stop retailing solution. None of these groups, however, has experimented with a monolithic retailing format such as Walmart, Safeway, Best Buy or Costco, where their own corporate brands act as mega malls.

Indian retail may experiment with one more concept of stores within stores. Large behemoths like Hindustan Unilever and P&G may create sub-stores within the stores where all their products can be offered as integrated solutions. This is a trend that is apparent in electronics with displays organized as per product categories and brands with dedicated sales personnel. It is the value proposition of brand loyalty and product loyalty that could determine the drive for, and success of, such a store within a store concept. Extending it further, these giants could have their own exclusive sales plazas or malls. There is, therefore, likely high scope for further evolution of the physical retailing format in multiple models. Whichever retailing model is adopted, the development of a marketing personality would be foundational for the retail success.

Marketing Personality

The success of the physical format depends on the marketing personality of the shop and its salespersons. Marketing personality, like all professional personalities, gets developed based on personal attributes, education, and experience. While Indian institutions are focused on developing marketing managers, little infrastructural support is available to develop the needed marketing personality in frontline sales personnel. These persons do not need statistics for market research or strategy for market penetration. They need, however, a deep understanding of consumer psychology, a thorough knowledge of product attributes, an inquisitive mind for customer needs, an empathetic approach to striking a conversation, and above all a commitment to deliver value for the customer. They are relationship managers more than sellers or marketers. Figure 12.1 illustrates the needs of marketing personality.

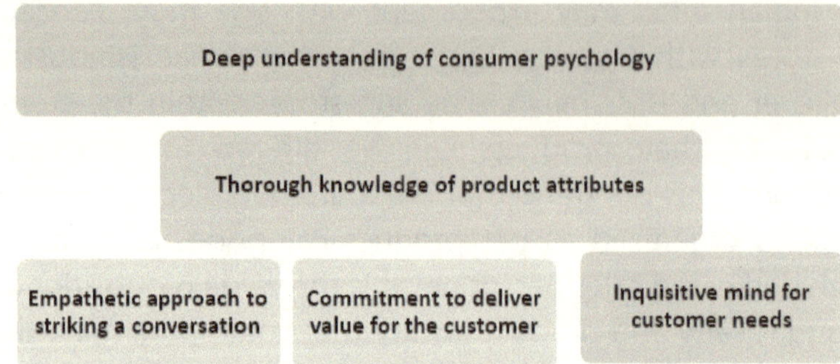

Figure 12.1: Needs of Marketing Personality

Larger hotel and hospitality chains have been quick to realize the need for frontline customer interface and have established dedicated in-house training institutions and on the job training and apprenticeship programs. Shops and malls as well as a host of other customer-facing organizations have perforce to depend on the general pool of talent from educational institutions. There are, however, only a very few institutes in India that impart the right kind of education and training for developing a well-rounded marketing personality. National Institute of Sales, founded by NIIT has been one but the country needs a lot more. On the lines of Industrial Training Institutes offering technical apprenticeship training, the country needs Marketing Training Institutes to turn out sales and marketing personnel who can support the retail revolution. A retail outlet that has persons of appropriate marketing personality tends to acquire a customer-friendly personality of its own. If retailing format would owe its success to marketing personality, the latter in turn would need customer service as the key driver.

Customer Service

Customer service has several components. The first is a warm greeting; whether a salesperson welcoming a customer to the store or a field sales person greeting the homemaker or doctor, the warmth, smile and connectivity of the welcome greeting sets the tone for a customer friendly ambience. The second is a polite enquiry on what the customer is looking for. The ability to distinguish between focused and unfocused customers as well as between impatient and languid customers is the key to guide them appropriately to the required store location. The third is to provide transparent and authentic product information; informed decision making by the customer leads to customer satisfaction. The fourth is to understand customer indecisiveness as an opportunity for need discovery rather than to force a buy through canvassing. The fifth is an ability to commit to getting the right product after the need discovery. As products range from high generic to high technology, the need to understand consumer psychology and align the store philosophy becomes progressively more important.

As products move higher in specificity and technology, as illustrated in Figure 12.2, two factors become important. The first is the ability and willingness to offer pre- and post- sales support; this is essential to ensure complete lifecycle support to the customers. The second is the ability and willingness to transform each sales transaction into relationship development; this is essential to ensure a value proposition for Indian retailing beyond products and brands. To succeed in this, the ratio of customer service executives to the customer base becomes important. Investment in people and technology would be an important component of the new retail format. People investments must focus on adequate numbers of trained marketing people. Investments in technology should focus on understanding the consumer needs better and forming a long-lasting relationship with them. When Google and Facebook can collect huge amount of information on the preferences of the site visitors simply through their browsing habits, the physical stores should be able to supplement customer databases with physical connectivity and emotional rapport.

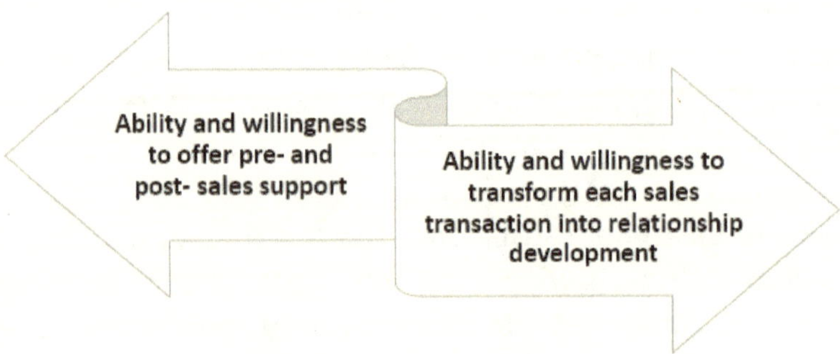

Figure 12.2: Two Factors for High-Specificity and High-Technology Products

In the emerging Indian retailing milieu, as discussed in this chapter, while the choice of an appropriate and differentiated retailing format would be a key strategy consistent with each retailer's vision, development of marketing personality and integration of customer service would be universally required to drive sustainable growth.

Chapter 13

Positional Monopoly: Ten Management Lessons

Positional monopoly occurs when a retailer is exclusively present in a geographically defined marketplace, with no other competitor with similar products or services being present in that geographic area. The classic case is that of Higginbothams, the famous heritage bookstore that has its book stalls in several railway stations of India. While books can be purchased anywhere and anytime, the exclusive positioning of the bookstalls in the railway stations without any competition helps planned and impulse buying by train passengers. The need to spend time in long journeys by the passengers and the accessibility of the bookstore as well as the captive pool of passenger-readers create positional monopoly for such bookstalls. Food catering by the sole catering agent of the Indian Railways, IRCTC, in railway trains is another example. The same can be said of sole selling shops that are situated in isolated areas, say a 'kirana' shop in the Himalayas!

Positional monopoly occurs at a product level too. Certain retailers may choose to stock only one brand of a particular class of products forcing customers to buy that product as part of a larger bundle of products from that retailer. Similarly, certain manufacturers may choose to retail their products only through certain channels (including only e-platforms). Positional monopoly makes customers forsake their brand loyalty in favour of purchasing convenience or inevitability.

Positional monopoly gets reinforced when the demand for a product is a natural and integral part of a society's lifestyle and culture, and the demand can migrate from one brand to another easily. Positional monopoly does not, however, mean that there would be unbounded demand. This chapter attempts a study of positional monopoly through the case optics of a famous sweet shop of Chennai and seeks to develop some key management insights. Figure 13.1 illustrates the instances when positional monopoly occurs.

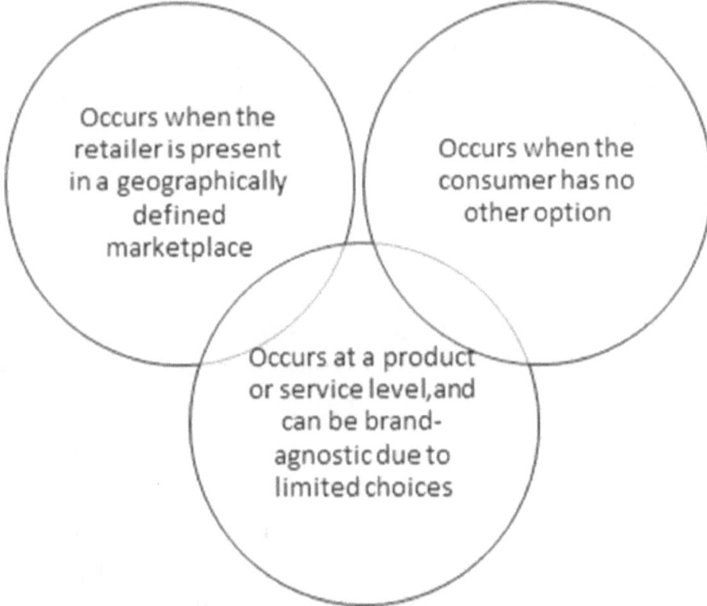

Figure 13.1: Instances When Positional Monopoly Occurs

Sweet Tooth

Most Indians have a sweet tooth. They also have a fascination for 'branded sweets' and 'signature sweets'. In Chennai, famous sweet houses such as Aggarwal, The Grand Sweets & Snacks (GSS), Sri Krishna Sweets (SKS), Archana Sweets, Adyar Ananda Bhavan (AAB), Shree Mithai, and Nithya Amirtham are some of the branded sweet houses, with an amazing array of mouthwatering sweets. All these houses have their signature sweets, Aggarwal's Jangri, Grand's Fruit Halwa, SKS' Mysorepa, Archana's Badam Halwa, AAB's Sonepapdi, Shree Mithai's Kaju Katli, and Nithya Amirtham's Motichoor Laddu are some such signature sweets. Of course, in each case, the formidable range of sweets is accompanied by an equally tasty set of snacks. In this respect, GSS probably is the best-known brand. Like geographic indicators, the sweet houses have their locational niches in important shopping districts, with distinctive taste profiles.

While the sweet houses have their proprietary and distinctive tastes and flavours, they have no monopolistic power. They have their loyal customers, but the sweet shops are substitutable too. If one were to imagine a situation where only one of these sweet houses were to be present in an area, it stands to reason that the substantial demand of the seven brands would flow to the brand that monopolises that area. That is the sweet pulling power of the distinctive sweet houses! In recent years, SKS embarked on a store positioning drive that positioned SKS retail shops in traffic flow spots such as airports and fuel delivery stations. Of these, SKS sweet stalls in the Chennai airport have been unique and distinctive, strategically positioned with high visibility. The ideal situation of 'positional monopoly' has thus been secured by SKS. It, therefore, offers an interesting case study to understand the nuances of positional monopoly. The information on shop placements and other statistics mentioned in the case may not be accurate or up to date as the airports keep undergoing spatial changes. However, the data and propositions are certainly directional and relevant.

Tested Taste

SKS sweet stalls are situated, one each, in the arrival and departure halls of the Chennai domestic terminal (Kamaraj Terminal). They are small, compact stalls offering the full portfolio of sweets and snacks, in ready-to-carry boxes as well as in open trays for on-the-spot assorted selection and customized packing. SKS has also made special efforts to cater to the perceived unique needs of air travellers by offering special multi-product packs and ready to eat foods as well. Some of these custom packs are not available in its downtown city stalls, making the airport shopping for sweets unique. All the products in the airport stalls are served in a hygienic manner by courteous staff. The stalls also provide flexibility to have packs of just one or two sweets. Customers are even provided with a generous opportunity to test the taste of different products, a unique customer-friendly feature of SKS in all its locations!

Given the sweet tooth that passengers have, the special role sweets play as gifts by travelling public, the service atmosphere created, and the general demand portability for sweets across brands, the positional monopoly should have secured a demand of several thousands of packs to the SKS airport stalls. That is because the airport, combining the domestic and international terminals, handles 15.3 lakh passengers approximately in a month, which works out to approximately 51,000 passengers per day. In marketing and sales management, brand recall and footfalls are considered essential to generate sales. SKS stalls which capture 100 percent passenger eye-views and are supported by thousands of walk-pasts are ideally positioned for maximal footfalls and hence for maximal business, reaching up to as many passengers as handled by the airport, at least in a theoretical sense.

Bitter-sweet Position

In contrast to the above positive indicators of positional monopoly, however, not more than a couple of hundred packets are possibly sold in each of the SKS stalls in the airport daily. The high brand visibility and the excellent product range of SKS in a uniquely exclusive airport positioning is contrasted, unfortunately and surprisingly, by weak sales. Applying some general management and industrial engineering principles, certain factors can be identified for the bitter-sweet result. Strategic positioning for effective sales is more important than visible positioning for branding. The stall in the departure hall is located near the gates before the check-in counters and before the security area. Fundamentally, the departing (boarding) passengers would be in a preoccupation to take boarding passes and in a hurry to undergo security check rather than purchase sweets in a languid manner. Clearly, if the sweet stall in the departure hall is in the pre-boarding waiting lounge there would be a greater possibility of relaxed purchase.

Similar positioning issue affects the sweet stall in the arrival lounge too. The arrival sweet stall is located near the exit gates after the taxi booking counters. Here again, fundamentally the arriving (homebound) passengers would be in a preoccupation to get into their cabs once the cab booking is done rather than purchase sweets delaying the homecoming further. Clearly, if the sweet stall in the arrival hall is in the baggage claim area, there would be a greater possibility of purchase while the passengers wait for their baggage. To aggravate the issue for the arrival lounge stall, the choice of sweets is on a lower scale, compared to what exists in the departure stall. The arrival stall, on the contrary, should have a much better USP than either the pre-boarding departure stall or even the city stalls (as the homebound passenger could always think of the city alternative). The lesson here is that positional monopoly by itself does not confer any significant advantage unless it is strategically secured and creatively deployed to be effective.

Multi-level Business Potential

Every business (in fact, every human endeavour) would have a maximum level (driven largely by the total customer universe), a potential level (driven largely by customer demand preferences), a constrained level (in fact, most times self-constrained by infrastructure and organization!), and an achievable level (which may work best when it is also aspirational). The case of SKS sweet stall illustrates the point tellingly. Given that 51,000 passengers pass through the Chennai domestic airport daily, the potential for SKS is to sell as many as 51,000 packs at least. However, demand preferences and perceptions on time trade-offs as discussed above set a potential business level which can be quantified only by consistent consumer research. This can lead to a figure higher or lower than the magical 51,000 mark. Let us assume in this case that it would lead to a potentially lower level of 25,500 (50 percent of the maximum). Here comes the catch; most businesses and organizations are not set up to capture even the potential business; they are self-constrained by their own infrastructural, operational, and organizational templates!

Take the case of the airport sweet stall. Combining both the departure and arrival stalls, it has four dispensing and billing customer sale points. The stall itself can accommodate only two queue lines, keep in mind also that every customer would have luggage with him or her, making the queue lines complex and making it difficult for more people to join. Each selection in the sweet store by the customer from the first look to final delivery through all the steps of iterative choice, communication, packing, billing, and payment takes on an average five minutes. As a result, every five minutes four packs can be delivered (because we have four customer points in the aggregate). Assuming that the stalls are run round the clock 24 hours (which is not a reality and is not relevant as domestic flights do not operate round the clock), we have 288 slots of five minutes each. Given the delivery rate of four packs every five minutes, the feasible number of packs that can be delivered on any day is only 1,152 which is 9.2 percent of the potential daily business and just 4.6 percent of the maximal daily business.

Various other logistical and behavioural issues would determine if even the constrained business of 1,152 packs can, in fact, be achieved. These could relate to queue lines not accommodating more than a handful of passengers, mismatch between flight times and wait times, bunching of flight and people arrivals and departures, mismatch between customer wants and sweet availability, and the need for sales personnel to have rest times and breaks. The achievable business would be clearly lower than 1,152 packs, and it is not, therefore, surprising that the sweet stall manages to sell no more than half of even the self-constrained demand. Clearly, there could be limitations (imposed by the airport authorities or the leasing charges) in terms of owning a larger space that accommodates additional display space, more queue lines, and more billing points. The Multi-level Business Model illustrates how the typical businesses are planned to inherently operate hugely below their maximum potential and what can be done to bridge such huge gaps.

Management Lessons

The objective of the chapter (and the embedded case study) is not to discuss SKS Sweets per se, a respected and efficient entrepreneurial institution in its industry. Rather, the objective is to develop certain insights as to how businesses are unknowingly planned, established and operated not to reach their full potential (and, in some cases, even to fail!). For all we know, SKS airport sweet stalls may have been established just to establish brand visibility and not with business economics in mind. Again, as with all case studies, quantitative or qualitative factors are less important than the concepts and insights such analysis brings out. There are several management lessons that can be gleaned from the case study. The same is illustrated in Figure 13.2.

1. As illustrated by the study of positional monopoly, monopoly by itself does not guarantee a maximized business. Several strategic and operational positioning initiatives are required to achieve the full potential of even a monopoly.

2. The total market ecosystem should be thoroughly studied to determine the maximum as well as other demand levels. The Multi-level Business Model suggested in this chapter provides a powerful tool for the study. It could be a real eye opener in terms of what can be achieved.

3. It is important to realize that even apparently well-established or well-run operational models tend to have significant unseen and unknown constraints that severely limit business realization. Industrial engineering and business management principles must be utilized for an introspective analysis and follow-on improvement actions.

4. Customer connect is a vital factor, whether for physical or virtual businesses. In this case, for example, a simple repositioning of stalls could provide higher customer connect and better business while signature packs, advertised in advance for their features, could minimize the transaction times.

5. There would always be additional lateral solutions even if constraints cannot be avoided in toto. For example, the sweet stall can be a part of an SKS restaurant in the airport. Or, SKS may enter alliances with select other food points in other strategic locations of the airport to display and sell at least the signature SKS packs.

6. Reticence, even in respect of known institutions and visible brands, is not an acceptable marketing option; active marketing, including market research, is essential for all types of firms and all kinds of brands.

7. In today's context, a networked business can provide a huge competitive advantage. For example, a departing passenger can be facilitated to log in his product requirement ahead of his travel which is delivered fresh at the airport neatly packaged as desired at the time of departure; or, an arriving passenger in a hurry may be encouraged to leave his request at the arrival sweet stall which is delivered at his home by one of the city branches nearer to the customer home.

8. A business maximization approach needs, more than numbers, the right business and operational insights. As can be seen from this case study, a simple retail outlet can throw up valuable management lessons.

9. The right business insights would never develop from complex boardroom models; they result from simple *'gemba'* (real place) observations by open minds. And finally, there can never be a limit to improvement; it is a continuous and perpetual process *('kaizen')*!

- Structural monopoly alone isn't enough
- Study the market ecosystem
- Analyse constraints for improvement
- Customer connection is vital
- Look for lateral solutions
- Active marketing is essential
- Networked business is advantageous
- Need the right insights for maximisation
- Improvement must be in the workplace and continuous

Figure 13.2: Management Lessons from Positional Monopoly

Positional monopoly is helpful but not sufficient for capturing the full marketing potential. Strategic marketing excellence is required to capture the full potential as brought out by the above nine management principles.

Chapter 14

Indian Retailing and Shopping: Need to Restructure Spatial Paradigms

Indian retailing industry is one of the most important pillars of the Indian economy, together with agriculture, manufacturing, and infrastructure. Without retailing, what is produced or value added can never reach consumers. Indian retailing sector is one of the largest in the world. In 2022, the retail market size in India was approximately USD 836 billion, and it is anticipated to increase to USD 1.7 trillion by 2026. It is also one of the most unorganized sectors with over 95 percent of the shops being in owner-seller format and dotted all over the urban and rural urban landscape. In FY 2022, shoppers from Tier II and Tier III cities accounted for over 61 percent of the total e-commerce market share, which is an increase from 53.8 percent in FY 2021. The growth rate of e-commerce in Tier I cities was 47.2 percent, while Tier II and III cities experienced a growth rate of 92.2 percent and 85.2 percent, respectively. Most importantly, it is one of the most valuable employment generators, providing jobs for as many as 43 million Indians. Over the last couple of decades, supermarkets and large format markets and shopping malls have made an increasing presence felt but it is unclear whether these are any more planned and futuristic than the unorganized ones, as this chapter brings out.

What is retailing (selling) for sellers is shopping (purchasing) for buyers. Shopping can be classified into two types; the essential daily needs and the lifestyle needs. It can also be classified as planned and impulsive. Availability of appropriate shopping formats is essential for generation of consumer interest and conversion of interest into actual purchase. As illustrated in Figure 14.1, the shopping and retailing process is so complex that it requires the best of management processes, from supply chain management to customer relationship management, with digital and data analytics being an integral part. While retailing is a growth engine for India with more purchasing power being placed in the hands of the burgeoning middle class, with cascade down to the indigent sections too, flux and mortality in the retailing sector are a matter of concern. There is a need for a relevant hybrid model of retailing and shopping in India. This chapter discusses a few issues and proposes some approaches based on certain examples from the Chennai retailing and shopping space.

Figure 14.1: Requirements of Shopping and Retailing Process

Off the Mark

Three decades ago, Landmark was the most popular bookstore in Chennai. Its first and most favoured store in Nungambakkam, a downtown shopping district was indeed a landmark. Landmark no longer is a store there. Landmark's other two outlets in Spencer's Plaza and City Centre have also disappeared. Many would attribute Landmark's disappearance to the emergence of online reading habits on one hand and the departure of the original promoters and indifference of the new investors on the other hand. Part of the truth is that Landmark's decline also corresponded with the decline of the host-malls. Many book lovers of Chennai feel sad about the disappearance of Landmark. Yet, a new bookstore called Starmark (of Emami Group), established in Chennai's premier and popular shopping multiplex cum shopping mall, Express Avenue has become quite a favoured place for book lovers. Even this has changed ownership to Crossword. This seems to be a case of brand ceding importance to location.

Viveks had, for decades, a flourishing retail business in whitegoods and electronic goods in Chennai, located strategically in important traffic intersections. Once famous for its store expansion and thronging crowds for New Year sales, Viveks has scaled down its operations due to lower customer visits. Tata Group has its Croma chain of electronics stores in all major cities. Of all the stores in Chennai, not all locations have good footfalls. In contrast, Croma stores in Mumbai airport seems to have the highest footfalls. Westside, Viveks, Croma and such other retail brands continue to be well known with high recall. Some of these are also well located. The declining consumer interest is, therefore, more than a matter of ordinary concern. These trends are not company or retailer specific but are symptomatic of an emerging urban shopping trend.

Urban Constraints

Surprising it may seem, Indian cities are not planned for an expansive retailing and comfortable shopping experience. Indian cities and towns are essentially mixed-use districts with residential, office and commercial entities located jowl to jowl. The concept, as in America, of segregated shopping districts, residential communities and business districts does not exist in Indian cities. The shopping districts in USA provide for huge parking areas that can cater to parking of several hundred cars, without any parking fee. In contrast, old-age shopping pioneers like Viveks have practically no parking space while the newer ones like Reliance, Croma and Girias have very limited parking space, just for a few cars. Shops located in shopping complexes such as Express Avenue and Phoenix Shopping Mall have general parking space of the respective malls but it is all paid parking space. In other words, most standalone city retail shopping places are designed only for shoppers who can put up with shopping inconveniences while in respect of newer shopping malls even window shopping would cost something!

While this restriction and bottleneck has not caused any specific migration from physical shopping to digital shopping, the potential for exploiting the full shopping potential and enhancing shopping ease is completely compromised. Logically, this restriction should lead to construction of more shopping malls with adequate parking slots and the conversion of standalone shopping spaces into residential or building spaces. Possibly, shops located on roads with high parking space (like those in Pondy Bazar) may be able to still manage but shops in arterial roads with non-stop traffic (example, Anna Salai) or in traffic intersections (like Viveks) have little hope. As several thousand jobs and lives are dependent on the continued prosperity of vintage shopping spaces, urban constraints need to be addressed. Radical it may seem, firms like Viveks may gain business if they convert their ground floors into parking lots and move businesses upstairs!

Penny Wise, ...?

The Indian urban shopping crisis is symptomatic of lack of 'design thinking' in planning and setting up social utilities. When Viveks acquired additional land space in one of the showrooms, it has chosen to use it for product storage and display rather than for parking. One of the leading hospitals was planned in Chennai with the least possible parking space causing enormous hardships to doctors, hospital staff, patients, and caretakers, besides vendors. Even when a new hospital was set up by the same group several years later, lessons of parking insufficiency were not incorporated. Most other corporate hospitals too followed in a similar restricted mould. The way facilities are planned in India, the premise is simple but not wise; land is considered premium, to be utilized to the last square centimetre to create business assets. This is indeed a myopic view of business, a view that does not put people first.

The purpose of business, depending on its nature, tends to be one or more of the following, illustratively: caring, diagnosing, curing, entertaining, provisioning and educating. People are core and central to all these activities. Unless people can access the location safely and easily, enter and exit the premises comfortably, park their vehicles securely and move around purposefully, people would be diffident to enter the malls unless essential. In trying to maximize space for business assets, firms are only sub-optimizing their own business potential. Indian service providers as well as service receivers believe in 'touch and feel' physical form of buying and selling. With India set to increase its dependence on personal transportation vehicles, the pressure on parking space is only likely to increase. This characteristic can only be protected by better spatial planning that balances people and assets.

Shopping Districts

Fundamentally, India should come up with its own native concepts of shopping districts where roads are out of bounds for vehicles and are dedicated for pedestrians. Chennai's upgraded Pondy Bazar is an example of a potential shopping district. More such districts are possible with some innovative thinking on creating parallel vehicular ways, having elevated ways, mass parking lots and comfortable connecting paths. This will not only reduce vehicular transportation, congestion and pollution but also provide a clean shopping experience to citizens. In addition, all large format shops should be asked to create free parking spaces at land level and move the businesses up (both literally and figuratively). New malls and supermarkets should, of course, come with either ample basement parking or supplemental vertical parking.

There must be special arrangements for direct-to-consumer sales by setting up farmers' markets and small and medium manufacturers' markets in major halls, public grounds and stadiums in urban areas. This would enable a significant level of disintermediation and give fillip to niche producers, for example producers of organic products and handicrafts. As new highways and industrial corridors get constructed, it should be a part of the planning agenda to construct integrated mini shopping malls and food courts alongside the highways at critical points. Planned purchase and impulse purchases could be fully exploited with such spatial planning. Taking a balanced approach on shelf space, movement space and parking space, malls and retailers can create a win-win for themselves and their customers. Figure 14.2 illustrates the ways for developing shopping districts in India.

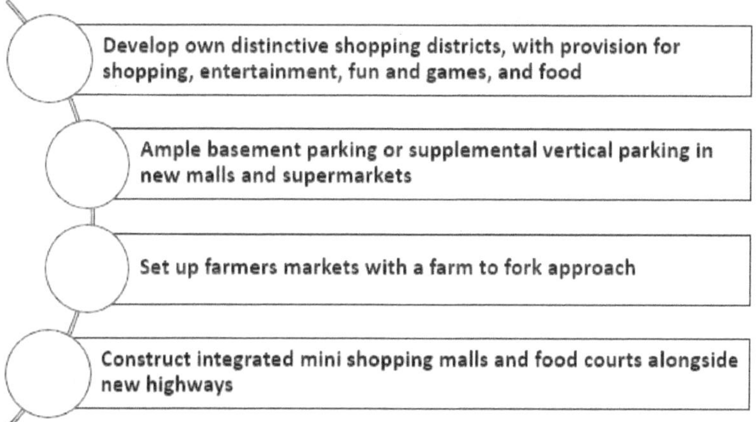

Figure 14.2: Ways for Developing Shopping Districts in India

Rural Planning

Shopping should not be solely for elite consumer needs in urban areas. Rural areas require significant retailing and shopping emphasis. In fact, rural areas offer considerable potential for creating exchange platforms and shopping districts. As development is sought to be brought to rural doorstep with the adoption of villages, it makes sense to allocate certain amount of expenditure to create producer cum marketing yards and retailing cum shopping platforms. This again would enhance urban-rural connectivity. It is today considered appropriate to create bypasses that skirt villages and towns. This is cutting them off from the highway of development. To mitigate the situation, recanalization of highways to the newly proposed yards would be helpful.

One of the many ironies of life is that space is not usually where demand is. Yet, human habitats have grown as much horizontally (moving demand to where space is) as vertically (creating space where demand is). What is applicable for human living is applicable for retailing and shopping too. Any new construction in city should provide for excellent parking avenues. Creation of multi-brand retail stores in outskirts and earmarking a space in all gated communities for shopping malls that meet captive and external needs are some needed measures. A few decades down the road, existing urban areas will connect with the existing rural areas. That should not be through existing unplanned urban chaos, exploiting every square inch of space; rather, it should be through a more scientific expansive spatial planning that puts people first.

Section 3
Marketing

Chapter 15

Four User Factors (4U's): The New Age Market Definers

Classical marketing hypothesized the importance of 4P's in how marketing is positioned and made successful in the marketplace. As illustrated in Figure 15.1, these 4P's are Product (or Service), Place, Price, and Promotion. Together, these constitute the marketing mix that would influence the success of marketing. Many of the successes of marketing (as also failures) are related to the way a company manages (or mismanages) its marketing mix. That said, not all the 4P's are equally important for all types of products and services. For example, for a product like cake, the taste, variety and freshness of cakes and the location which favours instant cake purchase are far more important than price or promotion. However, in the case of a restaurant the culinary offerings, the location of the restaurant including the parking space, the pricing of the dishes over a spectrum, and the novelty as well as the intensity with which the restaurant is promoted are all equally important.

Figure 15.1: The Traditional Marketing Mix (4P's)

Classic marketing, therefore, incorporates a three-phase approach to successful marketing comprising (i)market research to define the 4P's, (ii) a product and service development plan, and (iii) a marketing strategy that designs and executes the marketing mix. The issue with this approach is that it has been developed in the pre-Internet and pre-globalization era wherein the 4P's offered considerable leverage for differentiation. The Internet and globalization have completely altered how the products are designed, developed, and used. The 4P's while continuing to be relevant at a product level are overtaken by another set of user related factors. These are user expectations, user experience, user loyalty and user prosperity (Figure 15.2). The contemporary marketing mix moves the centre of gravity towards this set of factors internal to the user, from factors that are external to the user. These contemporary factors are discussed in this chapter as the 4U's of marketing in the Internet era.

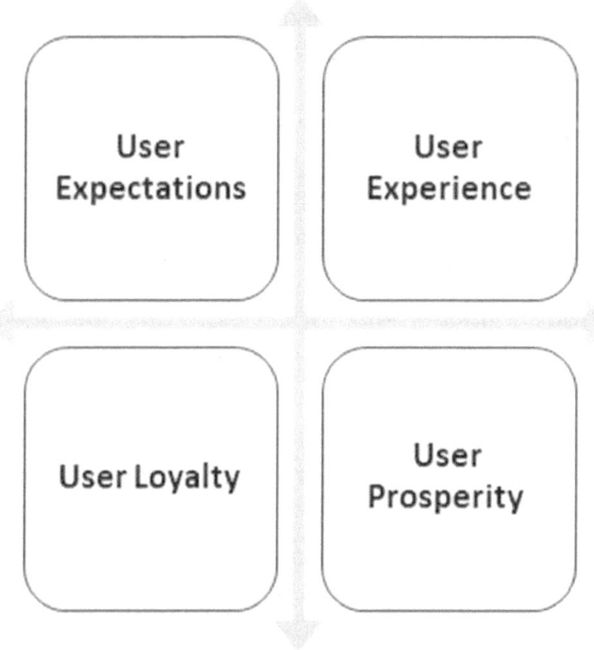

Figure 15.2: The New Supplemental Marketing Mix (4U's)

User Expectations

The earlier era required companies to deploy a posse of market researchers to approach potential customers with sets of questions and hypotheses and develop a required product or service profile based on the research. Today's user, however, is much more well informed of what is likely to emerge out of technological trends and even has a better awareness of his or her own expectations. A plethora of industry exhibitions and events as well as company announcements and indications build up user expectations. Today's product development tries to lead rather than follow any latent consumer needs. User expectations are set ahead of product launches than as a result of product launches. As companies outline their emerging technologies and future products far ahead of launch, user expectations also build up exponentially. There are several examples of such lead times.

Even the sober automobile industry has begun announcing its models under development. Trade magazines are full of new automobile features, months ahead of the likely launch dates. Movie houses are no longer secretive about their new productions. Launch and audio events are held months ahead, with openness. Futuristic generations of smart phones are announced even as the latest ones are launched. Even infrastructure projects highlight the upcoming architectural features proudly, for example Mori Tower in Tokyo or Burj Tower in Dubai. Product definitions, ahead of launches, set user expectations. There is now a new responsibility on corporations to define what they can deliver in future, by accelerated design rather than by accidental default. The free availability of information on the Internet has immeasurably helped this process of setting user expectations, universally without any distinction of rural or urban, or even the poor and the rich.

User Experience

Products and services are governed by features and specifications which provide functionality and performance. In the Internet era, a whole new concept of user experience has emerged. Whether it is improvement of hardware or software, user experience has a whole new definition for users. There are expectations out of not only the product but out of each of the components. The expectations of an automobile user today are manifold, from the starting and gliding ease to power and fuel economy, from strength and safety to style and elegance, and from comfort and convenience to capacity and connectivity. Products of new generation technologies have even more exacting expectations; the scrolling and swiping smoothness of a smart phone must be matched by the processing and multi-tasking capability, the connectivity capability by the imaging competence and the hardware strength by the application count.

User experience, however, is much beyond features and specifications. The ultimate user experience is achieved when a product design enables the most complex operations to be performed in the most simplistic fashion. This, in turn, is achieved when innovative features of a product are capable of being handled by the user in an intuitive manner. The first use of an equipment or device must, by itself, act as a guidance manual for the user. Apple products score impressively on this nature of user experience dimension. The look and feel, and the overall user experience of any Apple device clearly set it apart from any other device. User experience is based on the designers imagining the way users are likely to use a product and converting the user functionality into user experience. This is a higher-level challenge than just designing a product. User experience, being a design factor rather than a marketing factor, it is likely that future battles in intellectual property domain will be fought on the platform of user experience.

User Loyalty

User loyalty is the third of the U factors. Promotion, the fourth P of the marketing mix, is the factor that develops a brand around a product or service, creating perceptions around it. However, sustainable user loyalty is a function of the user experience and the corporation's marketing mix, especially price in respect of products and price as well as location in respect of services, including product retailing. In general, promotion helps a firm more to switch customer loyalty than to retain customer loyalty. However, promotion also can reinforce user loyalty if it is able to skilfully weave perceptions around user experience. Promotion is more than advertising. It is simulating user experience, and connecting products and services through user experience. The emphasis of the automobile industry in advanced countries on display of vehicles, and the test drives shows how user experience can make a difference to user loyalty, ahead and independent of purchase.

There are two concepts that are at the core of user loyalty as new products, especially the new electric vehicles, get launched by the typical firm and its competitors. The first is the loyalty-retaining user experience. The second is the loyalty-retaining user price. Tata Motors has, a few years ago, launched a plan to retain customer loyalty on these two dimensions. First, it has substantially upgraded all its car models, integrating several high-end features and stylistic elements into the car models. Second, the company also presented unusual future-ready trade-in options for current purchases. In certain product categories, a third dimension of operating assurance would be required. Automobiles, white goods, and other equipment subject to wear and tear over time are particularly supported by continued after-sales service. As opposed to product-specific user experience, after-sales service tends to be a firm level capability; Toyota, for example, scores over most competitors in terms of after-sales service.

User Prosperity

User prosperity is the foundation on which marketing segmentation and market skimming strategies have been based ever since marketing evolved as a management discipline, decades ago. The real definition of user prosperity, however, must be in the universalizing of prosperity, rather than its isolation. In emerging markets, especially, the concept of user prosperity has become opportunistic and, in some cases, even exploitative. Burgeoning prices of luxury products is a clear example of this unhealthy trend. One may say that there is nothing wrong in inherited rich and nouveau rich buying an imported luxury car at a million-dollar price. One may even argue, rather speciously, that the price of an imported car which bears over 200 percent of duties and taxes helps the buyer add revenue to the government exchequer! The argument is intrinsically flawed because not only such purchases increase conspicuous extravagance but also reduce employment generation. The purchase of one such large car takes away from the hands of the purchaser the power to purchase as many as three to five cars or use the money thus released for other productive purposes and generate additional employment.

This trend of extravagance is becoming rampant across ages and generations, unfortunately. A sum of Rs. 40,000 to Rs. 80,000 represents one equated monthly instalment (EMI) on a home loan of a young person, depending on the nature of the apartment. In this age, the typical young person of Young India is willing to sacrifice one EMI every year on a smart phone! And so is a gadget-enslaved older generation that is following such a trend. Unfortunately, neither generation uses even a fractional amount of the 'smartness' that a smart phone possesses. Real user prosperity occurs when each product or service helps the user become more productive and thus generate more national wealth. The key for firms here is a focus on the productive aspects of technology rather than the cosmetic aspects of technology. User prosperity that gets generated out of productive technology is far more enduring than that is generated wholly out of cosmetic technology. It is important that firms and users focus on productive leaps in technology than incremental cosmetic improvements to support the market skimming strategies. It is also equally important that such productive technology is diffused into the low-end products as well so that productivity driven prosperity is facilitated across income and demographic levels.

4U's, with 4P's

Classic thinking positions the product or the service as the focus, with the 4P's as the core of marketing mix. Neo thinking must position the user as the focus of the marketing mix, with 4U's as the enablers. It is important that we realize the continued importance of 4P's of product, price, place, and promotion even as we shift the paradigm around the user with the 4U's of user expectations, user experience, user loyalty and user prosperity. The result would be an enhancement of user productivity, universally enabled alongside generation of national wealth, equitably distributed.

Chapter 16

Saturated Launch Versus Silent Launch: An Agenda of Quality and Innovation

Product launch is the critical starting point in the lifecycle of a product. Next to product development expenditure, product launch expenditure is the single largest expenditure component of a company. While the scale and scope of launch determines the scale of revenues, a splurge on product launch which is expected to provide a launch revenue boost could also have an adverse cost impact. Several options are available to the new age marketers to achieve saturation marketing through a media mix. The loudness of some of the product launches including multiple full-page advertisements raises the question if the maximal deployment of the promotional resources has become commonplace in today's competitive marketing scenario. The view could be that promotional resources are well spent in that manner to garner attention and mind share. In fact, some of the promotional characteristics of high technology products like consumer electronic products are focused more on visual aspects than on technical points. Even in respect of iPhone there is nothing more than a strong product visual and a price buyback offer in a full-page advertisement!

While this excessiveness is an offshoot of free market competitiveness, the trend of saturation and intense advertisement of product launches is also related to the shortening product lifecycles. It has probably become important for firms to aim at the fastest possible recovery of investments, sometimes in periods as short as 3 to 6 months. The movie launches of recent times which aim at not only maximum number of screens in the home state or home country but also simultaneous multilingual and multi-country launches is a striking example of saturation launches. While the automobile industry in sellers' market conditions was accustomed to pre-launch booking of cars, firms in other businesses, especially cell phone and tablet firms, are vying with each other in taking pre-orders although such industries are not exactly in sellers' market conditions. Saturation marketing for the benefits listed above carries with it the possibility of making the customers insensitive to the messaging. It is time to consider if silent marketing could be an alternative to the current trend of vocal marketing; however, prior to that, an examination of what could constitute saturation launch would be appropriate.

Saturation Launch

Saturation launch involves launching a new product through a well-conceived and well-coordinated advertisement campaign on the new product involving all the media (almost like a blitzkrieg!). Typically, it starts with teaser advertisements in the pre-launch phase and full-blown advertisements in print (newspaper and journal), radio, television, cinema, and social media immediately prior to and after product launch. In respect of certain products (such as automobiles and electronic gadgets) exposure in exhibitions of products at prototype stage itself is a given phenomenon. The benefit of saturation launch is that it captures the attention and imagination of the widest possible potential buyer and influencer base. It caters to diverse attention spans and mood scenarios, from early morning to late night exposure and flexibility of weekdays or weekend coverage. Given that each medium has its dedicated following as well as transient and random following, an exposure strategy can be designed based on product features and target customers. Saturation marketing is expressive in multiple ways; in fact, it attempts to capture the imagination of the customers through multiple human senses.

Pictorial, reading, listening, touching and simulation are the ways in which saturation marketing works. Saturation marketing can attract a potential customer to a product through pictures, educate through written explanation, convince through sound bites, motivate through feel, and integrate through experiential simulation. Movie trailers, product displays, model homes, architectural walkthroughs, self-selection options and automobile test drives are examples of how pilot experience options can be deployed by firms to propagate the features of products as an effective launch cum marketing experience. Next to such holistic experience, pictorial launch and marketing has been the most effective, and popular, medium of launch communication in India, even in this digital age. Sky hoardings, wall posters and wall paintings, rain and sun canopies and painted displays on transport equipment continue to be the most expressive launch media in India. Packaging and carry-bags as well as flyers and leave-behinds or product leaflets enable communication of the messages in a more ambulatory fashion. It is estimated that a saturation launch campaign on all these lines together with maintenance marketing would cost anywhere between 5 to 10 percent of sales revenue for a product that achieves a viable scale. This is not a small allocation by any yardstick. Figure 16.1 summarises the benefits of saturation launch.

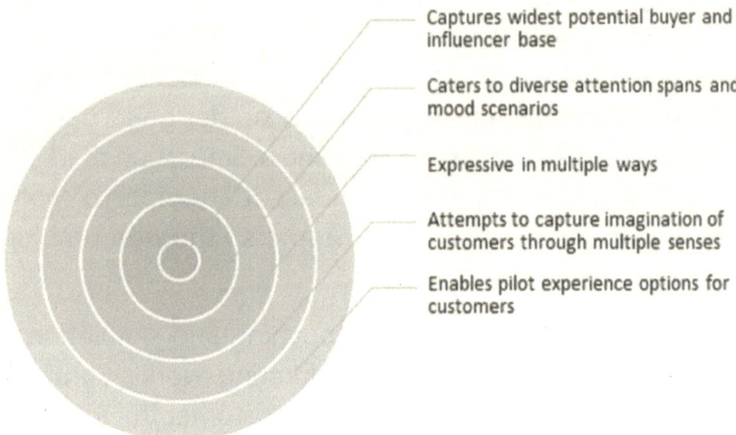

Figure 16.1: Benefits of Saturation Launch

Silent Launch

Silent launch, on the other hand, could save the firm a considerable amount of such expenditure which can be passed on to the customers in terms of lower prices for the products. However, what exactly could be a silent launch has no formal definition. A silent launch may be defined as the launch of a product without advertisement or publicity of the banal kind. One of the recent silent launches in India has been the re-launch of Air India after its ownership transfer to Tata Group. Tata Group has resisted the temptation of going saturated on this epochal event, and for right reasons. In practical terms, silent launch tends to be the only option for products launched by micro, small and medium enterprises (MSMEs) and self-help groups

(SHGs) which cannot afford launch resources. That said, a silent launch need not be, and cannot be, a nondescript launch. Silent launch could involve quiet but effective product display at points of sale with efficient sales executives explaining the product features, and wherever feasible, enabling the touch and feel experience. Display of new automobiles in luxurious shopping malls is an example of silent launch. Even in the FMCG sector, consumers are often surprised by new products which quietly take shelf space alongside established products. Some of the MSMEs and SHGs tie up innovatively with leading hotels and retail chains to gain display and marketability as a component of the corporate social responsibility of such large enterprises.

Silent launch is particularly appropriate under five conditions. The first is when the product is such a runaway hit that it needs no special publicity. An iPhone, whose attributes of use and symbolism of possession are well known, qualifies for such a silent launch position. The second is when the product is likely to be a low volume niche product whose sales would not bear a proportionately elastic relationship with the advertisement and other launch expenditure. Tata Aria, which though a good product could not capture the imagination of the market, falls in such a category. The third is when a product is launched under marginal costing principles leaving no scope for launch extravaganza. The fourth is when, as discussed earlier, the firm by its very ownership or operational structure has no resources to support launch activities. The fifth is when the product is of a neighbourhood variety; for example, local produce or local eatery. Word of mouth, including product reviews by independent reviewers, plays a strong role in the success of silent launches. Silent launches can occur in any industry though! The movie industry is prone to successful silent launches made possible by positive word of mouth.

Products which are highly visible in use (like automobiles) or in display (like televisions) and products which are a common part of daily use (like fountain pens) gain by word of mouth or ease of use communication. Some industries like pharmaceutical industry or insurance industry may find themselves appropriate for (relatively) silent launches given the regulatory restrictions. Figure 16.2 illustrates the five situations where silent launch is appropriate.

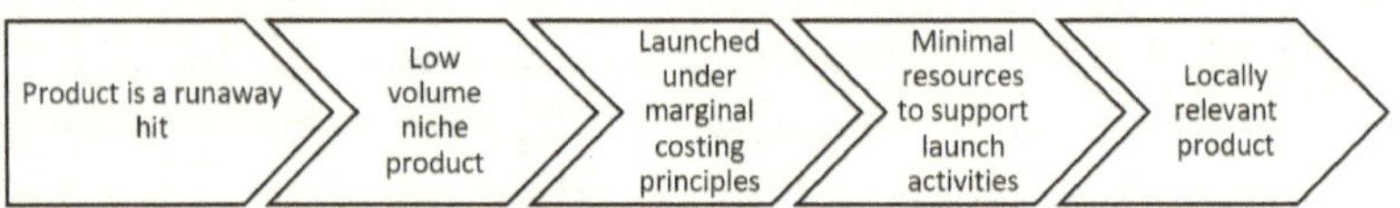

Figure 16.2: Five Situations Where Silent Launch is Appropriate

Quality, Innovation

Saturation marketing, by definition, is cost-intensive. In contemporary marketing in India, it has become cost-excessive due to several high voltage attempts to grab attention. The practice of having a celebrity brand ambassador (a successful movie actor or an accomplished sports person, for example) has been the biggest cost driver of saturation marketing, on a rather universal basis. Sponsorship of major sporting events such as Cricket IPL and Football World Cup are the significant seasonal cost drivers. Taking full front page advertisement space in newspapers and multi-fold front page advertisement space in journals and magazines has been another extravagant cost driver. Sponsorship advertisements in popular television serials or sporting event telecasts are also major cost drivers. Influencer marketing, with its related risks, is a new cost driver. In terms of sunk costs with recurrent expenditure, exclusive company sales plazas have emerged as the trend to capture consumer imagination. Big firms tend to utilize all these elements to ensure, in their view, strong enterprise and product line recall. However, does this recall automatically translate into consumer preferences for specific products? The answer is probably in the negative.

If Samsung, LG or Sony would launch a curved super high-definition television, the consumers would be interested in evaluating purchase of such a new product based on the novelty of features and the prestige value associated with such purchase rather than on whether any of the companies was associated with any great event or celebrity. It may be argued that when the market is crowded with many competitors, such high voltage and saturation marketing enables some differentiation and recall. That said, it is a moot point if there exists a direct correlation between such saturation marketing investments and actual product purchase decisions. Many of the concepts underlying saturation launch and marketing need to be validated by research on the revenue effectiveness vis-à-vis cost extravagance. In the earliest stages of mechanical revolution, in the middle years of electronics revolution and in the contemporary digital age, only quality, as evidenced by predictable and reliable performance, remains as the robust consumer draw while only innovation, as evidenced by premium, futuristic product design, remains as the unique product differentiation. As competition gets tougher, firms would do well to seriously reconsider marketing extravagance and re-evaluate relative allocation of expenditures between sustainable quality and innovation on one hand and saturation launch and marketing on the other. From the author's view, the balance must tilt strongly tilt in favour of the former! In such a quality and innovation driven scenario, silent launch would provide more value for the consumer than saturation launch could provide.

Chapter 17

Digital Marketing: Instant Satisfaction or Virtual Nirvana?

Economic and social development is based on exchange transactions; more specifically, buying and selling transactions. As part of our lives, we buy or sell something or the other most of the times. Such buying and selling transactions generally cover tangible products and services but they also cover, occasionally, intangible factors such as goodwill and brand equity. Many times, buy-sell transactions get known under different nomenclatures. A common example is a banking transaction, whether a deposit or a loan; but a closer look will reveal the embedded buy-sell nature of even a banking transaction. In certain other times, the presence of intermediaries and channel partners obscures one from the realities of buy-sell transactions. From the very established situation of physical buying and selling that has been in vogue till recently in an exclusive manner, electronic commerce has brought in completely varied hues to buying and selling. Two ubiquitous variables, one an outcome variable called value and the other a process variable called bargaining, influence the arithmetic of buy-sell, leading to either profit or loss.

The buy-sell transactions are a key aspect of human, organizational, social, and national behaviour. Like a coin has two sides, all these entities have buying and selling as the two sides of their personalities. Resources, especially natural and financial resources, are finite. It is, therefore, impossible to specialize and excel only in buying or selling. One needs to be adept at both simultaneously. Organizations tend to believe that buyers and sellers have characteristics that are different and differentiated; rarely one does see a head of procurement becoming a head of sales, and vice versa! There are some who believe that the underlying characteristics are the same, and the differences are caused by the respective universes that the buyers and sellers operate in; the buyers operate in a limited supply pool and the sellers operate in a huge market place. In respect of a bank as an example, the buyer of a fixed deposit has only a few banks to choose from while the bank has millions of customers to sell its deposits to.

Buy-sell Characteristics

Buyers do not exhibit homogeneity. A buyer who is part of an organization tends to be methodical, seeking high quality for low cost. The same person as an individual tends to be less analytical and more emotional while exercising his or her buying decisions. An organizational buyer tends to operate within a fixed budget while an individual buyer prefers to be influenced into purchasing with relatively elastic budgets. An organizational buyer tends to be a responsible and accountable buyer while the individual buyer tends to be a responsive and self-empowered buyer. The organizational buyer is motivated to save costs and increase profits for his or her organization as part of an integrated organizational goal system. The individual buyer is inspired to fulfil needs and increase esteem as part of a diversified social aspiration system. Industrial buying and individual buying have completely different ecosystems and behavioural triggers even if the operating person is the same. Figure 17.1 compares the characteristics of a business buyer and an individual buyer.

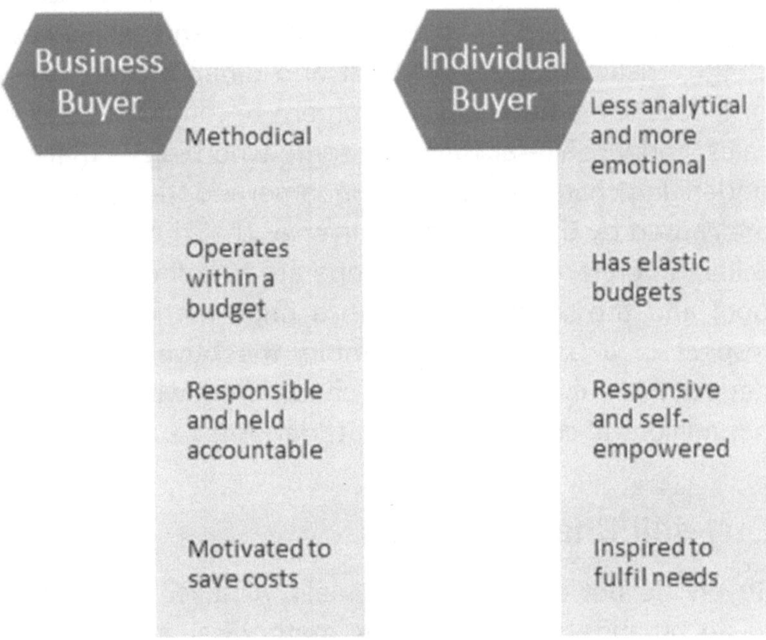

Figure 17.1: Characteristics of a Business Buyer and an Individual Buyer

Sellers also do not exhibit homogeneity. A seller who is part of an organization tends to be methodical, seeking high price despite low cost. The same person as an individual tends to be less analytical and more emotional while exercising his or her selling decisions. An organizational seller tends to operate within a budget while an individual seller prefers to be influenced into selling with a view to deleverage, save or buy something else. An organizational seller tends to be a responsible and accountable seller while the individual seller tends to be a maverick and self-compelled seller. The organizational seller is motivated to offer discounts and raise volumes or prices for given volumes, with a view to increase profits for his organization as part of an integrated organizational goal system. The individual seller is inspired to fulfil needs through better perceptions and increase esteem as part of a diversified social aspiration system. Industrial selling and individual selling have completely different ecosystems and behavioural triggers even if the operating person is the same. Figure 17.2 illustrates the characteristics of a business seller and an individual seller.

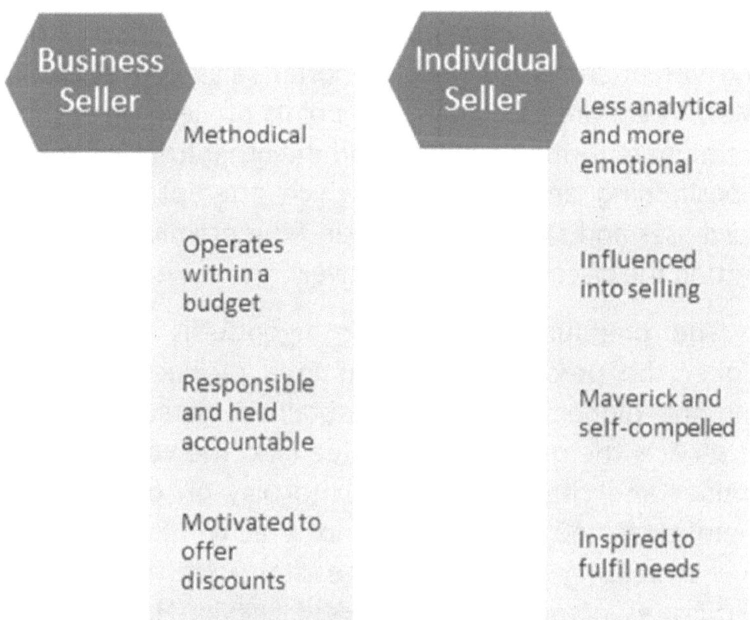

Figure 17.2: Characteristics of a Business Seller and an Individual Seller

Premium-discount-loyalty-volume mix

A trained organizational buyer and an experienced individual buyer have one common characteristic though. He or she invariably seeks premium at a discount. A trained organizational seller and an experienced individual seller have also one common characteristic in a similar manner. He or she invariably seeks volumes at a premium. Both premium and discount generate loyalty. Loyalty, in turn, generates volumes. The buyers and sellers have a convergence play in how premiums and discounts are structured for a given specification and quality level. The selling strategies of organizations and the buying strategies of individuals vary depending on how the premium-loyalty, discount-loyalty and loyalty-volume relationships are structured. It appears that within this convergence, a divergence is developing between physical stores and virtual stores (or brick & mortar sales and electronic sales). There are essentially two points of view; one from a premium repositioning angle and the other from a discount repositioning angle, both of which attempt to increase purchases and sales, without losing the premium image or getting the discount tag, respectively.

The premium repositioning hypothesis is that the higher the perceived premium in a product or service and the higher the discount obtained on such product or service, the greater is the value (and the volume). Even entities and channels that wish to play on premium are therefore forced to simulate, if not exactly offer, discounts. The increasing trend of same store gift or discount certificates of premium retailers (Lifestyle, Home Centre, Shoppers Stop) or the same channel loyalty points of premium corporations (Taj Hotels, Sheraton Hotels and Lufthansa) are designed to encourage long-term repetitive buying behaviour on premium products without sacrificing the short-run profitability that could have come with discounts on premium pricing. The discount repositioning hypothesis is that the lower the perceived premium and the higher the discount obtained on such product or service, the greater is the value (and the volume). Even channels which wish to play on discounts are, therefore, forced to continuously enhance the discount experience. The increasing trend of flash discounts by e-commerce channels, e-pharmacy chains, and Uber style cab services are designed to continuously refresh the value-volume equation, even with discounts.

Close Touch to Virtual Scan

Electronic commerce, including electronic auction, has redefined the buy-sell characteristics. The first-hand look and trial performance of physically available goods have been the solid foundations of physical buy-sell experience. These are now partially replaced with the 360-degree compasses of universal scan and analytical evaluation of endless arrays of portal-linked goods. The physical buyer has become a more focused and circumspect consumer while the digital buyer has become a more empowered and impulsive consumer. The physical seller is challenged with the task of re-establishing the relevance of brick-and-mortar store while the digital seller is challenged with the task of delivering to the promise of digital platform. The physical buyer and seller are in a state of rediscovery for the next level of interaction, with the physical sellers attempting to find other value enhancements besides look-feel (digitized shopping follow-up, for example) and the digital buyers seeking to find other credibility alternatives besides direct interface (digital price matching, for example). The digital buyer and seller are in a state of evolution with the digital sellers attempting to find other value enhancements besides discounts (same day delivery, for example) and the digital buyers seeking to find other credibility alternatives besides discounts (reseller warranties, for example).

The big corporations and the small consumers in both physical and digital buy-sell relationships are thus in a state of evolving expectations. As the chairman of Hindustan Unilever, Harish Manwani, stated once, electronic commerce cannot be wished away. The physical sellers may decide or influence their channel partners to list what can be sold through digital channels; the long-term success may, however, lie in supplementing and complementing rather than in competing and substituting one for the other. This could include own e-commerce sites or contractual tie-ups with independent e-commerce sites to make available what is not physically available in quick time. As the consumers of e-commerce sites recently experienced, what is most sought after digitally is rarely available freely. The digital buyers may patronize the digital portals for instantaneous buying gratification; the long-term satisfaction may, however, lie in bringing in some of the discipline and practices of physical buy-sell to digital platforms. This could include more voice-verification opportunities, product reservation facilities, cancellation options and product return policies. Both flash sales in digital platforms and progressive sales in physical platforms require media advertisements, a trend likely to continue for long time – until a time point is reached when buy-sell is a phenomenon that is as embedded and as contractual as a family, school, college, club, or job relationship is. A completely integrated buy-sell ecosystem, complete with digital payment systems, is what the future evolution would be.

Digital Nirvana

In the extended digital age of the future, buy-sell will undergo a major transformation. A few principles of buy-sell nirvana will determine the evolution. Firstly, all buyers will be sellers, and vice versa. Buying intentions will be to buy as of now but only to use temporarily and sell eventually. Selling intentions will be to sell as of now but only to induce repetitive buying through a variety of means, including buyback. Secondly, all physical will be digital and all digital will be physical. Buyers will seek seamless transfer between digital and physical buying and selling. Sellers will redesign and throw open their call centres and warehouses to buyers (akin to factory outlets). Thirdly, modularity and scalability will be used to extend product lifecycles. Designers will be encouraged, or even required, to use as much portability as possible. Fourthly, value will be determined by neither premium nor discount; it will be determined by exchange feasibility. Fifthly, buyers and sellers will weave themselves into integrated ecosystems in which phones, tablets and computers with banks and telecommunication providers will connect the buyers and sellers.

These principles could lead to a new ecological logjam. The more one buys the more one will sell, and vice versa. With digitization while paper and trees are saved more plastic, metal and rare earths are potentially being generated, consumed, and wasted. If this trend accelerates, as it looks to, the planet could be burdened with profligate consumption of resources and excessive hoarding of products of multiple generations. As buyers keep looking at the earliest points of sale and resale, rather than maximal points of use and extended use, and as sellers keep looking at the earliest points of purchase and repurchase, products will only multiply exponentially. Accelerated buy-sell (of a range, from physical goods to financial instruments) is seen today (and possibly for several years, and even decades to come,) as an inevitable driver of socio-economic development. This will soon be a fit case for accepting some philosophical and spiritual caveats relating to the limitations of the planet. A buy-sell nirvana could be a theme that would encourage 'optimum development–optimum conservation' (if not, 'minimum development–maximum conservation'). Nations would have ombudsmen, corporations would have offices, societies would have crusaders, and families would have thinkers who will reflect the principles of a responsible universal digital age that focuses on design optimization and resource conservation.

Chapter 18

Testing and Homologation: 'Make or Break' for Firms

The history of the automobile industry has examples of certain automobile firms occasionally failing to be in full compliance of regulatory standards. For example, there have been news reports stating that the famed Japanese car manufacturer, Suzuki, found discrepancies in its fuel and emissions testing but denied any cheating. Suzuki said that its testing method did not comply with Japanese regulations, but the results are not materially impacted. Earlier, Mitsubishi of Japan, another famous automobile leader, admitted that it had been manipulating fuel economy record of its automobile models for several years, a news which caused a serious erosion of its market capitalization. Consequent to that, Nissan of Nissan-Renault alliance announced a 34 percent strategic stake in Mitsubishi to stabilize the company. These follow the infamous emission scandal at Volkswagen, a global automobile giant, that came to light in February 2015 involving tampering with of software code of engines fitted on millions of cars to show the vehicles to be in compliance of regulatory standards. A few other manufacturers are reportedly involved in such errors, discrepancies, or manipulations. Figure 18.1 illustrates the consequences of non-compliance.

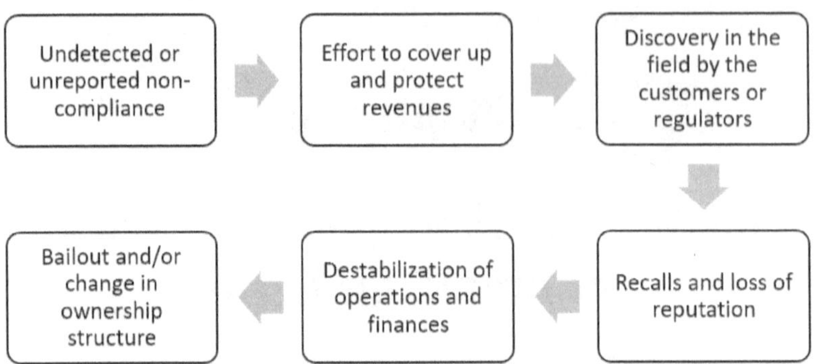

Figure 18.1: Consequences of Non-compliance

Such high visibility incidents pertaining to product quality come on top of several recalls that have been prominent in the automobile industry, covering both vehicle manufacturers (GM, Toyota, Honda etc.,) and component makers (Firestone, Takata etc.,). Nor is this a new trend. A review of available literature reveals that automotive manufacturers including the Big 3 of USA and other European makers were beset by problems of quality and non-compliance since the 1940s. India had its own incident when Standard Motor Products had to close shop in the late 1980s as a result of alleged violation of fuel efficiency norms and concessional customs duties. Most of the compliance issues pertain to fuel economy and safety. At another level, electric two-wheelers of certain models caught fire over the last twelve months either while charging or in operation in India. This has been attributed to the inadequacies in electric batteries, thermal management systems and harmonization to the Indian operating conditions. Flouting of governmental regulations is by no means confined only to the automobile industry. Nestle has been in the eye of a perfect storm in India in 2015 because of alleged non-compliance of its lead product, Maggie, with the label claim. These incidents which make or mar not merely reputation but even the very existence of a company bring out the importance of testing and homologation in industries.

Testing and Homologation

Testing is the process of evaluating a product, system, or their components with the intent to find out whether they satisfy the prescribed specifications or not. Testing is an integral part of an overall quality system which comprises a series of policies and procedures to identify compliance to specifications, identify gaps and potentially suggest measures to remediate and improve. Testing is just not an internal commercialization requirement for a company. It is required for homologation, usually of an end-product. Homologation is the official confirmation and approval by the regulatory authorities of a country that the product meets the prescribed regulations and laws besides the company's own specifications and claims. Every nation tends to have its regulatory agencies, rules and procedures, and testing agencies. A manufacturer based in India and marketing in India must necessarily meet the Indian regulations. The manufacturer must also meet testing and regulatory protocols of all the nations to which its products are exported. Testing and homologation could be proactive too. From time to time, news reports suggest that certain Indian cars fail to comply with the standards of crash test conducted by Global Car National Car Assessment Programme (GNCAP). While some of the requirements may not be mandatory, it is helpful for companies to have proactive testing and homologation programmes that are best-in-class, and futuristic.

In addition to the above, in case technology is imported, the standards of the country supplying technology need to be followed. In certain cases, as brought out above, certain desirable global standards need to be met voluntarily for establishing product and brand equity. In today's globalized and networked production system, fine-tuning design and manufacturing to meet the requirements of multiple nations is a critical requirement. The requirements of testing and homologation vary across industries. They are most complex and long drawn in the pharmaceutical industry relative to any other industry. Regulators in the pharmaceutical industry, especially of US, EU, and Japan, focus on development and manufacturing controls through physical inspections of facilities and processes. Such agencies provide product approvals based on exhibit batches, dossier reviews and inspection outcomes. In other industries, product certifications are all that are required. That said, given the critical importance of testing and homologation, and emergence of testing and regulatory agencies in various countries, companies must evolve new approaches for the domain. Some suggestions are made below.

Six Principles for Effectiveness in Testing and Homologation

In most companies, regulatory affairs, new product testing and homologation are parts of R&D setup, mainly because of the developmental nature of these activities, and the impact these three departments have on specification setting and product development. That said, there should be a strong interface between mainstream functions such as manufacturing, sales, and service with R&D and each of these with related departments to ensure that results are interpreted in terms of actual site manufacturing and field usage conditions. This collaboration needs to be more than just baton passing; it must be more in the nature of interactive handholding, while challenging the proceedings and providing solutions, based on every perspective. Six principles, as illustrated in Figure 18.2, for assuring effectiveness and integrity in testing and homologation are discussed below.

Figure 18.2: Six Principles for Effectiveness in Testing and Homologation

Developmental Quality Assurance

While quality is generally considered paramount in companies, quality is not fully understood and executed well in an R&D context. This paradox arises from the fact that most of the R&D work is experimental and developmental, and not standardised and repetitive, in nature. The paradox can be resolved through developmental quality assurance (DQA) which understands the specific uniqueness of R&D but imposes the rigour of quality on development and testing. To ensure that testing and homologation absorbs the full rigour of mainstream quality function, DQA professionals must be from the mainstream quality function but with an exposure to the uniqueness of R&D. The focus needs to be on calibration of equipment, prescription of standard testing procedures, cross-calibration of equipment, processes and conditions encountered internal simulators, external simulators, and real-life operating performance of products.

Concurrent Quality Management

The developments that happened with the automakers indicate the need for concurrent quality management as a concept that is as important as concurrent engineering. Just as quality cannot be inspected but needs to be produced, it also must be an integral part of design to delivery process, from specification setting to homologation, and performance in the real world. This requires that the focus of concurrent engineering must change from current 'first to market' to 'right and first to market.' Most designs involve incremental changes, with an eye on performance improvement or cost reduction. Some of the best practices of change management such as justifying a change and making an exception report when it fails to meet up to the expectations would help in ensuring concurrent quality management.

Global Product Development

Many of the homologation issues are both a corollary and a fallout of globalization imperatives. Globalization enables customization of products to meet different markets but it also carries certain risks when cross-platforms are used across countries. An evolved global product development system which designs products for the minimal and maximal conditions of testing and performance that are globally relevant ensures that such products are backed by globally sustainable product platforms. These could relate to meeting more stringent crash tests, using cleaner fuels, operating under punishing operating conditions, and so on. Global product development will also require a very strong global regulatory department which is well-versed in the operating conditions, and homologation requirements of different countries.

Software as Hard-stop

Today's products, especially the automotive products, incorporate more software than in the past. This trend, including deployment of new digital technologies, is only likely to increase in future. As the examples quoted in the early part of this chapter demonstrate, software is one aid for manipulation too. It is important to develop not only bug-free and hack-proof software to ensure safety and privacy of automobiles and their users but also make it traceable and manipulation-proof. CXOs in charge of R&D and product development must integrate software development and error-proofing, including artificial intelligence, sensor technologies and robotics as an essential part of R&D tool kit.

Quality as Board Audit Function

Importantly, there is a need to make quality as an important responsibility of the functioning of the board of directors of a company. All boards today have audit committees to review finances and financial governance as also monitor internal controls in a company. Keeping mala fide intentions aside, financial outcomes are nothing but a resultant of operational integrity. Quality is the sentinel of operational integrity. The link between quality and integrity is thus evident. It is, therefore, important that the boards take upon themselves review of quality as an essential board responsibility. Product testing and homologation processes in global diversification strategies must logically merit attention in quality-centric board functioning.

Organizational Positioning

The above discussion brings out the importance of testing and homologation in making or breaking the reputation of a company. As Volkswagen episode demonstrates, slippages in this vital domain can put paid to global leadership ambitions of a company. And, the Mitsubishi episode demonstrates that the very survival and ownership of a company could be at stake. There is every reason, therefore, to bring testing and homologation, from the current side play in R&D departments to the forefront of cross-functional commercialization of new products.

This requires that testing and homologation is treated as a high technology endeavour and not as a tail-end activity of R&D. This also requires that this function is positioned with the brightest technical talent which is also exposed to the requirements of different countries, and is taken up as a key delivery by the chief technology officer of a company. Integrity and competence in testing and homologation are akin to the role of safety in operations. Its effective presence is the greatest insurance for the success and sustainability of both performance and reputation of companies.

Chapter 19

Last to Market but Smart to Grow: Five Management Principles

Not every company can be the first company to hit the market, whether the product is an innovation or improvement. In today's world of wider competencies, it is not uncommon for many companies to work simultaneously on new products, model changes and facelifts. Different companies choose different months of a calendar year to launch their products. In respect of certain product categories, the launch of a new operating system or a new semiconductor is positioned as a major product upgrade although the product may remain the same in the overall look and feel. Smartphones and personal computers are products in this category. In certain other products, the look is altered, keeping everything else the same. Automobiles fall under this category. The overall idea behind contemporary market launches is to imbue certain freshness to the portfolio of the products.

Being the first-to-market is not an easy task; it requires advanced engineering, smart manufacturing, and agile marketing. The DNA of such firms tends to be unique. Over time, however, as technology becomes relatively more accessible, the market starts becoming more populated with several follow-on players. As market expands and firms can segment their markets based on unique features and combinations, the first-to-market concept could morph into first-to-market-segment concept. Not surprisingly, in a free-market economy there would be firms wanting to always enter an industry. It is easy to appreciate that the first-to-market company, and early followers will have the bulk of market share. However, firms that enter an industry despite being the last or near-last to enter also have their motivations, and must have an appropriate toolkit to succeed.

Last-to-market

Being the first-to-market is measurable and understandable as a well-merited aspiration. Being the last-to-market, however, is less measurable as it is difficult to forecast who else will join the late party. Being the last-to-market is also less understandable, and tends to be arbitrary. For example, any share less than 1 percent could be one measure in one type of industry for being the last company in the race, but even 5 percent may not be the right one for being the last company in the race in another industry. Any production level less than the minimum economical production quantity could be another measure. However, this level could vary across companies based on their overall cost structures. As costs keep coming down, the sustainable minimal production quantity and minimal viable market share should be coming down too. Still, it would beat one's imagination as to why a firm should, in a manner of speaking, be the 100th firm to enter a market when the same effort could be expended to be in the first group of entrants in another field. There are, of course, valid reasons for the last-to-enter firms as well.

For example, the industry itself could be so fragmented that there may not be much difference between the first-to-market and the last-to-market. Secondly, the entry barriers could be so low that there is enough scope for even marginal players to make an entry. Thirdly, there could be so much outsourcing and contract manufacturing occurring in the industry that being the 100th manufacturer would be easy. Fourthly, certain firms have resources that can be marginally deployed in the easy-to-enter industries without big expectations. Fifthly, managerial mind-sets of operating in highly established market segments prompt such late-stage entries. There are many examples with varied technological and marketing characteristics that confirm to the above criteria. Examples are the Indian pharmaceutical market, global smartphone market, Indian processed food market, and so on. Figure 19.1 summarises the valid reasons for the last-to-enter firms.

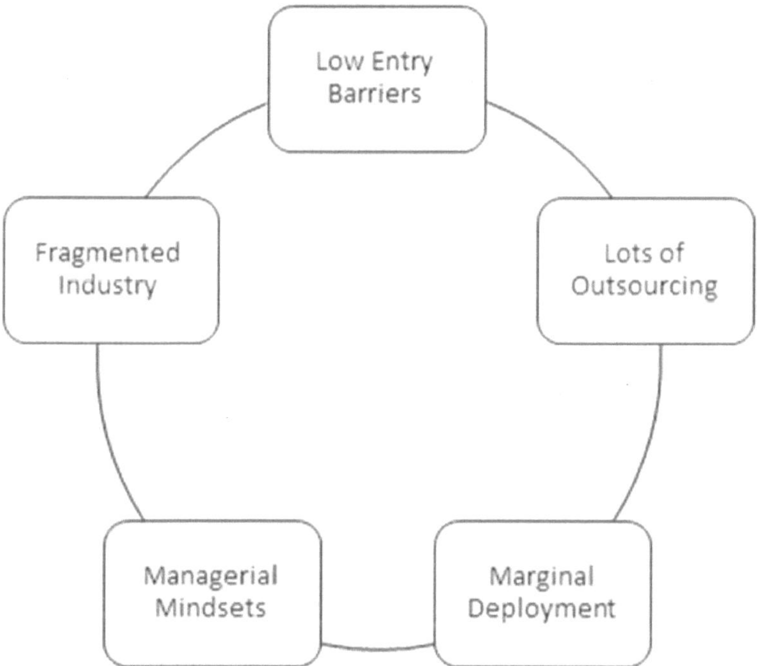

Figure 19.1: Valid Reasons for the Last-to-enter Firms

Turning the Tables

Admittedly, a pioneering company has many strategic advantages which can be further sharpened to snuff out competition from the late entrants. These include lowering of prices, cross-subsidization, differentiation, geographical expansion, securing distribution channels, buying up retail spaces, aggressive advertising, product extensions, product innovations, market segmenting, sales discounts, service offerings, aggressive advertising and so on. As a result, the later one enters a market, the smaller one's market share could be, empirically. A 1995 study by Gurumurthy Kalyanaram and others in Marketing Science suggested that the new entrant's forecasted market share divided by the first entrant's market share equals, very roughly, one divided by the square root of order of entry of the new entrant. It is evident as a market gets crowded the last entrant would have miniscule market share. Yet, empiricism may not always be the only guidepost.

In normal social life, we have countless stories of backbenchers in schools and colleges becoming top rankers as well as the poor and underprivileged reaching top positions in society. A combination of aspiration and optimism, diligence and commitment, grit and energy, knowledge and application, and positioning and a bit of luck helps in such amazing accomplishments. Late entrants to industries and markets similarly have opportunities to prove their mettle and turn the tables on the incumbents. Admittedly, whatever 'magic' late entrants can spin, the incumbents can also carry out with their superior resources and manage to maintain or expand their lead. However, performance is not always only a function of increasing size and scale. Incumbency also leads to complacency of invincibility while late entry is backed by the passion of the underdog to upstage the favourite!

Late Entrants

Late entrants are of two types. The first type is a well-endowed corporation which has decided to make a belated entry into an industry which is already catered to by the existing players. Entry of Reliance Jio into telecommunication services is an example. Such companies have all the resources to achieve any of the typical pioneering advantages despite the late entry and secure a market space. Such firms are not a subject of this chapter. The second type is a humbler entity or individual with just the necessary resources to make a modest entry. These companies may not have the resources to claim any of the advantages that the large late entrants have but are skilful in securing a market hold. Such firms typically would adopt the following five principles as summarised in Figure 19.2.

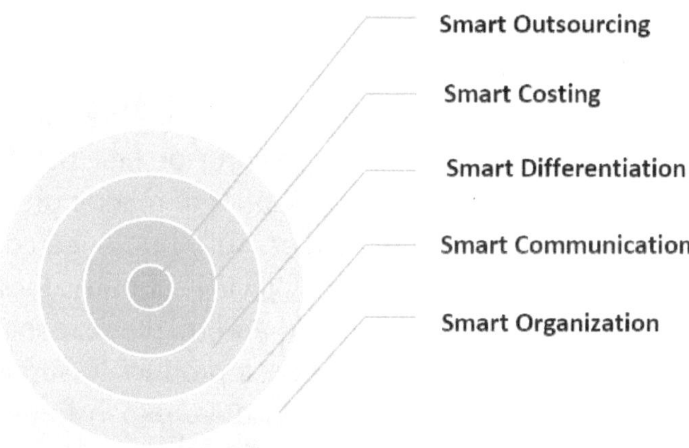

Figure 19.2: Five Principles of Late Entrants

Smart Outsourcing

Every company needs design, manufacturing, and marketing capabilities to put a product into the market place. Typically, each of these domains takes 25 to 30 percent of total available investment, aggregating to 75 to 90 percent, leaving 10 to 25 percent of the available investment for other activities. A late entrant deploys smart outsourcing in as many areas as possible to reduce the typical investment to just a small proportion of what an integrated corporation would need. The smartest outsourcer would outsource all operations, close to 90 percent, and focus only on strategy and oversight. The typical outsourcer, however, may choose to invest in one of the three key areas, be it development, manufacturing or marketing, and strategy, in addition. Smart outsourcing requires smart selection of the outsourcing partner, and providing a compelling value creation to the partner to break into the market together.

Smart Costing

It is not so well recognised that costing, and consequently pricing, can make or mar a product. Purist accountants who fully burden a product with all the functional, site and corporate overheads and management inefficiencies literally kill the new product. In a pioneering or first batch entry, there could be scope for recovery prior to market growth but for late entrants to mature markets, fully burdened costing is a sure way to defeat the very objective of entry. Strategists must realize that market toehold and market expansion are the fundamental requirements for a product to survive. It is necessary to secure an entry and drive expansion, even at a loss, to be able to recover later. Smart late entrants focus on smart costing and smart pricing, and in most cases carry their outsourcing partners along in this strategy.

Smart Differentiation

Differentiation is more common today than envisaged. Differentiation is, often, confused with having variety. Having just a few products does not lessen differentiation (e.g., as in the case of Apple) nor would a profusion of products provide differentiation (as in the case of certain Chinese smartphone makers). Amidst a smartphone clutter, Oppo's selfie phone with industry-leading 16 MP front camera was an example of focused differentiation, a few years ago. By leveraging the scientific validation of Indian herbs and spices, a late entrant to the Indian masala product market could create new formulae for differentiation. An ice cream maker may capitalize on the seasonality of fruits to develop seasonal special entries. Late entrants would need to focus on micro differentiation to make a smart entry.

Smart Communication

While incumbents, pioneers, or fast followers may focus on aggressive advertisement, late entrants must focus on smart communication to be seen as providers of products which are qualitatively feature-rich, affordable, and differentiated. Outsourcing helps the late entrants to assimilate the best-of-breed product features, from ingredients to packaging, and deliver them through multiple channels. Brand recall can be maximized with smart communication rather than just aggressive advertising. Out of several advertising campaigns, one normally recalls only those which convey a central message in a creative fashion. Airtel 4G advertisement, for example, communicated a lot without saying anything explicitly about the widest cellular coverage.

Smart Organization

In all cases, the 'organization' is important to secure and sustain market superiority. Late entrants, however, can bridge a lot of gaps with an organization that is agile, flexible, and adaptive with the right culture. Managers of a smart organization will have a first-hand feel for the marketplace as well as the manufacturing base. They should have a keen understanding of what makes customers switch brands and select outsourcing partnerships that provide such advantages. Smart Organization tends to be lean and non-corporate in structure and systems. Their relationships with product partners and retailing channels help the late entrants secure competitive advantage for the firm.

Scaling Up

Late entrants certainly have a chance to enter a crowded market, and grow with the smart formula discussed above. However, such firms must contend with the fact that the incumbents are bound to hit back after experiencing the initial disequilibrium while even later entrants would try to replicate the success of the (earlier) late entrants. The challenge for the reasonably successful late entrants is in terms of continued strategic momentum to move up to the next trajectory; solutions could emerge from new business and value chain models rather than established ones.

Simple successes lead to industry and private equity community taking notice. They are brought into a higher trajectory through mergers and acquisitions and/or external financing. The typical late entrant may thus gain huge power based on the late-entry success but could become a typical incumbent through the step-up process. That would be a bit unfortunate for the established firms that were smug in the thought that they were well-ensconced but for the ecosystem it would be a benefit. As late entrants turn incumbents, and new late entrants join the industry, and the early entrants try to retain their spaces, the whole market would expand and the product line-up would improve, keeping the ecosystem rich and bright.

Chapter 20

Indian Automobile Marketing: A Three Layer Demand Model

The Indian automobile market is one of the largest and fastest growing markets in the world, with a registered peak annual production of 31 million vehicles in 2018-19. The domestic sale comprises over 24.50 million two-wheelers, and nearly 4.0 million cars and utility vehicles, with other categories of vehicles constituting the balance. The rapid growth has put an enormous pressure on the already congested and inadequate road system in India but that does not seem to deter either the customers or the manufacturers. A combination of rising incomes and increasing number of players with a liberalized policy regime has led to the growth in the market. Compared to other developed markets, however, the scale and scope of the market has not motivated either the customers or the manufacturers to seek or introduce more relevant marketing approaches, respectively.

It is not an exaggeration to say that the automobile dealerships in India typically have showrooms no bigger than what white goods manufacturers have (after adjusting for the size and variety of products). It is also commonplace to have only a few representative models on display rather than comprehensive product range. The approach of having large sales yards through which customers can have walkthroughs and have reviews of multiple models briefly is also non-existent. Salespersons typically speak about only the broadest of the features and let the customers decide on purchases on their own. Much emphasis, on the other hand, is placed on media advertisements, often with celebrities to build corporate brand equity and develop product differentiation. The explosion of information on the Internet has equipped the customer with more information. Even so, even a better prepared customer must make do with a narrowly equipped dealership to make a purchasing evaluation without much choice.

Constituents of Demand

This chapter hypothesizes that most consumer goods, including the automobile, have three layers of demand. The first is a steady state replacement cum augmentation demand which is related to the economic factors of the society in terms of population growth, GDP growth, job growth, purchasing power, urbanization, rural modernization, transportation needs and infrastructure growth. This may be called the economic demand. The second layer of demand relates to the pull of new products and models whereby superior technology as expressed in several design and performance parameters, including the styling of the car, create additional demand, for both replacement and augmentation, over and above the economic demand. This may be called the technology demand. The third layer of demand is purely seasonal related to festive seasons, New Year sales or simply discounts. This may be called the promotional demand. In an ideal industrial situation, the bulk of the demand should be driven by the economic demand with the technology demand and the seasonal demand providing impetus to move the overall demand to the next trajectory. Figure 20.1 illustrates the three layers of demand.

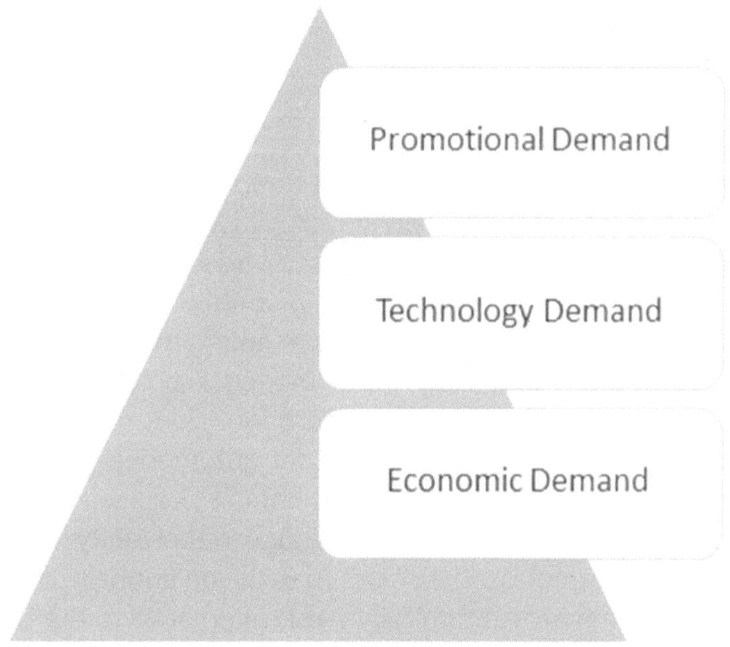

Figure 20.1: The Three Layers of Demand

In the context of India, with a population growth rate of 0.9 percent per annum and a GDP growth rate of around 8 percent, and with all other parameters following a growth trajectory, the automobile demand can comfortably cruise at a rate of around 12 percent. This has, in fact, been the trend too. However, the inter se ratios of economic demand, technology demand and promotional demand are sub-optimal. I would postulate that the economic demand must be 60 percent, technology demand 30 percent and promotional demand 10 percent of the total demand in an ideal socio-industrial situation. In India, though not empirically established, these proportions are at 60, 10 and 30 percent respectively. In other words, there is a strong manufacturer induced push to demand, which also tends to be seasonal. While the effectiveness of the marketing departments in creating such seasonal push is commendable, it needs to be further titrated in terms of its constituent push factors.

Economic Demand

The economic demand for automobiles in India, in quantitative terms, is heavily driven by two-wheelers, given the nature of income patterns, narrow road conditions, low parking spaces, and inadequacy of public transportation. Nevertheless, passenger cars have emerged as a strong growth sector aided by new models. Looking to the future, there are both gloomy and bright sides to the likely movement of economic demand for automobiles in India. The bright side is that the huge annual peak sales of 21 million two-wheelers presents a huge opportunity to the car makers to double their sales to 8 million annually if only they can offer an economically viable alternative to the two-wheeler usage. In addition, the trend to possess a second farm home or opt for weekend travels boosts the demand for a second car, especially in the utility vehicle segment. The gloomy side is that with the roads highly congested and parking spaces severely restricted, potentially the limits to growth in automobile population have already been reached. From an ideal perspective, the public transport must really be boosted in terms of both quantity and quality so that excessive use of automobiles, the two-wheelers at least, is moderated.

Given the current restraints, the economic demand can be sustained only if a significant part of it is taken over by replacement demand rather than augmentation demand. This paradigm is also closely linked to the industrialization or professionalization of the used car market, and the strict implementation of the vehicle scrappage policy announced by the Government of India. Rising oil prices, growing environmental concerns and the stricter emission norms (BS VI and beyond) would serve to enhance the demand for new cars as replacement with better performance characteristics, especially emission, fuel economy and drive. At the same time, unless more manufacturers and dealers come into the used car market and vehicle scrappage ecosystem in a big way, it would be difficult to make replacement demand a meaningful demand option (rather than a customer exigency option as is currently in vogue). The shape and scale of the replacement demand can only be sparked with appropriate technology strategies of the company, which would be reflected in terms of technology demand. In an ideal scenario again, the technology demand should funnel itself equally into replacement demand and augmentation demand.

Technology Demand

Technology driven demand is what keeps the economic demand buoyant. While economic demand grows on socio-economic factors (cars were indeed sold in India even when technologically the models were outdated), it is the technological profile of the automobile that determines the level of technology demand. The smaller size (sub-four metre length) and fuel economy of the cars are incentivized through excise duty concessions by the government. This, often, presents a skew in the development of cars with relatively price-inelastic larger models having higher import content and only the lower end, mass produced cars being indigenously manufactured from the component stage. While at first glance this may seem appropriate for India's economic and road conditions, lack of a manufacturing scale across the models does deter the Indian automotive industry from becoming globally competitive for the long term.

The Indian car industry is driven mostly by global names. The good thing about this is the ready access of models and the establishment of modern manufacturing plants. The challenging thing about this is the lack of indigenous R&D to the extent desirable. There is evidence from the track record of Tata Motors and M&M that investments in indigenous research and development do contribute to product development. Toyota Etios and Maruti Suzuki Ertiga are pointers to what customization to a market can accomplish in terms of product portfolio. If the parent corporations and the Indian subsidiaries arrive at a paradigm by which annual product updates and refreshes are developed locally and new model introductions are done globally, there could be benefit to local and global corporations as well as local and global consumers. The Indian industry should view local development as a clear strategy to achieve a larger technology induced demand, enhance replacement demand, and finally keep integrating the technology demand into economic demand. Figure 20.2 summarises the strategy to leverage the technology demand.

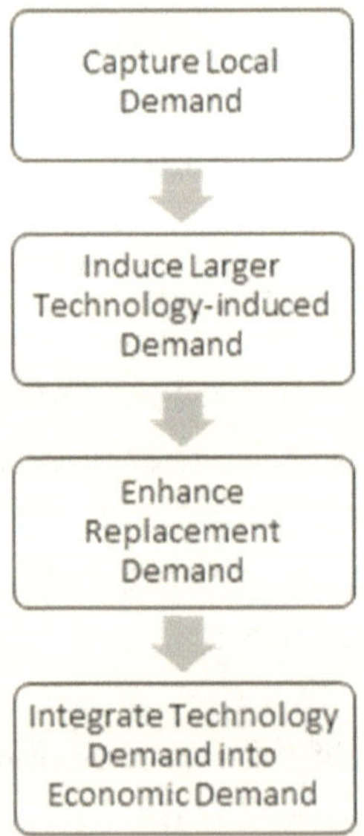

Figure 20.2: Strategy to Leverage the Technology Demand

Promotional Demand

Promotional demand to stimulate sales, clear stocks, or even pave the way for model upgrades is not unique to India. Even the most developed markets deploy promotional tactics most vigorously. The practice of effecting sharp drops in prices of current products ahead of the launch of the next-generation products is a clear trend of firms realizing that customers are alive to new technologies taking shape. That said, long festive season promotion is an approach which is probably unique to India. The months of September to January typically emerge as the manufacturers' sweet spot in terms of promoting higher demand on the plank of celebrations and auspicious occasions. When the seasonal promotion is combined with new product introductions, the marketplace can, in fact, turn lively. Every festive season, the Indian car manufacturers introduce scores of new models, some of them brand new introductions. Intensity of competition and increase of demand, coupled with lower prices could boost a seasonal increase in demand.

The manufacturers, however, must seriously consider if the Indian automotive dealer infrastructure is geared to do justice to the promotion of multiple products. As mentioned earlier, most Indian dealerships have little or no display yards as the dealerships in the West have, or the way even a space-constrained country like Japan has. The dealer showrooms can hardly display four or five models as compared to ten or fifteen which most manufacturers would have in their portfolio (ignoring the variants). The companies are also unwilling to display all their models nationally as a promotional write-off. The approach of a salesperson explaining the full features on a dedicated basis is also, by and large, absent. Most dealerships do not have customized sales and service solutions which recognize that a substantial proportion of cars in India is driver-driven. This emerges as a blind spot given the increasing sophistication of the new breed of cars that are being introduced in India. Most promotion is done by manufacturers that too through newspapers and television advertisements, oftentimes with movie celebrities as brand ambassadors. The manufacturers would need to relook at dealer economics and enable a more holistic marketing, sales, and service paradigm to integrate the dealer-level selling into the economic demand and technology demand processes.

The Three-layer Demand Model

Automobile marketing is a complex amalgam of socio-economic factors, technological factors, and consumer need factors. While the sheer power of economic development provides the motive force for the expansion of the Indian automobile industry, understanding the demand paradigm in terms of economic demand, technology demand and promotional demand as proposed in this chapter would help the automobile manufacturers, global and Indian, to develop proactive and responsive strategies that optimize the long-term demand-production models. There is considerable talent in the country, economic, engineering and marketing, to model each of the demand layers and come up with firm-specific strategies which could collectively foster healthy competition in the Indian automobile market, and enable the Indian automobile industry achieve global competitiveness.

Chapter 21

Common Branding: Uncommon Power

The research company Kantar provides an illuminating annual report on the top 100 global brand power list, BrandZ. In its BrandZ 2022 listing, the firm reports that Apple has topped the list of the world's most powerful brands with a whopping USD 947.1 billion valuation. Apple's notable strength lies in its remarkable level of differentiation and consistent diversification across its extensive range of hardware, software, and services offerings. The follower 9 brands and their valuations have been Google (USD 819.6 bn), Amazon (USD 705.6 bn), Microsoft (USD 611.5 bn), Tencent (USD 214 bn), McDonald's (USD 196.5 bn), Visa (USD 191 bn), Facebook (USD 186.4 bn), Alibaba (USD 170 bn) and Louis Vuitton (USD 124.3 bn). Over the past year, the collective value of the Top 100 most valuable brands globally has surged by 23% to reach a staggering USD 8.7 trillion. This growth underscores the significance of strong branding in successfully navigating through an increasingly volatile global economy. More than half of the total value of the Top 100 ranking is contributed by the Media & Entertainment, Business Solutions & Technology Providers, and Retail categories.

The computation of brand value, of course, is a complex subject and could lend itself to varied methodologies.

BrandZ, for example, allocates a company's intangible earnings to a brand, determines the percentage attributable only to the brand and then determines the brand earnings multiple based on market valuations, brand growth potential and brand dynamics, all using its proprietary and alliance databases and methodologies. These three factors are multiplied to arrive at the brand valuation. The Kantar analysis shows that American brands accounted for 56 out of the World's top 100 brands for the last two years, consecutively. American brands' share of Top 100's total value has increased by 24%. The number of Chinese brands in the top 100 fell by four from last year while the European brands have maintained a steady aggregate count at 18. Brands from Argentina and Saudi Arabia have made it to the list for the first time ever.

Top 100 Brands

A summary of the top 100 brands of BrandZ as listed in Kantar's web site (http:// www.kantar.com/) offers informative insights. The brands as listed by the site, in the descending order of brand power (value) are: Apple, Google, Amazon, Microsoft, Tencent, McDonald's, Visa, Facebook, Alibaba, Louis Vuitton, Nvidia, Mastercard, Nike, Moutai, Verizon, Aramco, Coca-Cola, IBM, Adobe, Instagram, UPS, Oracle, AT&T, YouTube, The Home Depot, Accenture, Hermès, PayPal, Tesla, Netflix, SAP, Telekom/T-Mobile, Qualcomm, Intel, Starbucks, Xfinity, Walmart, Disney, Marlboro, LinkedIn, Cisco, Texas Instruments, Salesforce, Samsung, Chanel, Tata Consultancy Services, Intuit, Costco, Spectrum, L'Oreal Paris, Meituan, AMD, TikTok, American Express, Wells Fargo, Xbox, RBC, Gucci, J.P. Morgan, JD, HDFC Bank, ICBC, Haier, Infosys, Vodafone, Toyota, Huawei, Chase, Bank Of America, Mercedes-Benz, Mercado Libre, TD, Siemens, Snapchat, UnitedHealthcare, BMW, Ping An, DHL,

Uber, Commonwealth Bank of Australia, Dell Technologies, Kuaishou, Zara, NTT, FedEx, Lowe's, Lancôme, China Mobile, Adidas, Target, Ikea, LIC, Budweiser, AIA, KFC, Adyen, Xiaomi, Aldi, Airbnb, and Morgan Stanley.

The Kantar Sustainability BrandZ Index highlights Microsoft, Zara, and IBM as the leading brands in terms of sustainability, which accounts for 3% of brand equity and is expected to increase. Tesla is a notable success story, rising to No. 29 from No. 47, reflecting the growth in the sales and importance of electric vehicles globally. Louis Vuitton has become the first luxury brand to enter the global Top 10 since 2010, with a 64% growth in brand value. The index also features new entrants, such as Kuaishou, Aramco, Infosys, and Mercado Libre, from various categories. Chinese brands, such as Tencent and Alibaba, continue to hold strong, with WeChat and Douyin/TikTok rivalling the US's dominance in the Media & Entertainment category. Haier achieved a 33% growth in brand value while facing unique pandemic challenges. Four Indian brands, Tata Consultancy Services, HDFC Bank, Infosys, and LIC, figure in the list.

Corporation Versus Product

It has always been a matter of debate as to which constitutes the real brand – the corporation or the product. While the debate may not have an answer yet, it is evident from the listing that whichever corporation has achieved a complete alignment or integration between the company and the product brands has reached the top of the top-ranking list. Apple and Google as well as Microsoft and IBM, AT&T and Vodafone, and McDonald's and Coca Cola are proof enough of this. However, this seems to apply more in technology and fast-food space, where there is intense customer contact, than in basic and other infrastructure sectors such as oil. By the same token, banking and financial sectors which tend to have an integration of the corporate and product brand, should have ranked higher; however, their low ranking could be due to the aftermath of the global meltdown and the role of global banks and financial institutions in that. Companies such as GE, Toyota, Samsung, and Sony, each of which has a powerful corporate brand as well as several product brands, seem to have slipped a tad. More powerful integration of corporate and product brands is being attempted by these firms to reassert their overall brand power. Figure 21.1 summarises corporation versus product branding.

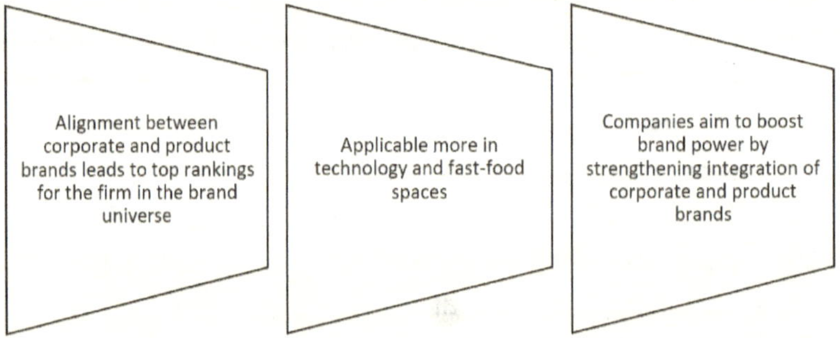

Figure 21.1: Corporation versus Product Branding

A comparison of the BrandZ 2022 report with the previous BrandZ reports brings out the relentless march of technology and growth of Internet behemoths in global brand power. Apple has regained its top spot in the BrandZ global ranking that it last held in 2015. Apple stands out even among the top brands due to its high level of differentiation and control. By manufacturing its flagship processing units in-house, Apple has gained greater pricing power and logistical flexibility in the market. Apple's hardware advancements have enabled breakthroughs in computing speed and camera processing, which are then effectively communicated by its best-in-class marketing communications team. In the regulatory landscape, Apple's new data-collection policies for its iOS software have significantly impacted the advertising and social media industries. Google has risen to the number two spot, with 79% year-on-year growth, making it the third-fastest riser in the Global Top 100. Amazon has fallen to third place after Apple and Google's exceptional growth figures allowed them to leapfrog the retail giant. Microsoft remains at the number four spot, thriving as the world's most valuable Business Services brand under the CEO Satya Nadella's leadership. Despite tech brands remaining a dominant force in the Kantar BrandZ Top 10, they are more susceptible to regulatory headwinds than brands in other categories. Nonetheless, nine brands from last year's Global Top 10 have returned to comprise this year's elite upper tier of brand value, joined for the first time by Louis Vuitton at the number 10 spot.

Brand India

Several of the global brands already operate in the Indian markets. As a result, the country brand power would have been computed into the global brand power in a nominal manner. That said, once the Indian economy reaches the super power status it is likely that Indian regional brand power would be a major proportion of the global brand power. That expectation, however, is of little consolation for a country which has built an impressive product range of its own in various sectors. Notably, several FMCG, pharmaceutical, automobile, oil, infrastructure, airways, banking, steel, and other basic industry brands have built up a brand momentum of their own and must therefore qualify for global competition. The acquisition of certain Indian brands in the 1970s and in the 2010s and 2020s by multinational corporations in fields as diverse as beverages and pharmaceuticals points to the importance of building brand equity. India Inc must give a serious thought to enhancing the scale, scope and reach of Indian brands so that they could figure in the global brand listing more prominently. It would appear that at least 3 to 5 brands in each of the important sectors of the Indian economy can make it to the global league of top 500 powerful brands by 2035.

The question then is the basis on which a true and sustainable Brand India can be built. A hypothesis is that Brand India would need to be built not only on the arithmetic of sales and reach but also on something that would be more intrinsic to the Indian market. From design to delivery, there could be ways in which an Indian hue can create a distinctive Indian brand. While Tata Motors, Titan, Taj and ITC hotels are examples of Indian corporations building globally visible brands, Toyota Innova MUV, Nissan Micra and Hyundai Santro are examples of customized Indian designs being generated by multinational corporations with global visibility. Particularly, in areas where India has natural comparative advantage such as basmati rice, jewellery, clothing, herbs, spices, tea and coffee, and more recently market-scale advantage such as steel, automobiles and devices, creation of Brand India would be desirable and feasible. To be able to do this, Indian corporations would need to integrate modern technology with native heritage, and achieve higher levels of product quality and service delivery. As it takes time for the products to come on to their own in the global branding arena, the high brand power of the Indian corporate groups needs to be utilized for the purpose.

Unified Versus Split Branding

The strategy of branding has a significant impact on the power a brand will be ultimately able to generate. Empathetic and evocative naming of brands provides great connectivity to the user. Indian truck and bus maker Ashok Leyland named its medium duty truck as Comet and medium duty bus as Viking in its early years, a branding which has grown from strength to strength over the decades due to the simplicity and connectivity. So has been its naming of its heavy duty truck range as Hippo and Rhino! Apple's simple "i" became universally evocative for a range of gadgets. Companies such as Samsung which revelled in name and brand proliferation started discovering the virtues of polarizing the branding of smartphones and tablets around the most successful Galaxy brand line-up. Brands also benefit from supplanting across product divisions to inject energy into tepid product or business line-ups. Sony successfully resorted to extension of its successful Walkman and Cybershot brands of music systems and cameras respectively, and more recently the Bravia TV brand to reenergize its cell phone range. On the other hand, Nokia, once a market leader in cell phones, slipped in leadership with unhelpful operating systems and impersonally numbered brands. To qualify as an empathetic and evocative brand, the brand should have an ability to create a physical image, and usher in a virtual experience the moment the brand name is mentioned.

Companies in India, it appears, follow no unified or calibrated strategy on brand building. The Tata Group which has the highly successful hotel brand "Taj" decided to remove certain lower- and mid-level hotels from the umbrella brand. As a result, brand segmentation in perceived alignment with customer segmentation has been affected. This trend contrasts with smartphone makers spreading the high-end brands all the way down to lower price and value points to enhance user perception of prestige. The potential to establish umbrella brands is, in fact, huge in a growing economy like India. For example,

Zydus Wellness has established and grown a brand of sugar substitutes called Sugar Free. Initially, an aspartame-based formulation was named Sugar Free Gold. Later, a sucralose-based sugar substitute has been branded Sugar Free Natura. Now, a plant (Stevia) based sugar substitute has been introduced under the name Sugar Free Herbiva. It is easy to hypothesize that sooner than later, a strong umbrella brand of Sugar Free would be built up with immense potential not only as a broad-spectrum sugar substitute brand but also as a potential umbrella for a large variety of dietetics and wellness options. Clearly, different industries and different products offer multiple options, from unified to split options, to develop a larger brand power.

Uncommon Power

Brand power is a strategic hedge against the vagaries and vicissitudes of economic and business environment. A strong brand helps a company coast through lean patches with enough entropy left in the wheels of business. The iconic brand power held by Sony as an electronics super brand helped the corporation manage the opportunity miss it had on flat panel televisions until it could develop its own panels. Sony's loyal customer base was disappointed but was willing to return to its fold at the first opportunity of Sony coming up with its own flat panels. Toyota's iconic quality image has been so strong that despite the unprecedented recalls in 2009, the corporation continued to be accepted as a leading marquee brand. In fact, in the BrandZ analysis of 2022, Toyota jumped up several notches in brand power, and remains the leading global car brand. Brand power, once established, provides a surrealistic continuity to businesses. For example, despite lack of progress or even setbacks in drug discovery, a few Indian pharmaceutical firms continue to be branded as innovative discovery driven companies.

The insurance provided by brand power must be utilized in a judicious manner by companies. It cannot be seen either as an optical façade or as an easy reprieve. Those companies which have recognized the responsibility that comes with established brand power and exerted to get back to innovative track with other new product lines as well as the affected core product lines reasserted their positioning. Sony, for example, continued to innovate in gaming devices and a host of other electronics products during the time it grappled with flat panel setback, thus enhancing overall brand equity through supplemental channels. Microsoft fought back on its Cloud, Surface, and other newer platforms, jettisoning its failed mobile operating system and cell phone business. Properly strategized and prudently utilized, brand power acts like the flywheel of business, smoothing the energy flow for growth. India Inc must recognize the need to build a massive Brand India for global visibility, and work on appropriate strategies. Figure 21.2 illustrates the benefits from brand power.

Figure 21.2: Brand Power

Chapter 22

Products, Brands, and the Firm: The Five Laws of Branding

The relationship between products and brands has been an exciting and fascinating area of research in marketing strategy. As illustrated in Figure 22.1, products represent performance and functionality while brands represent experience and assurance. Typically, products build brands but once built, brands outlast products. Marketing strategy, oftentimes, must face the intriguing dilemma of new products riding on the existing brands or steering off to develop new brands. The more interesting question is also whether the firm itself represents a brand, and in some cases the product as well. In the recent years of technological innovation and marketing acceleration, the relationship between products, brands and the firm has demonstrated multiple facets. The relationships could vary across firms and industries but certain generic principles represent the essence of such relationships.

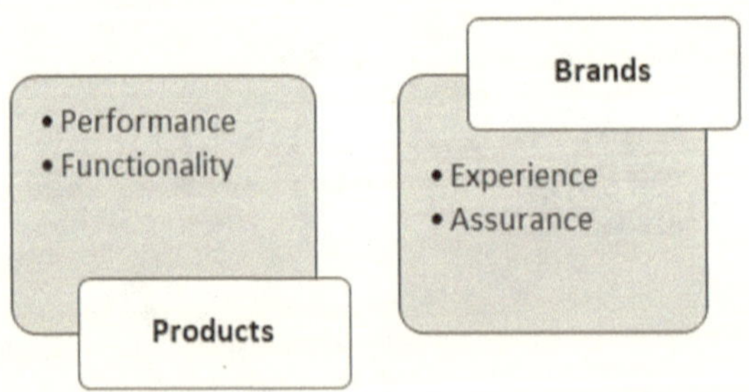

Figure 22.1: Representation of Brands and Products

There could be a view that products, brands, and firms are not standalone phenomena but are dependent on certain other critical foundational factors. For example, products may be seen to be embodiments of technology while advertising and product experience may be seen to build brands. Firms may be expected to be built not merely by products but also by a variety of tangible resources like assets and finance and intangible resources like culture and values. While this reality need not be denied, products and brands represent the final outcomes of all efforts of a firm and represent respectively the tangible and intangible assets that together drive the competitive advantage of a firm. This chapter proposes certain simple laws of product and brand performance as influencers of firm performance. Like Newton's laws of motion, these laws are simple but universal and immutable. The five laws are illustrated in Figure 22.2.

The First Law: Distinctive Products make Sustainable Brands

Products help consumers fulfil their needs. Products offered by several firms may have similar characteristics, but only certain products end up building themselves into real brands. Products get transformed into powerful brands when they offer functionality, reliability, durability, maintainability, affordability, and differentiability on a consistent basis to the customers. From an organizational process point of view, these product features are an outcome of innovation, quality and competitiveness in design, manufacture, and service. Firms should direct their efforts to develop products that offer the six-feature bundle through requisite organizational processes.

Firms with global leadership or national leadership, in any product category, reflect the above theorem. They master the organizational processes to provide the six superior product features, consistently, product after product. Brand building is a phenomenon that clearly goes beyond advertising. It is a total organizational paradigm. Toyota, Nissan, Honda, Sony, Panasonic, Apple, GE, and any of the top firms with strong brands have organizational processes that enable exceptional products. There exist no shortcuts for building brands but there exist well proven multiple methodologies to achieve functional excellence and integration. Each of the firms listed above has relied on functional excellence within organizational integration to reach its respective pole position.

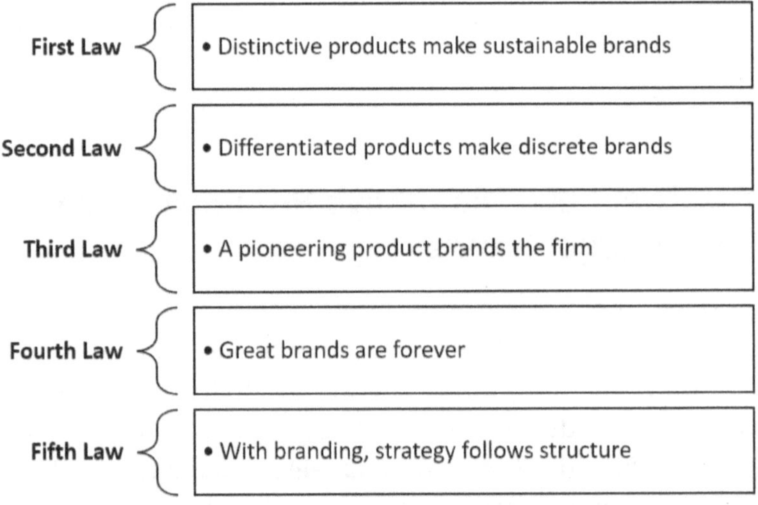

Figure 22.2: Laws of Product and Brand Performance

The Second Law: Differentiated Products Make Discrete Brands

Brands are expressions of product differentiation. However, overuse of singular brands on multiple products leads to monotony while underuse of a successful brand for product extensions wastes valuable resources. Samsung, it appears, has overused its successful Galaxy smartphone brand on multiple products. LG, on the other hand, has underused any of its brands to better represent its smartphones. Companies struggle with the right balance in brand-product nexus. Product differentiation is the key to discrete brand recognition. Weaving a unique brand around each unique design theme is a helpful approach.

In an automobile line-up, hatchbacks, sedans, crossovers, utility vehicles and off-roaders qualify for discrete brands. Each of these product segments may be known by integrated brands but each product segment can house further differentiated products, each with a discrete brand. Titan's Raga brand represents an ethnic uniqueness for ladies watches and the Edge watch brand represents slim design form factor. Both have been highly successful as they continue to preserve their unique propositions. However, Titan's sub-brand Fastrack which started as a youthful brand known for its funky designs could not attain the same brand equity despite India having a high proportion of young people. At times, sequential simplicity makes the brand-product bonding perpetual and continuously expanding.

The Third Law: A Pioneering Product Brands the Firm

Most companies have multiple products but just a few brands. However, it is left to a few pioneering firms to develop singular products with which respective brands, and even the firms, are completely identified. This is true in highly developed markets as well as naïve emerging markets. Typically, this happens when the product provides a unique need fulfilment and/or user functionality and experience like never before. Once this phenomenon happens, the world starts referring to products and use of products by the pioneering product itself. For a firm to be in such an unassailable position, it needs market-savvy innovative technologies.

Several examples, from the distant past as well as contemporary present, come to mind. Coca Cola representing sweetened beverage as a product, brand, and the firm, first in America and later globally, is a classic example. So does Xerox, the pioneering developer of photocopying machines, representing the process of photocopying as Xeroxing. Philips is still remembered as a company of bulbs. Even in contemporary times, people call searching the Internet as 'googling' rather than by any other name, with Google getting identified with its pioneering search engine product, in the triple formats of the product, brand and firm. Clearly, product pioneering needs to be the goal of firms that enter sunrise industries with leading-edge technologies.

The Fourth Law: Great Brands are Forever

The deep, and inseparable, bond between the consumer and the product as well as the brand has one downside. When the product becomes irrelevant, the brand too becomes irrelevant. That said, great brands that are made by great products have a truly mystique effect. Within reasonable generations of humans, the brands never wither away; they just remain frozen in a grateful and appreciative consumer memory to be thawed into life just at the right time. Firms that are engaged in divestments or acquisitions and firms that are phasing out technologically obsolete products must keep in mind that brands have lives far beyond the products that made them.

Sony's Walkman was synonymous with a music device running on taped music. With the obsolescence of that technology and the related product, Sony had to jettison the Walkman brand. That did not mean the demise of the Walkman brand, however – the brand came back to brand Sony music cellular phones as Walkman phones. Nissan phased out Datsun line of cars, and the Datsun brand itself, as Nissan's other automobile products became the mainstay cars for the company. However, when Nissan set out to launch a global low-cost car series, Datsun re-emerged as the ideal brand that brought back its mystique. It is no wonder that Nokia has only licensed, and not sold, its Lumia smart phone brand to Microsoft; Nokia could still do something with Lumia brand a decade hence!

The Fifth Law: With Branding, Strategy Follows Structure

One of the cardinal principles of the theory of the firm, as postulated by Alfred Chandler (1962), is that structure follows strategy. However, in respect of branding, strategy must follow structure, more specifically business-product structure. Firms, depending on the industry setting and their own strategy, require diverse business and organizational structures to deliver. This leads to a brand hierarchy that cascades down from the firm as an apex brand into multiple business brands, each of which will cascade down into further product-line brands. On the face of it, such a brand hierarchy makes branding complex but with logical definition of business and product lineage, simplicity can be achieved. It would also provide for future business optimization.

The 'strategy follows structure' branding theory is particularly relevant when different products cater to different markets. There exist certain businesses that run on discrete brands, for example, branded generic pharmaceutical businesses in emerging markets such as India which cater to different healthcare specialties; such businesses validate the theory of branding strategy following business-product structure. Conglomerates and diversified firms benefit from the structure-driven strategy route. One of the well-established ways to retain thematic simplicity in such structural complexity is to prefix the Group's name or the Firm's name to all the new businesses and product lines. The examples that come to mind readily are the Tata business structures (Tata Steel, Tata Motors, Tata Chemicals, Tata Power, Tata Consulting Services, and so on) and the Google product lines (Google Plus, Google Play, Google Drive, Gmail, Google Glass, and so on).

Lessons from Laws

Not many Indian companies appreciate the theory and practice of strategic branding. Either the firms see the brand as a target rather than as an outcome or they dissipate the potential power of branding in a crisscross maze of brands. The perfect brands are those which score a 10-10 on the dimensions of revenue and profits. Most firms, however, fail to appreciate that such a perfect branding is built on the product or service scoring a 10-10 on user experience and user trust. Apple, in several ways, comes closest to the concept of perfect brand in the above perspective. The organizational competencies and processes must blend into an optimal mix to achieve perfect brands.

Even more fundamentally, Indian companies should start cleaning up the brand clutter (for example, companies getting known by multiple and complex names, and product-brand overlaps confusing customers). Firms also need to identify areas in their business-product canvas where and how the five laws of branding postulated herein can be applied. Business leaders must see branding beyond advertising or even customer recall, essentially in terms of products and services that ride on technology, quality, and competitiveness to deliver on need fulfilment with the six imperatives that were mentioned in the preamble. It is worth recalling these six product or service attributes as being functionality, reliability, durability, maintainability, affordability, and differentiability.

Chapter 23

Products (or Services) and Firms: The Five Laws of Emotive Brand Loyalty

As the previous chapter discussed, six attributes of a product or service, namely, functionality, reliability, durability, maintainability, affordability, and differentiability, result in sustainable branding. Important as these points are, a brand is beyond these points. Many of the six points are tangible points, which a customer can experience in many "me too" products as well. A premium sedan such as Hyundai Verna may have all the six features to a rational mind but the said car as a brand may not be as powerful as BMW or Mercedes is. A brand is more of emotions, as a result of which the customer does not think of critically evaluating the above six points in respect of a product under the brand; the customer takes the presence of the factors granted. As another example, Mont Blanc pen may not necessarily score high on all the six factors but customers are willing to spend a fortune to acquire one. Such meaningful insights point to the need to supplement the previous chapter by developing appropriate constructs for the emotive aspects of branding.

Emotions and Loyalty

Emotions are strong feelings, and are characterized by positive ones such as respect, love and attachment, and negative ones such as anger, fear, and hatred. Emotions are independent of rational thought. An emotive act or product causes people to feel strong emotions. A strong brand, without doubt, is based on, and is capable of, evoking strong emotions. When Nokia decided to sell its Lumia smartphone business, several people responded more emotionally than analytically. The emotions were feelings of sadness that it marked the end of a historic Finnish brand, rather than feelings of optimism that a new owner with deep pockets and an emerging mobile operating system would infuse new life. The latter was probably based on negative emotions that Microsoft could not yet make a success of computing devices and, in addition, a concern that Microsoft Windows would never be an OS platform that could revive and ramp up Lumia. Clearly, future is somewhat imperfectly but popularly prejudged based on emotions rather than rational thought. At times, as in this case, emotional judgements would turn out to be right. Figure 23.1 explains the positive and negative emotions that a brand can create.

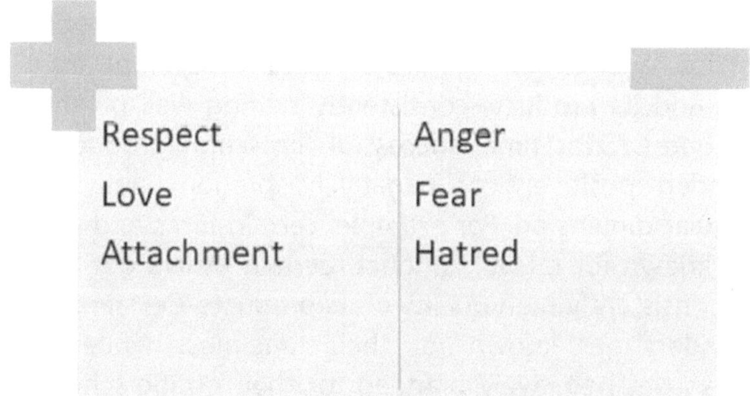

Figure 23.1: Positive and Negative Brand Emotions

At the same time, despite Nokia trailing other firms and brands in product features and customer acceptance, millions of Nokia handsets continued to be sold globally, the reason being brand loyalty. Loyalty is the quality of being faithful in support of someone or something. Like emotions, loyalty is also not necessarily based on rational thought but at the same time has necessarily a history of the customer benefitting in the past from the product or service in terms of the six factors discussed in the previous chapter. Emotions and loyalty reinforce or erode each other contextually. The objective of all marketing generally, and advertising specifically, is to cause positive emotions and build brand loyalty. That said, it is to be realized that both emotions and loyalty cannot materialize in thin air, and, on the other hand, require a record of past performance based on the postulated six factors. This chapter postulates (as summarised in Figure 23.2) five immutable laws of emotive brand loyalty to deepen the understanding of these processes.

The First Law: An Emotive Brand is "Product Plus Trust"

Certain products and firms evoke trust; a belief and an assurance that they reflect quality, dependability, goodness, service, and ethics. The trust typically develops from a firm and its products consistently scoring well on the six attributes. Over time, successful firms and products get branded positively, or negatively, predominantly on a singular dimension. For example, certain firms and groups get known for ethical conduct. Certain others get known for consistently high quality of its products. Certain service providers get known for their timeliness while some others get negatively branded for their erratic schedules. Consistent delivery on product attributes leads to brand equity and sustained brand equity leads to brand loyalty. The leading and lagging brands of the world have their instructive lessons on compliance to this law.

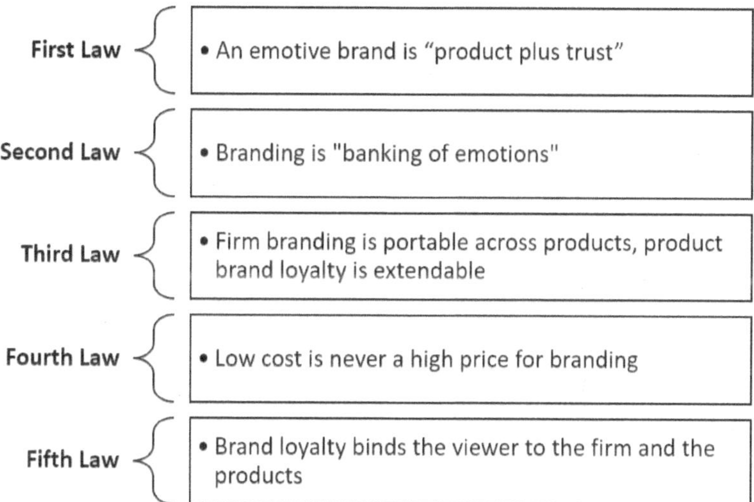

Figure 23.2: Five Immutable Laws of Emotive Brand Loyalty

The Second Law: Branding is "Banking of Emotions"

A firm must provide products of quality to be a player of any standing in an industry. Yet, some firms and their products gain a higher level of customer trust within an industry. This may be considered firm level aggregate branding. Once a firm achieves collective superiority in all of its products, occasional or isolated setbacks are taken in stride. For example, Toyota, the world's leading manufacturer of automobiles had, a few years ago, a series of product recalls in one of the most stringent markets of the world. Yet, the company could tide over the crisis rather comfortably, and even achieve higher sales in the years after. Apart from an unassailable reputation of quality, a humbled and focused response to addressing the quality concerns protected the Toyota brand. Branding is like a savings bank of emotions for the firm. The larger the account, the more secure is its future.

The Third Law: Firm Branding is Portable, Product Brand Extendable

Firms which are fortunate to develop brands tend to be anxious to leverage the success of brands to drive success of new products. While doing so, firms tend to fritter away the opportunity by an inadequate appreciation of the scope (opportunities and limits) for brand reformatting. As a principle, product branding can be extended in a product family but cannot be ported across products. Any attempted portability across product lines could be suboptimal compared to developing distinctive line-specific brands. For example, Samsung could extend its Galaxy brand to all its smart phones but its porting to a camera line-up was not as successful. On the other hand, a firm which has high firm level brand equity can port its equity into new product lines. Conglomerates and firms with high brand equity are well positioned to achieve this. New firms of Tata and Reliance groups as well as new product lines of electronic giants are indicative of this.

The Fourth Law: Low Cost is Never a High Price for Branding

Theories of marketing teach us that features with underlay of technology and overlay of luxury come with a price. Premium products demand higher price. That said, price competitiveness of a product buys brand loyalty, the other attributes remaining the same. A customer who prefers a Mercedes SUV to a Toyota Innova (also an SUV) typically has such preferences based more on the reputation of Mercedes as a luxury brand even if it is pricey. That said, the same customer who prefers the Mercedes SUV may not prefer a Land Rover SUV, despite Land Rover being a better SUV brand because of the much higher price tag that a Land

Rover has (Rs 2.5 crore versus Rs 1.5 crore of Mercedes). The practical application of the six attributes of functionality, reliability, durability, maintainability, affordability and differentiability varies from customer to customer based on the nature of the customer, the social and economic demographics and the product itself. Apart from the customer's own preferences, the overall social infrastructure influences brand acceptability.

The Fifth Law: Brand Loyalty Binds Consumers

Brand loyalty takes many forms. The reasons why a product, firm or brand commands loyalty varies from customer to customer. For someone who understands the entire spectrum of automobile industry, Toyota could be the most favoured brand for its innovative accomplishments in manufacturing management, and not necessarily because of the quality of any particular model. For someone who understands aseptic practices, a hospital that has state-of-the-art aseptic practices could command respect while for many others the association of top-notch medical consultants could be the decider. It is for this reason that some brands, "super-brand" themselves to ensure higher brand loyalty. While Aquafina and Kenley mineral (pure) water brands command brand loyalty for purity, Evion and Himalayan evoke further connect with the emphasis on bottling at source of Alpines or Himalayas as the case may be.

Emotional Connect

The relationship between a seller (the firm) and a buyer (the customer) is neither a selling relationship nor a purchasing relationship; it is one of human relationship. In an organization, for example, people may deliver on performance and may get rewarded in terms of compensation, and teams may share bonuses amongst the members; however, unless there is an emotional connect or an empathetic rapport amongst the team members, the team may not be reaching the fullest potential. Even though a sales transaction between a seller and a buyer may be a onetime occurrence (or even a periodic occurrence in respect of retail transactions), the multi-factorial emotional feel of getting to know a brand, exercising a reasoned choice, being sold with care, experiencing the functionality and after-sales service care, and having options to upgrade to next generation products all add up to building the emotional connect around a product, firm and brand.

Wise companies, therefore, do not consider their responsibility fulfilled with delivery to the retail chain; they pursue a diligent and caring connect till the point of contact with the customer, at the time of potential sale and thereafter. While a firm cannot be present at all points of contact, the firm would choose associates and partners who are aligned with its own emotional code of connectivity. The emotive brand loyalty of a firm and its products is probably the most important determinant of sustainability in a hyper-competitive market. The emotive brand loyalty does, however, get built on the foundations of the six fundamentals that characterize a product or service to the customer: functionality, reliability, durability, maintainability, affordability and differentiability.

Section 4
Strategy

Chapter 24

Customized Product Design: The Next Wave of Competitive Advantage

Exponential technological development has contributed, from the 2010s, to a massive increase in product lines and products. Companies typically run hundreds, if not thousands, of store keeping units (SKUs). The more global a company is, the greater is the proliferation of SKUs. SKUs typically define product variations to meet country and customer specific homologation needs. It is, therefore, tempting to hypothesize that there is a huge wave of customization that is sweeping the industrial scenario. Unfortunately, SKU proliferation ends up adding to complexity with variations rather than meeting multiple customer-needs with real customization. Product variations do not necessarily mean customer customization. The nature of variations, oftentimes, tends to be as per design templates rather than customer needs. Product variations, as are commonly found irrespective of product or country, tend to fall broadly under three main categories: category driven, performance driven, and price driven. There are, however, two other influencers that are esteem driven and policy driven.

Category-driven is exemplified by broad and dominant product configuration; for example, smartphone versus non-smartphone and sedan versus utility vehicle. Performance-driven is exemplified by hardware and software differences which together set performance differentials between products. Price-driven appears rather easy to understand in terms of different price points at which a product can be positioned but is more complex; specifications-driven costs and brand-driven premiums impact price. Esteem-driven is reflective of product-market niches that are created by companies. Policy-driven is the outcome of the influence of regulatory policy on product design. The preference for 660 cc mini cars in Japan or sub-four metre cars in India which qualify for lower excise duty reflect that category. Despite five such categories and influencers, and hundreds of SKUs, rarely do products get designed around customers.

Customer Choice; a Mirage?

The interests of the customer and the corporation are conceptually aligned but practically tend to be misaligned. As an example, the hundreds of apparels in retail stores are designed with certain standard sizes and ruling fashions as of the date of manufacture in mind. In fact, factory production, ipso facto, tends to promote standardization and reduce customization in any field. Reverting to the example of apparel, decades ago when there used to be no readymade apparel, tailoring represented the only and complete form of dress development, which was truly customized to the individual. In the tailoring paradigm, the consumer had the choice of selecting a cloth and getting it tailored to his or her measurements and stylistic requirements. In the current paradigm, mass production of multiple designs does not necessarily translate itself into real customer choice. Probably, the right phraseology for the current scenario is product choice rather than customer choice.

Mass production in factories, of course, vests several other advantages of quality in design, manufacture and delivery, use of superior material and methods, reliability, and adoption of global trends. Henry Ford's assembly line manufacture of a standardized car in a single colour in the 1910s represented a pioneering model of mass industrialization while General Motors' competing strategy of differentiation was an alternative approach. Figure 24.1 illustrates the advantages of mass production in factories. In contemporary times, Apple represents a Ford-like approach in smartphones with not more than a couple of products in each product line while Samsung with its scores of smartphones represents an amplified version of General Motors. Customer choice, however, is not a matter of numbers either; there need not necessarily be a proportionality between SKUs and customer choice. A simple question clarifies: Is a large smartphone equally ergonomically optimal to hold and operate for all ages and for all types of palms? The answer is a 'no', which implies that a person of a small palm has to either bear the burden of an oversized state-of-the-art phone or a right-sized smaller screen phone of lower specifications.

Figure 24.1: Advantages of Mass Production in Factories

Customer Choice Defined

True customer choice occurs when a customer can secure a product that meets his or her expectations on all specifications and at all price points. This is an awakening that is occurring slowly, but surely, even in some of the more stable category manufacturers. Luxury vehicle manufacturers such as Mercedes Benz and Audi began moving down the categories to B class and A class cars as well as towards compact SUVs to provide their customary luxury specifications across all categories and price points. Becoming a full-length manufacturer is seen as the solution to providing customer choice. Probably, this is a beginning and still not a full resolution of the trend. The concept of full-line manufacture as it exists today is one of positioning products at different price points, which almost invariably translates having a range of products from low-spec to high-spec. True customer choice, however, enables the design of a product around the customer needs, with a very open and flexible mix and match approach.

Dell, the computer maker was long seen to be a leader in customers designing their computers by selecting the configuration of choice. Even the Dell model is not representative of true customer choice. Changing the processor, adding RAM capacity or battery power, or providing operating system (OS) options and accessory choices are more in the nature of upgrades rather than product redefinition. True product definition would occur if a customer can, in the case of Dell for example, mix and match the specifications of Inspiron, Latitude and XPS models as well as those of laptop, ultra-book and tablet. Similar is the case with automobile manufacturers who try to customize marginally based on power train options or interior trim. The day when a hatchback can be grown proportionally into a compact utility vehicle at customer's choice is probably still futuristic even globally. Service industries, which are not manufacturing oriented and therefore should be better placed for flexibility, find it difficult to offer multiple services in flexible formats.

Customized Product Design

The challenge in achieving true customer choice lies in combining the benefits of mass factory production with the rigour of fulfilling individual customer choice. Reverting to the example of readymade apparel, there could be two ways by which the manufacturer can achieve customized service. This would require a digital measurement system in each retail shop. By taking the measurements and communicating the measurements to the central factory along with the requisite cloth and style codes through the company information technology system, the retail shop can provide the custom-stitched, yet factory made, apparel to the customer rather than try to force-fit or re-tailor the available options at the retail store. This approach leads to the building up a database of thousands of people measurements and developing a more customized size and style classification that could combine the advantages of factory design and production with the benefits of custom tailoring for the customer. Over a few months, the database would exponentially expand and provide a competitive advantage to the apparel manufacturer relative to the others.

The concept can be extended virtually to any sector with appropriate modifications. Given the openness and the lead time of 6 months in designing and manufacturing a smartphone, the smartphone makers can encourage customers to pre-book their phone requirements by taking a picture of the buyer's hand (palm lines and finger prints can be covered to avoid risk to personal details) and an inventory of his choices in terms of screen size, screen type, pixel resolution, on-board memory, micro-card memory, processor speed, operating system, camera pixels, flash type, battery power and build type, to quote just a few parameters. This customer database can facilitate the design of a truly ergonomic and operationally customized smartphone. Like with apparel, as the company builds up a database of millions of customer profiles, smartphones can be smartly, rather than presumptively, designed for the widest possible focused fulfilment. This approach can be leveraged for any product or service with appropriate data capture and analysis systems to move towards mass customization.

Mindsets and Competencies

This chapter has proposed a radically different way of conducting product design. The proposed paradigm makes the customers the product designers by enabling them convert their individual experiences, thoughts and desires into millions of specifications which can be sifted through, using high speed processing technologies, to develop histograms of customer choices. With Artificial Intelligence, the paradigm can take a quantum leap in creativity and optioning. The paradigm requires a major shift in the mindsets of corporations. They must resolve to understand and fulfil customer requirements first hand by asking intelligent questions, providing meaningful options and redeeming the customer hopes with products that are better customized. Customers also must change their expectations and behaviours for the paradigm to be successful. They must be aspirational, discerning, responsive and responsible. They must be demanding but also patient. To enable the initiative, achieve widespread awareness and expand to achieve self-sustaining capability, corporations could do well to form customer clubs which can become the nuclei of customer creativity and design enablement. Figure 24.2 summarises the major shifts required in the mindsets of corporations and customers.

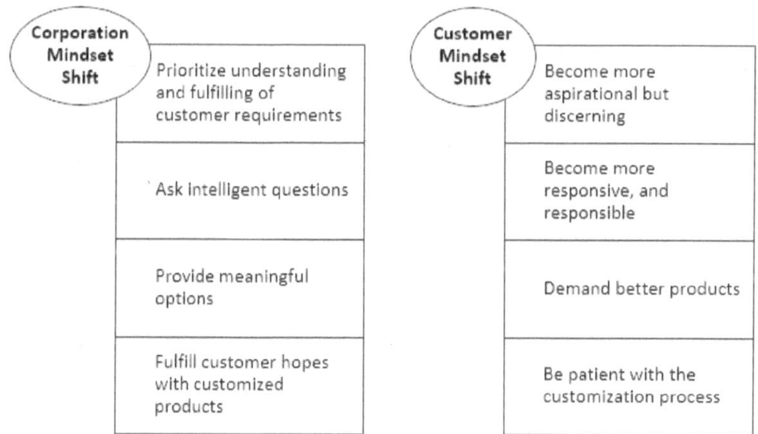

Figure 24.2: Corporation and Customer Mindset Shifts

Corporations need also competencies to be able to successfully pilot the customized product design initiative and institutionalize the customer integration. Companies need to identify and establish the essential digital infrastructure that is required to connect the customer to the corporation. As with the apparel company, it could be the ubiquitous tailor for taking measurements of customers in the apparel retail store, supplemented by style manuals or style portals. As with the smartphone company, it could be palm scanning and product design kiosks in the phone retail stores. At the central level would be a very strong information technology backbone that connects all the primary data collection hubs with a powerful central Cloud server system, a high-speed algorithmic processing system and a multi-faceted analytical capability. Organizational design must provide for structures and processes that enable continuous interactions between the market and product design divisions of the company. Talent that is technology savvy and customer friendly as well as analytical would be essential. Customized product design (CPD) would be the next wave of competitive advantage for corporations if backed by appropriate mindsets and infrastructures.

Chapter 25

Common Production and Dual Branding: A Case Study of Renault Nissan India

Something unique happened in the Indian automobile industry with Renault and Nissan, entering India jointly in 2005. Renault Nissan Automotive India Pvt Ltd, which has a major presence in India with a large manufacturing plant in Chennai and an all-India marketing presence, implemented a unique business model. Cars and utility vehicles developed and supported with components from Renault and Nissan global network are manufactured in Renault Nissan state-of-the-art manufacturing plant in Chennai and are sold under different brands through Renault and Nissan marketing networks, each product being offered with minor specification variations. Nissan Micra small car was offered as Renault Pulse hatchback, Nissan Sunny sedan was offered as Renault Scala upscale sedan and Renault Duster SUV was offered as Nissan Terrano. Nissan Evalia utility vehicle was launched as Style by the joint venture partner, Ashok Leyland.

Common product and dual branding in a homogenous market is not uncommon in other industries such as electronics and FMCG but is certainly a new feature in the automobile industry. That India is home to this experiment through Renault and Nissan is a matter of interest to the observers of the Indian automobile industry. The industry has witnessed shared marketing (Tata and Fiat), and shared components/ aggregates (Maruti Suzuki and Fiat), but the example of one company marketing a common product with minor modifications as two products has been unique. This clearly is different from multiple marketers sourcing the same product for sale as different products, a feature common in the branded generics market of the pharmaceutical industry of India, and in the branded white goods and electronics industries of India. Renault Nissan unique business model certainly necessitates greater examination of the business model of common production and dual branding.

Benefits of Scale

The crux of sustainability in any industry is scale. Scale is of even greater importance in the automobile industry which requires lakhs, if not millions, of product runs to recover the costs of machine tools and dies, especially those related to high technology components and systems such as engines and transmission boxes and stylistic parts such as body panels. While sharing of components across the globe is commonplace in the automobile industry, setting up plants in specific countries is a high-cost endeavour, requiring country-specific strategies. Renault Nissan earmarked huge funds for its India expansion but the disruption to the Alliance at the global level between 2019 and 2021, decelerated the India plans. However, restructuring of the Renault Nissan global alliance in 2023 and the success of Nissan Magnite have injected new vibrancy into Renault Nissan India operations. More impactful operational integration and brand restructuring are on the cards. Figure 25.1 illustrates Renault and Nissan as a unified corporate alliance.

Having common design platforms and common manufacturing infrastructure enables Renault Nissan as a unified company, and as two different companies – Nissan of Japan and Renault of France – reap significant advantages in a volume-constrained and competition-intensive country like India. In 2023, Renault and Nissan have revealed their latest strategic plan for India, which involves a substantial investment of USD 600 million to boost production and research and development activities, implement electric vehicle technology, and shift towards carbon-neutral manufacturing. It is evident that this strategy provides economies of scale. Potentially, this strategy can be utilized by Tata Motors in respect of Jaguar-Land Rover up-market model range, although the product overlap is unlikely to be anywhere near that of Renault Nissan. This brings us to the question of whether common production and dual branding should cover non-overlapping, partially overlapping or fully overlapping product portfolio. In other words, should economies of scale be accompanied by economies of scope?

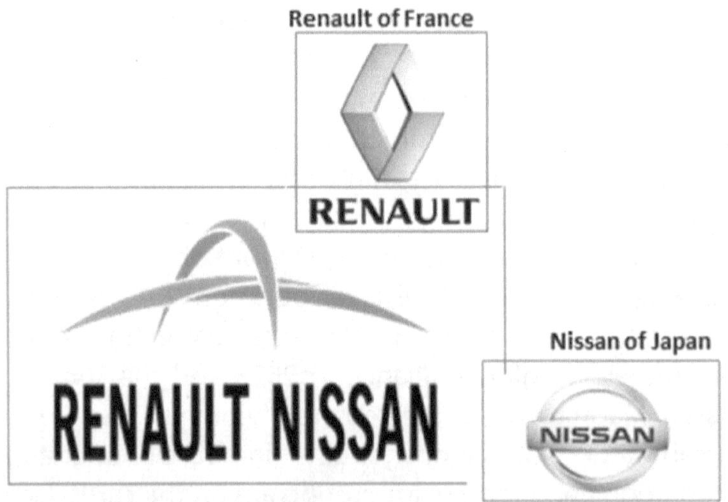

Figure 25.1: Renault and Nissan as a Unified Corporate Alliance

Options of Scope

Given that most global car companies are full-line producers, the true economies of scope accrue when both the brands offer the full portfolio. In this approach, differentiation becomes tenuous and requires ingenious solutions. Renault Nissan sought to adopt a strategy of minor upgrades serving as differentiators even as both companies offer the same product platforms. Sunny car of Nissan was upgraded, for example, as Scala sedan of Renault with a minor luxury touch. Any strategy of splitting the product range, for example small cars and sedans with Nissan, and luxury vehicles and SUVs with Renault would not provide the same level of economies of scale and scope, according to Renault Nissan. There are, of course, arguments for and against this hypothesis, again based on the experiences of the Indian automobile industry.

Marketing focus could provide an alternative view. The experience of Maruti Suzuki has proved that it is possible to be a mass producer of small cars and A, B and C segment sedans. The experience of Toyota Kirloskar has proved that it should be possible to touch a sale of 200,000 units per annum just on the basis of a well-designed utility vehicle, Innova. There is, therefore, the possibility that Renault and Nissan could adopt completely different marketing foci, and still derive the economies of scope at the plant level. The reintroduction of Datsun brand by Renault Nissan helped in such differentiation to an extent. In a sense, it could be seen as existence of two companies of non-overlapping product portfolios in one company. Potentially, this could be seen as a choice between maximizing production economies (common full-line product portfolio) versus maximizing marketing differentiation (split product portfolio).

Design, the Integrator Cum Differentiator

If the possibilities of economies of scale and scope must be combined, only design offers some significant potential. There are two considerations of design that have promoted the trend of exclusivity amongst the diverse car makers, as illustrated in Figure 25.2. The first one is the proprietary nature of designs which is prompted by business considerations. The second one is the customized nature of designs which is aimed at performance optimization. The first barrier can be overcome by cross-licensing of technologies and sub-products, a trend that is widely seen in the electronics industry, and could be emulated by the automobile industry. The second barrier requires creativity of design with design platforms that are applicable not just for one model but more for a small group of contiguous models. This means that a 1500 cc engine in naturally aspirated, turbocharged and turbocharged-intercooled options should power three distinct car models which require power of 100 PS, 130 PS and 160 PS and torque of say, 140 NM, 200 NM, and 260 NM. While the nature of diesel engine and heat recovery/ recharging technologies make the paradigm within grasp in respect of engines, the challenges could be higher in respect of other vehicle systems, but not impossible.

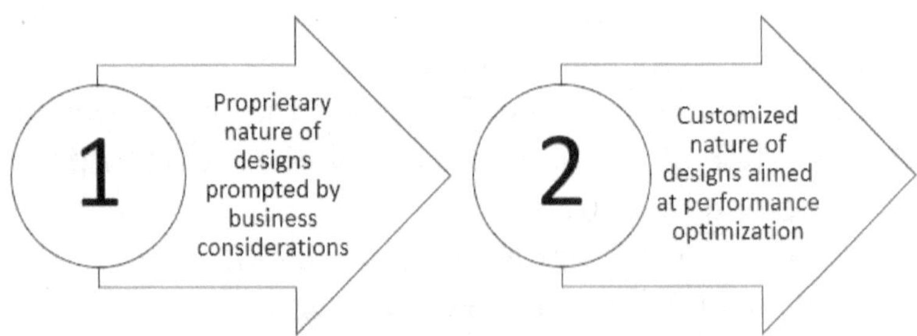

Figure 25.2: Considerations in Promoting Exclusivity in Car Design

The first of the challenges pertains to the chassis. A typical ladder type chassis provides maximum flexibility to change wheel base, front track, rear track, height, and width while a typical monocoque in situ welded chassis has the most inflexibility as every curve and anchor point is pre-formed. The new trend of hydro-formed chassis could offer a mid-point. If the designers keep in perspective that the typical length of automobiles in A, B and C segments would range between 4000 and 4600 mm and width would range between 1400 and 1600 mm, and the length in B, C and D segments would range between 4400 and 4800 mm and width would range between 1600 and 1800 mm, it would be possible to design and develop chassis that are trended out of certain common profiles.

The second of the challenges pertains to ensuring structural strength and overall form factors appropriate to different segments. The consumer acceptance of "family look" across the full portfolio (as in the case of Audi Q3, Q5 and Q7) favours design exponents to be creative and effective with flexible C Post and other designs. Development of flexible stamping systems has enabled the Japanese automobile firms develop panels and stampings of different shapes, thicknesses, and strengths with efficiency. With the greater spread of aluminium as a material for automobile manufacture, greater flexibility could be achieved in this domain. As technologies for cross-metal welding develop in future, the possibilities could be immense.

The third of the challenges pertains to design of flexible transmission, suspension, safety, and steering systems. Probably, this would be one area where compulsions of customization would override the benefits of design flexibility, as these systems must be matched finely with engine power and torque profiles, segment ride and safety criteria on one hand and traffic navigation conditions on the other. This rules out, for example, use of a 5-speed manual box across all models. Customization of transmission systems, in fact, enhances engine performance and overall vehicle performance. Fortunately, manufacture of these systems has become such a specialized activity that judicious resort to in-sourcing of such specialized systems provides economies of scale and scope to designers and manufacturers.

The fourth of the challenges is one of designing interiors such as seats, lights and trim as well as vehicle electronics. These are typically outsourced completely by vehicle manufacturers although the designs must dovetail with vehicle profiles. The availability of modern and flexible moulding technologies and clever packaging would help such component suppliers become scale- and scope-efficient. The challenge here is probably high as the vehicle designers frequently seek "product refreshes" which typically involve exterior and interior trim and lighting systems. The elevation of the component industry to mastering high scale and scope is a challenge by itself, regarding which enough attention has not been paid, at least in the Indian automobile industry. The relatively small and medium scale of evolution of the component supply industry in India has been a kind of structural limitation in the past but need not be so now with the increasing volumes of end-products.

Multiple Approaches

While Renault Nissan business model of common production and dual branding is an innovative way of reaping economies of scale, there is a need for more involved and design driven approaches to combine design customization and manufacturing flexibility to ensure economies of scale and scope that are structurally internal to the firms and the industry, rather than dependent on market branding. Firms could also pursue more flexible and collaborative strategies of sharing internal systems without compromising the overall differentiation and competitiveness. Collaborative ownership and alliances together with innovative design and manufacturing could help the Indian automobile industry achieve sustainable economies of scale and scope, and become globally competitive.

The partnership between Toyota Motor Corporation and Suzuki Motor Corporation, initiated in 2016 and further solidified with a capital alliance agreement in 2019, stands as a remarkable collaboration in the global automotive industry. This joint endeavour, aimed at fostering long-term cooperation in innovative domains such as electric vehicle technology and autonomous driving, brought Toyota to acquire a 4.94% stake in Suzuki valued at 96 billion yen, while Suzuki secured a 0.21% stake in Toyota worth 48 billion yen. The collaboration included mutual supply of vehicles for the Indian market to benefit both TKM (joint venture between Toyota and Kirloskar Group) and Maruti Suzuki (Indian arm of Suzuki). The first car as part of this JV was Toyota Glanza (rebadged Maruti Suzuki Baleno, launched June 6, 2019) and second was Toyota Urban Cruiser (rebadged Maruti Suzuki Vitara Brezza, launched September 23, 2020).

In 2023, TKM entered the midsize MPV segment by launching Rumion. The Rumion is the fifth model exchanged between TKM and Maruti Suzuki in four years, following the Maruti Baleno – Toyota Glanza, Maruti Vitara Brezza – Toyota Urban Cruiser, Maruti Grand Vitara – Toyota Urban Cruiser Hyryder and Toyota Innova Hycross – Maruti Invicto models. The partnership has brought benefits, such as Glanza attracting first-time Toyota buyers and Grand Vitara targeting mid-size SUV customers. Invicto received 7000+ bookings with a 2-month waiting period. Both the companies uniquely badged and sold thousands of each other's vehicles successfully.

Chapter 26

Analysing Competitive Moves: A New Market-Centric Framework

An industry is composed of multiple players who together define the structural dynamics of the industry. Whichever way the industry is defined, narrowly or broadly, it is not untypical to have at least two competitors. Monopoly is almost non-existent in the current times while duopoly could exist in certain sunrise or technology intensive industries. In most cases, however, oligopoly typifies the industry structure in contemporary era. An oligopoly falls in between a monopoly, where there is only one firm in an industry, and the perfectly competitive industry, where there are several firms. The entry and growth are the most challenging in a monopolistic industry structure where competitive moves are often dictated and overwhelmed by the monopolist firm. In the perfectly competitive industry, entry is relatively easy and the competitive moves of the firms are affected more by market conditions than by each other's moves. Growth, however, is tough in a perfectly competitive industry. In contrast, in an oligopoly which falls in between a monopoly and a perfectly competitive industry, firms tend to have several options in their pursuit of entry and growth.

Michael Porter in his work on Competitive Strategy (1980) prescribes a framework for developing and countering competitive moves. According to Porter, the firm in an oligopoly often faces a dilemma. It can pursue the interests (for example, profitability) of the industry (or of some subgroup of firms), and thereby not incite competitive reaction, or it can behave in its own narrow self-interest at the risk of touching off retaliation and escalating industry competition to a battle. A firm needs to resolve the dilemma by choosing a balance between industry level cooperation (to avoid profit eroding warfare) and firm level competition (to avoid giving up potential revenues and profits). Arguing that in an oligopoly, the firms are mutually dependent in respect of competitive moves, Porter outlines a series of competitive moves that firms could typically follow. These are broadly classified by him as being cooperative or non-threatening moves, threatening moves, and defensive moves. Porter also hypothesizes that the nature of competitive moves is influenced by the industry instability on one hand (influencing the likelihood of competitive warfare) and the commitment of the industry members to the industry (influencing the likelihood, speed, and vigour of competitive moves). Amongst the three types of competitive moves, Porter lists several competitive options under threatening moves. Figure 26.1 outlines the competitive moves outlined by Porter. While Porter's framework of competitive moves is quite useful in developing competitive strategy, this chapter suggests an entirely different and potentially more useful framework for analysing and developing competitive moves.

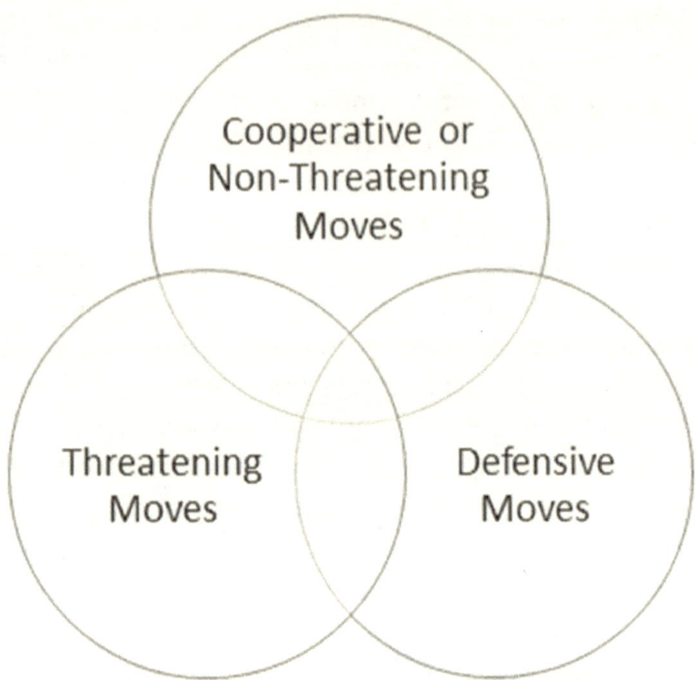

Figure 26.1: Competitive Moves Outlined by Porter

Listing Limitations

Porter's approach of listing competitive moves under different heads is centred on the firm rather than the competition. It also has the underlying theme of generic approach (which is a common theme throughout his Competitive Strategy Work), rather than an approach customized to the nature of competitors. For example, it talks of moves being offensive or defensive based on a judgment of whether the firm can make its moves on a pre-emptive basis or on a responsive basis. The framework proposed by Porter is limited to functional strategies such as Timex conceptualizing a different channel strategy than its Swiss competition could. While doing so, Porter rather simplifies the competitive paradigm by suggesting that retaliatory competitive moves could be lagging by the lead time that is required to implement them. He suggests, for example, that responding to a long lead competitive move such as a new automobile model or a new blast furnace would intrinsically carry a lag time in retaliatory response. This approach is deficient in the sense that even without having perfectly competitive industry conditions, the contemporary industrial scenario is marked by perfect information. In today's world, therefore, retaliatory responses to any competitive moves of the firm could take place with as small a lag time as a couple of months, which in fact could even be overcome with better execution by the competitors. Porter's theory also implies somewhat erroneously for the current situation that a firm's competitive move would have a similar advantage over each of the competitors and that each of the competitors makes a similar assumption.

In addition, Porter's framework is limited by the fact that today's firms are well anchored in concepts of continuous product improvement or yearly model changes. No firm, therefore, waits for the other firm to make a move. All firms in an oligopolistic industry structure would be capable of undertaking competitive actions in a simultaneous manner. For example, automobile makers not only undertake annual model renewals but also introduce multi-level product families (say, sub-compacts, compacts, sedans, and SUVs). Computers, mobile devices, and tablets have new product introductions on almost a quarterly basis. The differentiators for firms in the contemporary oligopolistic structure would, therefore, be more in terms of levels of innovation in product development, effectiveness in marketing, excellence in manufacturing, and efficiency in marketplace delivery. Certain core competencies of the firms, rather than generic functional strategies, distinguish the more competitive firms from the less competitive ones. This hypothesis leads us to the development of an analytical framework that does not start with the categorization and listing of competitive moves in a functionally generic methodology as suggested by Porter; rather it crystallizes a new theme of this chapter that the players in the industry must first be classified on the basis of their positioning in terms of their core competencies and the contingent business results. Understanding the competitors in a broad typology would be an essential foundational step in analysing and defining competitive moves in the new framework.

Competitor Typology

All the players in an industry can be categorized in terms of two critical dimensions. The first one is their ability to influence the market while the second one is the ability to compete with the other firms. On the dimension of market influence, firms in an industry tend to be one of the following: market creators, market maintainers or market destroyers. Market creators have their core competency in product innovation and create an entirely new market through their products. Apple is an outstanding example of market creator in the communication and computing devices industries. Market maintainers are competent enough to be successful product followers keeping the market live and expansive through their product followership. Most firms in an oligopolistic structure belong to this class. Samsung is a good example of a firm in this class, both in communication and computing industries. Market destroyers are companies which are faced with declining competencies and are unable to influence positive market development. Market destroyers through their dated or dysfunctional products cause customers to develop a negative image of the industry. Firms which flood an industry with cheap devices of low functionality constitute a striking example of market destroyers. Not every industry would have firms belonging to all the categories all through the years. One pioneering instance of a market creating firm may be followed by several annual instances of market maintaining firms and a few instances of market destroying firms.

On the dimension of competitive advantage, firms typically fall into one of the following three dimensions: share builders, share maintainers and share losers. Share builders are those firms which have their core competencies in marketing effectiveness, manufacturing excellence and delivery efficiency. Building on their product development capabilities, whether of innovation or followership, such firms achieve share building capabilities. Market builders are natural share builders as the market monopolistically develops around their innovative products. However, it is quite possible that market builders could fail to utilize the natural share building advantage if the core competencies in any of or all the domains of marketing, manufacturing and delivery are sub-optimal. Market maintainers, on the other hand, assiduously seek to create competitive advantage as share builders to compensate for the lower level of product innovation. Share maintainers are those firms which are in an equilibrium state in the oligopolistic structure. Many share maintainers possess a balanced portfolio of mid-range competencies that can maintain a reasonable market share in an oligopolistic market. Share losers are typically uncompetitive firms, lacking in any level of differentiation in product development, marketing, manufacturing, and product delivery. Figure 26.2 illustrates the dimensions of market influence and competitive advantage.

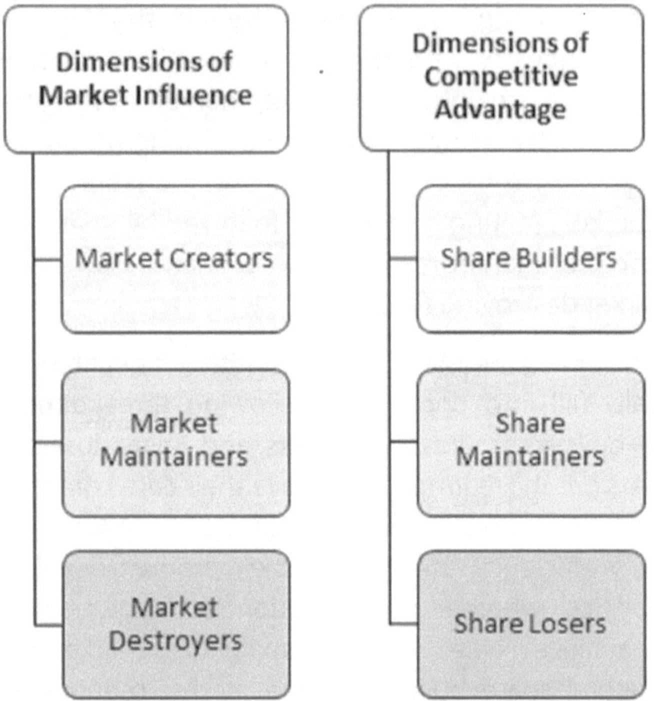

Figure 26.2: Dimensions of Market Influence and Competitive Advantage

The Firm in a Nine-grid Matrix

Typically, therefore, all firms in an oligopolistic industry can be categorized in various grids of the nine-grid matrix. The most competitive firm is the one which is both a market builder and a share builder while the least competitive firm is the one which is both a market destroyer and a share loser. While only a few pioneering firms fall in the most competitive grid, and a few in the least competitive grid, most firms fall in any of the remaining seven grids. The essence of competitive moves of firms would be to move to grids that reflect a higher degree of competitive advantage. It would not be possible for firms to achieve such mobility without first analysing where and how firms are positioned in various grids and then developing appropriate competitive moves. Once this grid is conceptualised and effectuated in the live industrial setting, Porter's competitive strategy framework can be effectively applied. Competitive moves can be designed around core competencies that are required to qualify for the superior grids. Similarly, each grid would have its own entry barriers and mobility barriers, raising resource bars and adding challenge to the execution of competitive moves. The concepts of industry level instability and firm level commitment articulated by Porter can also be appropriately fitted on to the nine-grid matrix.

The nine-grid matrix tends to correlate with revenue-profit as well as market size-market share markers rather well. The most competitive grid corresponds to high revenue-high profit markers as much as high manufacturing scale-high market share markers while the converse is true for the least competitive grid. Once the fact of the nine-grid matrix is recognized, it is easy to appreciate that simple defensive or offensive functional strategies would be inadequate. Tata Motors, for example, is an Indian automobile firm that belongs to the category of market builder-share builder. From 1985 onwards, Tata Motors has been adding new products and new markets in the truck and bus market qualifying for a near permanent presence in the most competitive grid. Its principal competitor, Ashok Leyland had, in the earlier years, been a market maintainer and a share maintainer, but has now aggressively transited into the share builder class through superior product, manufacturing, and marketing strategies. Volvo, on the other hand, has been an innovator in the coach segment through its high performance low floor buses but has just been a share maintainer despite having product innovation. New entrants into the heavy commercial vehicle industry such as Navistar and Isuzu have been market losers as well as share losers due to an inability to develop the required core competencies relevant to India. Competitive moves of firms in the superior grids tend to be a combination of offensive and defensive strategies while the firms in less competitive grids would need to follow a string of offensive strategies from model development to operational excellence and from channel building to brand building to transit to the superior grids.

Instability and Commitment

Industry structure sets the basic parameters within which competitive moves are made by the firms in an industry. Industry instability arises from evolution of technologies, processes, and resources as much as from entry of new players or exit of existing players. Industry instability is a relative term in the sense that a monopolistic structure faces mild instability as it transits to a duopolistic structure and a duopolistic structure faces significant instability as it transits to an oligopolistic structure. As an oligopolistic structure transforms into a perfectly competitive structure, however, the level of instability could reduce. Oligopoly offers an opportunity for competitive firms to dominate the industry, by way of a 20-80 rule (20 percent of firms dominating 80 percent of value), through appropriate competitive moves. The commitment of the firms to the industry, which is often demonstrated by investments in technology, infrastructure, capacity, and talent, has a major role to play in determining the relative industry instability and relative firm stability. The lack of commitment of firms to the industry, on the other hand, leads to a greater number of share losers and eventual exits, actually stabilizing the industry in the process.

The Indian domestic airlines industry offers a great example of the framework of competitive moves and the concepts of industry instability and firm commitment that are discussed in this chapter. Until the 1990s, the domestic airlines industry was the monopoly of only the State-owned Indian Airlines. However, with the economic liberalization, several private airliners were allowed to enter the aviation sector converting the industry into an oligopoly. For some years, it looked as though an industry shakeout would lead to a duopoly between the Indian Airlines and Jet Airways but eventually an oligopolistic structure emerged with different airlines becoming positioned differently (for example, Deccan Airways as a market maker through pioneering of low cost air travel, Jet Airways as a share builder with investments in capacity, technology and talent, Kingfisher and a few other airliners trying to be share maintainers while also being market maintainers on the plank of enhanced service). Despite the airlines industry being highly investment and lead time intensive, it is interesting to note that similar competitive moves (capacity expansion, aircraft modernization, trained crew, travel safety, price competitiveness, domestic reach extension, international routes, and electronic services) were being made by all the competitors to move to superior competitive grids.

The entry of Indigo into the Indian aviation scene in 2006 altered the industry structure completely. With its low cost and high efficiency model, Indigo achieved over 50 percent market share. Deccan Air got acquired by Kingfisher but Kingfisher itself went bankrupt. Sahara got acquired by Jet Airways but Jet Airways itself became insolvent. Indian Airlines got pushed to being a distant second. Newly launched Tata Group airlines Air Asia (in joint venture with Air Malaysia) and Vistara (In joint venture with Singapore Airlines) achieved nominal presence. The turbulence heightened with Covid-19 in 2020 and 2021, and the industry got almost grounded. Today, post-Covid, the industry is operating to full capacity and full fares.

Air India has been sold off to the Tata Group in January 2022, and the Group has placed a mega order for 470 new aircraft. Indigo also plans to add to its fleet strength in an equally significant manner. Akasa Air is a new airlines that became operational in 2022. In 2023, Go First declared voluntary insolvency. Jet Airways continues to be grounded despite the resolution of insolvency proceedings. The Indian airlines industry will witness significant competitive dynamics.

Core Competencies and Competitive Moves

Unlike the proposition made by Porter, competitive moves are not a set of functional actions or calibrated strategies that achieve superior position for firms. Competitive moves must be necessarily based on a sub-structuring of the industry on the dimensions of innovation and excellence, and then specifically woven around the core competencies required to move from inferior competitive grids to the superior grids or to defend their presence in the superior competitive grids.

Chapter 27

Porter's Theory of Market Signalling: Recrafting to Contemporary Times

Michael Porter in his work on Competitive Strategy (1980) proposes that reading of market signals be considered an essential supplement to competitor analysis and an important adjunct to making effective competitive moves. According to Porter, a market signal is any action by a competitor that provides a direct or indirect indication of its intentions, motives, goals, or internal situation. Porter accords major emphasis to market signals despite the recognition that some are bluffs, some are warnings, and some are earnest commitments to a course of action. Porter recognizes the opposite view that given the subtlety of interpreting market signals, too much attention to them can be a counterproductive distraction. Despite this feature, Porter considers that timely recognizing and accurately reading market signals is of significance to developing competitive strategy. However, like all of Porter's theories that have been crystallized in 1980 based on the research works of the period 1950s to 1970s, the theory of market signalling also needs considerable refurbishing to suit contemporary business times.

Contemporary business times are marked by a massive growth of information in public domain due partly to regulatory disclosure requirements, dissemination to meet the needs of investors and analysts, information requirements of stock exchanges, governance responsibilities, especially of listed companies, and competitive requirements of market making. This coupled with the growth of the Internet, Search Engines, Networking Sites, and now AI Platforms like ChatGPT, information sets on thoughts, strategies and execution of corporations are now more abundantly available than ever. Corporations are both mandatorily required and voluntarily eager to disclose as much information on their strategies and results as possible. This relative transparency is also aided by the fact that protection of intellectual property is now global, providing better protection to corporations for their pre-announced product and technology moves. The massive upsurge in information also exponentially enhances the load on corporate strategy departments should they start collecting, and reading all market signals diligently. The positioning of market signals in strategy formulation clearly needs a revision.

Forms of Market Signals

According to Porter, market signals come in varied forms such as prior announcement of moves, announcements of results, announcement of actions after the fact, public discussions of the industry and the firm by the firms, announcement by competitors on their competitive positioning and moves, discussion on tactics that could have been pursued, early implementation actions, comparisons of results and goals, cross-parry in related or unrelated areas, fighting brands and legal actions, including public and private antitrust suits. Amongst these, prior announcement of moves by a competitor is the most versatile form of market signalling. The purposes include capacity pre-emption, entry deterrence, threat of competitive response, setting or resetting industry-government equilibrium, testing of competitor sentiment, red herrings of strategic deflection, subtle or open brand building in the marketplace, image building amongst stakeholders. Today, several forums are available to generate such market signals, from routine stock exchange notifications to exclusive media events. Figure 27.1 illustrates the varied forms of market signals according to Porter.

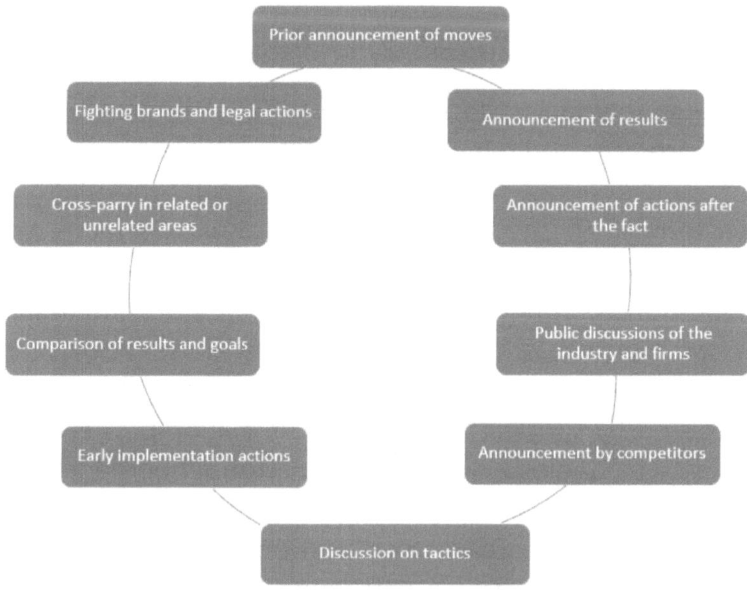

Figure 27.1: Varied Forms of Market Signals According to Porter

Annual reports of the firms and quarterly earnings reports as well as the analyst and investor calls constitute the other important source of market signals, often mandated by stringent regulatory and investor requirements. Indian regulations have always had certain unique additional disclosure requirements regarding capacity, production, imports, exports, R&D, energy consumption, technology imports and assimilation which provide valuable signals. Indian regulators require comprehensive management discussion and analysis of plans and results with additional information on risk management and internal controls, in the annual reports. As firms access global markets for funds through bonds or depository receipts, comprehensive prospectuses would need to be prepared with detailed treatment of all aspects of the firm. Disclosures on environment, safety, and health aspects as well as corporate social responsibility provide additional insights. Newly, the companies are required to furnish Business Responsibility and Sustainability Reporting (BRSR), which includes Environmental, Social and Governance (ESG) disclosures as well.

Customer facing information undoubtedly provides the most tangible and relevant source of signal information for firms. Increasingly, firms are choosing major international conferences to showcase their developmental plans and results. In addition, the concept of regular upgrading of models and technologies, occurring in as short timeframes as six months, is now commonplace. Technologies are openly discussed and debated as well as tested and evaluated by specialist agencies. Certification processes by industry technology bodies prior to product nomenclature provide additional valuable information. Examples are ISO certification, OSHA certification, FDA certification, Leed certification, TCO certification, CCF certification, SPC certification, and so on. These certifications are not merely product specific or plant specific but also reflective of an underlying or developing technological strength of a firm. To summarize, sources of market signals are more varied and more open than ever. The simple recognition and reading theories suggested by Porter on market signalling need to be significantly recast.

Volatility and Signalling

The theory of market signalling is further vitiated by the unprecedented volatility in global economic and geopolitical conditions. Typically, tactics requires a one-year timeline and strategy requires a three-to-five-year timeframe for effective execution. The economic developments that take place in today's globalized world are so profound that market signals, however well-intentioned and well-founded, are ceasing to be any firm indicators of a durable or sustainable strategy of a corporation. It is, for example, becoming impossible to predict with any degree of certainty the availability and prices of crude, metals, commodities, semiconductors, and agricultural products. Wild swings in the prices of basic inputs severely impact strategies that are built around such basic inputs. Market signals from industries affected by such globally volatile trends are not appropriate for any competitive analysis.

Volatility often brings in a herd behaviour, which overarches the need for study of individual competitive market signals and development of individual competitive moves. Economic volatility at times has a contagion effect on social attitudes and behaviour. For example, when incomes are threatened due to inflation in a recessionary environment, individuals drive up the demand for precious metals through hoarding rather than prudentially conserve cash. In the process, they ignore the illiquidity they are creating in their households or the potential losses they could sustain when prices soften in future. Irrational mass behaviour could extend to evolved corporations as well. For example, when recession is severe, all companies tend to be equally severe on cutting costs, including operational and futuristic expenses. Companies thus lose the equanimity to reassess their strategy based on their reordered internal strengths and weaknesses, and external opportunities and risks. Ability to read individual market signals differently from the overarching economic trends is increasingly becoming a new age requirement.

Public Discussions and Private Inferences

Reference has been made in Porter's work as well as in this chapter about public discussions of the industry as well as firm level developments in industry forums as well as conferences. The ability of the industry level public discussions to lead to meaningful market signalling has always been in doubt. Recent volatility in economic and political conditions has been further forcing public discussions into a format of herd behaviour. Public discussions, often, serve as industry signals for public policy formulation rather than for individual corporate strategy formulation. The strength of public discussions is often dependent on the extent to which the various stakeholders, including the governments and firms, are willing to share their experiences and perspectives in common industry forums.

The process of market signalling through public discussions is complicated by the fact that private inferences could be quite different from public postures. In an era of escalating fuel prices, an automobile manufacturer of a full line of automobiles, from small fuel-efficient budget cars to large gas-guzzling luxury cars, may be as vociferous as a dedicated luxury car maker in decrying the adverse impact of galloping fuel prices. In reality, the full-line manufacturer could be secretly planning a major shift in product mix in favour of fuel-efficient cars, including all types of clean energy vehicles. Similarly, public assurances of individual firms providing pan-industry services need to be reinterpreted based on their strategic moves. Moves of vertical integration or diversification may inject new competitive dimensions in the relationships amongst the parties. The views expressed by individual firms in public forums need to be interpreted in terms of technical and business characteristics of firms that express such opinions.

Signals Versus Strategies

It is not that market signals by themselves lead to major competitive moves. Often companies conduct futile searches for signals when strategies stare at them in all openness. When industries undergo transformations, the constituent companies articulate their strategies of transformation openly. This is happening in the field of clean energy and green mobility. The strategies of other companies to enter the new emerging domains would also be quite clear. Constitution of electric vehicle arms by most automobile manufacturers and entry of energy giants into green hydrogen are two examples. Oftentimes, therefore, by recognizing open strategies of competitors for their intrinsic competitive position, individual firms can derive a better understanding of the competitive landscape than a 'needle in the haystack' type of search for weak or confusing market signals.

This is not to say that signals have no relevance once the strategy of a competitor becomes visible. On the other hand, signals amplify the strategy for a better understanding. For example, the levels of capital commitment, manpower recruitment, product renewal, technology choices, infrastructure development and pricing competitiveness could all signify the vigour with which the strategy could be pursued. Lack of overt signals cannot, however, be taken to mean that the company has no commitment to the articulated strategy. Many times, signals also reflect a recalibration of strategy to be more successful relative to experience. For example, the sale by Reliance of fifty percent stake in its oil and gas reservoirs in India to BP or the sale of its shale gas assets in the US did not indicate a reversal of strategic commitment to oil and gas business; rather, it recognized the need to be more realistic in terms of resource and technology commitments for the stability and growth of that particular risky business as well as the conglomerate corporation in the overall. Figure 27.2 illustrates signal vs strategy.

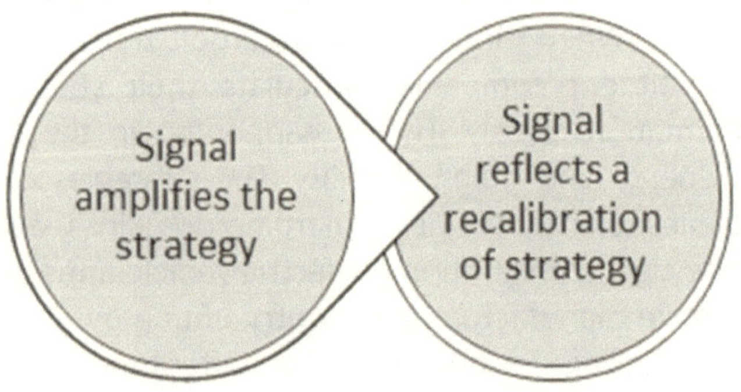

Figure 27.2: Signal versus Strategy

Surety from Subtlety

Given the emanation of market signals from multiple as well as newer and more varied sources in the contemporary business, the increased environmental volatility that dictates the fluctuating amplitude of signals, and the convergence between signals and strategies, there is a great need for subtlety in the theory of market signalling for the contemporary times. Subtlety in signalling theory enables greater surety in assessment. Subtlety arises from the adoption of a three-step process: first, focusing on the strategy rather than the signals to start with; second, evaluating the strategy in terms of the external volatility and internal competencies; and third, utilizing the signals to calibrate the strength of the strategy. As opposed to the scenario decades ago, it is no longer feasible or appropriate for firms to provide random signals without a well-developed strategy. Issues of materiality and corporate governance in public disclosures rule out intentional signal aberration.

Surety also emerges from the subtlety in the analysis of strategies and signals. For example, the kind of leader a firm selects to lead a new business provides a subtle but sure sign of its commitment to gaining leadership in the new business. The type of consulting organization a firm selects to chart a new growth strategy provides indicators of the firm's commitment to develop a high-quality growth paradigm. Continuance of key growth investments, say in R&D and manpower, in times of recession provide solid evidence of a firm's desire to up the ante in the post-recession period. The technological sophistication of equipment in new projects underscores a firm's focus on quality by design. The nature of structural changes in the organization and the pace of executive mobility in an organization reflect the firm's willingness to be adaptive and flexible. The insights that are developed out of the recommended three-step process of strategy-signal analysis would be much more useful than a vanilla reading of traditional signals recommended by Porter in his 1980 work.

Innocuous Signals and Incredible Strategies

Many times, seemingly innocuous signals are harbingers of resolutely incredible strategies. The exit of the chief executive of Google from the board of directors of Apple was a clear indicator of the strategy of Google to enter the cellular communication space, fortified further by its acquisition of the Android OS entity. Similarly, the company's strategy to make a Google phone Nexus was also indicative of the desire to enter the mobile device space, now finally established in no uncertain manner by the next-generation Pixel phones. Strategists must brood on seemingly innocuous signals of various companies for their strategic intent. Samsung's entry into the biologics business in 2011 was both a confusing signal and a measured strategy from the global digital giant. Today, one full decade later, it makes immense sense in the context of Industry 4.0, which is a fusion of physical, digital and biologic technologies. Companies need more than hard analytics to identify which one-off signals are clear indicators of incipient moves that are backed by immaculate strategies.

Start-up companies which are hardly noticed by the general industry represent another great example of weak signals turning into strong movements. Most times, the major firms are so preoccupied with the analysis of their peers that they fail to notice the major shifts in the industrial structure that could take place with the pioneering technologies and businesses that the start-ups pursue. Open AI and Chat GPT illustrate dramatically how new trends can be shaped by silent start-ups. If the mainstream companies do not notice such disruptive developments in time, they will have to make up for the missed opportunity by making expensive acquisitions. Reading subtle signals which are sound strategies is an intuitive flair as much as an analytical skill!

Chapter 28

Competitor Clusters: A Framework for Competitor Analysis

Michael Porter in his work on Competitive Strategy (1980) follows up the building blocks of structural analysis and generic competitive strategies with a framework for analysing competitors. He holds that analysing competitors in depth as per a detailed format prescribed in his theory provides a better perspective for formulating the competitive strategy of a firm. He considers that most firms conduct competitor analysis in a perfunctory manner as a result of which firms end up developing deficient strategies. He observes that many companies do not collect information about competitors in a systematic fashion, but act based on informal titbits of information making the competitor analysis desultory.

The framework for competitor analysis proposed by Porter comprises four diagnostic components in terms of future goals, current strategy, assumptions, and capabilities. However, he advocates an extensive canvas of study covering data from the parent corporation's vision and group strategy to the goals and execution plans of individual business units. Porter lays out a comprehensive database, comprising over 100 markers and metrics, to identify competitor profiles. Though Porter's hypothesis and framework for competitor analysis are interesting (he even commends it as an equally applicable model for self-analysis by companies), there are weaknesses in the Porter model from conceptual as well as practical points of view.

Challenges of Porter's Framework

The theory of competition is challenging in that there can be no singular definition of competition or competitor. At one level it is linked to industry definition, which is itself a moving target in the contemporary business environment. Secondly, competitors could be having individual businesses that compete differentially in diverse product-market combinations. The more a corporation is unitized and globalized, the greater could be the chance of multiple styles of competition from the same company. And, it goes without saying that the competitive profile of a single business firm, and the competitive profile of a single business within a conglomerate could be completely different. Figure 28.1 summarises the theory of competition.

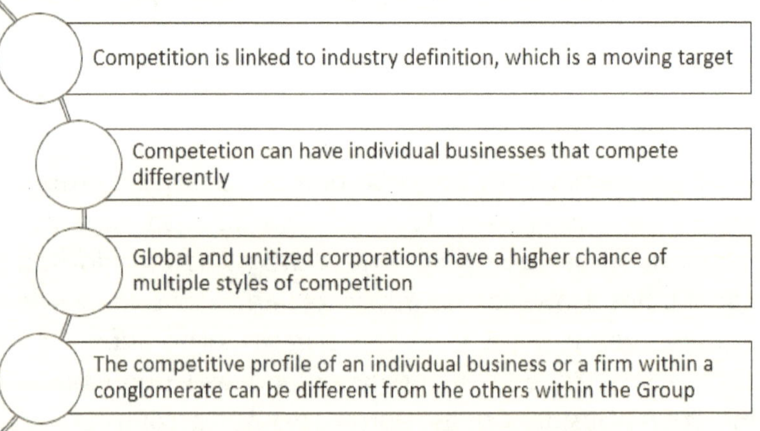

Figure 28.1: Theory of Competition

Porter throws in an important dimension when he hypothesizes that the study of competition should cover both current and emerging competitors. However, Porter does not indicate whether the study of competition needs to include all the competitors, a cross-section of them or only the top two or three. There could be two views on this, both with their own valid points. On one hand, it could be just sufficient if the best of the competition is benchmarked for superior performance. On the other hand, even a trivial competitor could destroy an industry structure by taking irrational actions that generate intense competitive forces. The above indicates that a comprehensive and insightful competitor analysis could be not only complex but also resource-intensive.

Outside-in Versus Inside-out

From a process point of view, Porter's methodology requires that the firm, especially its strategy department, train its telescope on what happens in the external marketplace. From a range of data, not limited to published industry statistics to competitive signals, and from supplier deliveries to equipment orders, the firm is expected to systematically receive inputs, which define the strategies of competitors. Obviously, while this could be an achievable task in the case of duopolistic and reasonably oligopolistic industry structures, it could be an impossibly people-intensive task in the case of fragmented industries, and a proprietary process in the case of knowledge industries. Porter himself admits the challenges of reliable data collection on competitors.

As opposed to the classic Porter's outside-in approach, the inside-out approach takes the view that, in large organizations and innovative firms especially, there would be enough knowledge within the company of industry shaping trends or enough inputs on the appropriate competitive trends from those employees who joined the firm from other competitors. The inside-out approach thus does not differentiate internal firm developments from competitive external developments. As a result, no specific resources are allocated for dedicated external competitive intelligence in the inside-out approach. In this approach, self-analysis and competitor analysis converge in terms of process mechanics.

Strategic Groups

Clearly, neither outside-in nor inside-out approach helps in establishing a robust and sustainable framework of competitor analysis that has a fair balance of resource deployment and information collection. When scores of competitors are analysed over several dimensions, each with multiple metrics, the emerging picture would be too diffused to lead to any meaningful conclusions. It would be more relevant to study convergent patterns of collective competitive behaviour than divergent profiles of individual competitive behaviour at the firm level. Porter's theory of strategic groups offers interesting insights in this context. Porter hypothesizes that firms in an industry can be classified into strategic groups, each comprising a group of firms following the same or a similar strategy along the strategic dimensions. The dimensions could be ones such as specialization and vertical integration.

The relevance and appropriateness of strategic groups in industry analysis had been tested by the author in his research studies conducted at the Indian Institute of Technology Madras, Chennai in the 1980s and 1990s, with the Indian automobile industry as the background. Dimensions such as import dependence, export competitiveness, product diversity and R&D intensity emerged as useful criteria to develop strategic groups, and predict their performance.

However, strategic groups may not necessarily be the sole basis for analysing competitive behaviour. Adoption of a particular strategy, and even its execution, merely indicates the competitive intent but does not necessarily reflect the competitive behaviour or competitive outcome. Competitive forces vary in their intensity and volatility depending upon how firms and strategic groups deploy their competitive capabilities. Strategic groups with an overlay of competitive behaviour could provide a simpler yet a more effective approach to analyse competition.

Competitor Clusters

Competitor clusters can be defined as strategic groups which deploy their competencies with a differential competitive intensity. A group that is R&D intensive could be low on the competitive use of such innovative intensity. Indian power plant producers as a strategic group are as innovative and cost-efficient as the Chinese power plant producers. However, Chinese power plant producers are much more aggressive in leveraging their systemic cost-competitiveness to gain a lead over the Indian power plant producers. Clearly, an Indian power plant producer would need to look at a different competitor cluster than it is used to while formulating its competitive strategy. The paradox of competitor clusters would be evident from highly competed domains such as consumer electronics and kitchen appliances. Companies tend to switch from their declared cost and differentiation positions from time to time.

A review of the Indian automobile industry (passenger vehicle segment) provides an additional example of competitor clustering. The industry comprises a fascinating array of companies with different strategic attributes; for example, a wholly indigenous company (Tata Motors), a largely indigenized company (Maruti-Suzuki), and different strategic groups of companies with American (General Motors, Ford), European (Mercedes Benz, BMW, Audi, Volkswagen, Renault, Citroen), Korean (Hyundai, Kia) or Japanese (Toyota, Nissan, Isuzu), Chinese (MG Hector), Skoda (Czech) technologies, and within each strategic group, strategic sub-groups of companies with high levels of import dependence and/or luxury orientation. While these companies could be grouped based on technological and business strategies as above, different competitor clusters would emerge when the competitive behaviour profiles are superimposed. When a new entrant plans to enter the Indian automobile industry space, the entrant needs to be conscious of not only the strategic group it could form a part of but also the competitor cluster which it would need to contend with. When the clean energy options are superimposed, the complexity only increases exponentially.

Dimensions for Clustering

While there would exist several strategic dimensions that firms could pursue, not all will be relevant for strategic grouping and many may not be appropriate for competitor clustering. Strategic strengths essentially are reflected in terms of new product innovation, manufacturing competitiveness, supply chain agility, market penetration and financial strength. Competitive behaviour is reflected in terms of the pace of new product introduction, pricing competitiveness, distribution flexibility, market spread and share, and profitability. A combination of strategic strengths and competitive behaviour would help develop relevant competitor clusters. While there could be thirty-six combinations of strategic strengths and competitive behaviours, only a few are significant for competitor clustering. The relevant combinations are those that are more inversely correlated than the others. Figure 28.2 explains strategic strengths and competitive behaviour for a typical firm.

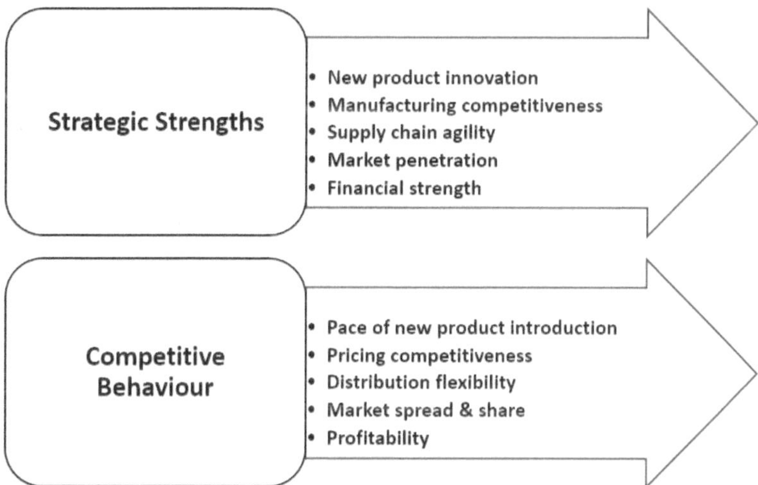

Figure 28.2: Strategic Strengths and Competitive Behaviour

The essence of competitive excellence is the ability to pursue strategies that are apparently contrarian but are equally result-oriented. One facet of competitive intensity is an ability to consume significantly high levels of resources (for example, an unceasing introduction of successive generations of products) and yet achieve outcomes that provide significantly high levels of financial strength (for example, high levels of product profitability). Another facet of competitive strength is an ability to pack maximal innovation into minimal product count (for example, just one or two products per year, each packed with breakthrough features) and yet achieve maximal market spread and market share (for example, global market footprint and over fifty percent market share). Yet another facet could be an ability to have the widest possible distribution capability with lowest product pricing (for example, mass retailing of budget products) and yet achieve high levels of financial strength (for example, corporate profitability). Toyota, Apple, and Walmart are institutional examples of the three facets of competitive profiling respectively.

Competitive clustering can be carried out in terms of simple integrated hypotheses as above (for example, most profitable innovation) or could be developed in terms of 2x2 grids (for example, high-low on select dimensions). In this approach, firms would be classified on appropriate scales in terms of innovation intensity and product profitability to develop four grids. The grids represent clusters which are high on both the dimensions of innovation and profitability, high on either innovation or profitability on one hand, and correspondingly low on either profitability or innovation on the other, and low on both innovation and profitability. Greater clarity would be achieved by adopting the grid approach to developing competitive clusters of firms. Because of the adoption of scaling technique, there could be multiple competitive clusters that could be positioned in quite a representative manner in each of the four grids.

Guidance for Entry

Any strategic framework should help firms achieve successful entry into or growth in an existing industry. The strategic formulations for entry and growth are, however, different. A new entrant to the industry needs to decide fundamentally on the strategic group to choose the right positioning within the industry, consistent with the available or accessible resources. For example, for a new entrant to the white goods industry, depending on the nature of the product and manufacturing technologies as well as the market plans and financial resources it would be necessary to decide whether the company should join a full-line, vertically integrated strategic group, or a narrow-line, outsourcing strategic group. As another example, a new entrant to the Indian automobile industry, depending on the ownership strength and resource allocation to region, needs to decide whether it would be a part of the import-dependent luxury car strategic group, a part of the indigenous component based low and midrange sedan strategic group, or just confine itself to only the newer electric vehicle space.

Choice of a strategic group provides an appropriate strategic focus and scoping to a new entrant. That alone does not, however, assure success to the new entrant. It becomes necessary to understand how the appropriate competitor cluster would respond to the new entry. When Nissan decided to enter the Indian automobile industry it chose the mass market oriented small car strategic group but decided to benchmark itself against luxury-oriented competitor cluster. Nissan sought differentiation through upgraded features, modern manufacturing, and niche marketing. In contrast, Volkswagen chose the strategic group of import-dependent, luxury car strategic group but has positioned itself on a competitor cluster that offers a wider range of automobile models with higher levels of technology. For new entrants, the choice of an appropriate strategic group is, however, of greater importance than the choice of competitor cluster.

Guidance for Growth

Each firm in an industry by the course of evolution falls into one or the other strategic groups. The successful growth of an existing firm in an established industry depends on the analysis of competitors and development of appropriate strategic responses. Such strategic reconfiguration could potentially move the firm into a different strategic group. Strategic reconfiguration by several firms could also lead to formation of new strategic groups with different strategic characteristics. An existing firm, therefore, needs to focus on an appropriate competitor cluster and on overcoming the competitive forces. Focus on competitive clusters would guide the firm onto the essential competencies that enable superior competitive advantage. Reverting to the case of the Indian automobile industry, the growth and the continued dominant play of Maruti-Suzuki is attributable to the company recognizing appropriate competitor clusters and responding to them. On the other hand, the modest growth of the other car manufacturers with American and European technologies is attributable to their being focused on strategic group membership rather than benchmarking themselves with competitor clusters.

An existing firm has the advantages of incumbency in that not all strategies need to be developed and executed from a zero base. It also has, as a corollary, the disadvantage of bearing the legacy of certain ineffective strategies that would have been pursued in the past. Overriding such advantages and disadvantages, the existing firms can realize, through the competitive cluster framework, a unique potential to identify the winning strategies to achieve industry leadership. Rather than get lost in a laundry listing of all the competitive parameters of all the players, the firm should simply focus on the essentials of the competitive strategies of competitive clusters. A range of six dimensions (sufficient in most cases) to thirty-six strategic dimensions (that may be required in highly competed industries with multiple players) as described in this chapter would be required for a meaningful competitive clustering framework.

Synthesis

Porter's theory of competitive strategy, first proposed in 1980, has continuing relevance despite the breakthrough developments that have been taking place in technology and competition over the last few decades. The competitive forces that exist in an industry are a cause as well as a result of the various actions taken by the incumbent firms. Rather than follow a unit level, multi-factor competitor analysis as proposed by Porter, this chapter has proposed a more efficient and more effective competitor cluster framework, which works well with additional deployment of the framework of strategic groups. Competitive clustering is more dynamic than strategic grouping and provides more frugal but more impactful dimensioning for firms to understand and respond to competitors' strategic behaviour in an industry.

Chapter 29

The Strategist's Challenge: Managing Choices and Options

The strategy of a firm is, by and large, collectively shaped. However, the strategist of a company, usually the chief strategy officer or, in some cases, the chief executive officer, has the primary responsibility to develop and drive the strategy of the company. With the environment becoming more complex and more volatile, the job of a strategist, which essentially involves taking bets on the future, has become more challenging. Fortunately, however, the complexity of strategy formulation also lends itself to certain simplicity of choices for each strategic direction a firm could take. To put differently, unlike in a scientific or engineering experiment which may have infinitely variable experimental conditions, strategy lends itself to fewer options and sharper selectivity.

For a truly professional strategist, the choice is never between doing something and doing nothing. Status quo is not an option for a strategist who loves his or her domain. The choice, on the other hand, is often between two or more options which can shape the future positioning of the firm in a more distinctive manner. For example, a decision between growth and profitability is a complex strategic choice. A decision between consolidation and growth is a more obvious choice. Again, the choices are not to be interpreted in generic terms. As an example, defining whether a firm should collaborate or compete in the industry is unlikely to provide any clear solution for the future. The options must be business and firm specific so that the impact can be perceived relative to the other players in the industry. Strategic choices are available as a generic tool kit; the strategist must customize the tool box to the firm's specific needs.

Simple Words, Significant Impact

The strategist's complex choices are often couched in very simple words and/or seemingly straight questions. Organic or inorganic in development, regional or global in expansion, specialization or diversification in business, penetration or diffusion for market share, equity or debt to drive investments, functional or business in organization structure, growth or profitability for dominance, generic or proprietary in technology, cost or value as niche, leader or follower in the marketplace, reinvestment or divestment for sunset businesses, integration or outsourcing in value chain, labour or automation in operations, private or public in constitution, and so on. Each strategic choice sets the company on a customized path of investment and growth which determines how the firm is positioned vis-à-vis other firms in the industry. Figure 29.1 illustrates the complexity of strategic choices.

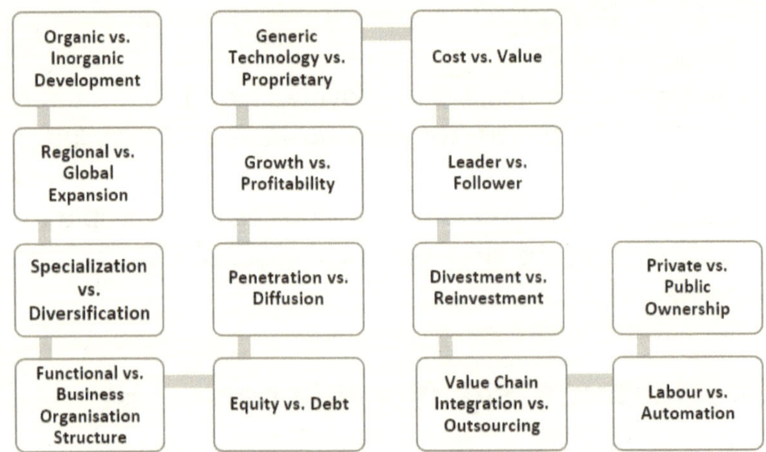

Figure 29.1: Complexity of Strategic Choices

While all strategic choices are theoretically reversible or changeable, some choices are much more rigid in terms of investment, asset and organizational commitments compared to others. For example, for a computer maker, backward integration into chip manufacture could be a move that is virtually irreversible except at a great cost. For an Indian developer and manufacturer of products, global marketing could be a highly investment-intensive gamble that may accommodate little chance of error. On the other hand, for a tablet computer manufacturer, reliance on one of the operating systems vis-à-vis another good one may not raise huge stakes. For a firm, a spin-off of an acquired entity may be easier than that of an organically built entity. The history of strategy is replete with examples of strategic choices delivering envisaged value as much as distorting established fundamentals.

Strategy: An Outcome or a Process?

Many a time, strategy is seen as an outcome; firms refer to expansion strategy, diversification strategy and acquisition strategy, for example. There would be explicit outcomes in each case. It is, however, incorrect to assume that strategy is all about outcomes. The outcomes are just strategic objectives; the route to achieve the objectives is, in fact, the core of the strategy. Except in the case of inorganic developments, outcomes rarely tend to constitute the total strategy. Even in such cases, the way the objective is described determines the central theme of strategy. If Tata Motors had the strategic objective of just becoming a global player in automobiles, its acquisition of Jaguar-Land Rover (JLR) is a good acquisition strategy in terms of an outcome. However, if the strategic objective of Tata Motors is described as building a sustainable global business in automobiles, acquisition of the ailing JLR was nothing but a first step in the strategy of building viable global automobile business.

Strategists have to view each of the strategies in terms of not only immediately visible short-term outcomes but also continuing strategic processes that deliver the envisaged long-term value to the corporation. Reverting to the example of Tata Motors-JLR, without a clear turnaround strategy in mind for the acquired JLR entity and a synergy plan for the group, the acquisition strategy would not have been a complete strategy at all. In hindsight, it appears that Tata Motors, in fact, had a total strategy laid out before them. Given such a perspective, the acquisition price that was seen to be high and the risk assumed that was seen to be bordering on adventurism were well-measured and successful strategic bets to redefine Tata Motors as a sustainable global player. Probably, the same may not be said to the same extent of Tata Steel-Corus acquisition in the steel industry, though belonging to the same group. Several overseas acquisitions by Indian pharmaceutical companies, in fact, failed to live up to the value generation objectives.

Extensibility and Reversibility

Like the theory of mobility barriers and switching costs that is formulated with reference to strategic groups in competitive strategy, the domain of strategy formulation must consider two important concepts: extensibility and reversibility. The concept of extensibility deals with the degrees of forward freedom built into the strategy to not only convert the first outcome into the first lap of a transformation process but also have enough flexible joints to integrate new pieces of strategy, which are not foreseen at the time of strategy formulation. GE's strategy of first entry into India with business process outsourcing and medical equipment joint ventures had enough flexible joints to foray into Indian R&D and manufacture and later diversify into many market-facing verticals. The same applies to the Korean groups of Samsung and LG and several other Japanese corporations which built their India strategies aggressively on the concept of extensibility.

Reversibility is a more challenging and complex concept to incorporate in strategy formulation. Both professionally and emotionally, no strategist builds a strategy to slide back in time. That said, reversibility need not necessarily have only a negative connotation. Unanticipated and more attractive new opportunities could encourage reversibility to generate revenues for investment. GE, for example, exited from its pioneering Indian BPO operation. This enabled the firm (Genpact) specialize in a rapidly commoditizing domain space to become a leader. In the process, the exit also generated revenue and space for investment in new businesses by GE. L&T's move out of the cement business despite the firm's deep involvement in construction as a core business reflected a revised thinking on cement as a vital, but not necessarily owned, adjunct to construction. Most times, however, reversibility could be triggered by basic faults in the initial strategy. These include lack of end-to-end strategic think-through, inexplicable failures in execution, and surprising adversities of competition and environment. Sahara and Deccan demonstrated reversibility and semi-reversibility by exiting unviable low-cost air carrier options in the airliner industry. Figure 29.2 summarises the characteristics of extensibility and Reversibility.

Extensibility	Reversibility
• Degree of forward freedom built into the strategy • Allows for integration of new pieces of strategy • Provides flexible joints for adapting to new opportunities • Enables expansion into new markets and verticals • Facilitates growth and diversification	• More challenging and complex concept • Not built with the intention to slide back in time • Can have both positive and negative connotations • Enables generation of revenue for investment in new businesses • Can lead to exiting unviable options and realigning with core business priorities

Figure 29.2: Characteristics of Extensibility and Reversibility

Solidity with Adaptability

The strategic choice is as good as the execution to achieve the intended outcome with the end-to-end enabling process. It is important that the strategist is involved and provided co-ownership in the strategy execution phases so that the outcomes and processes are either assured or modified to respond to any dynamic changes. Typically, the strategy is formulated by a high-level corporate team while the execution is carried out by several other stakeholders, who may have collateral objectives that are either complementary or contradictory to the basic outcomes.

Co-ownership of the execution phase by the strategist ensures that the primary objectives are not overturned by an expanded team. For example, in the case of Tata Motors-JLR while it may be appropriate for the Aria (cross-over vehicle) design team to derive synergy from the Land Rover team, it would be inappropriate for the Nano design team to try to derive synergy from the Jaguar team! The more the strategy remains true to its fundamentals, the greater would be its chances of success.

That said, responsiveness to a dynamic internal and external environment is also crucial to the success of a strategic choice. This requires that the strategy must have appropriate avenues for adaptability. L&T's move out of the cement business and GE's move out of the BPO business, though strategies in reverse, represented firm level response to commoditization at industry level. Definition of what is core and non-core in strategy is a feature of adaptability. Adaptability in terms of switching options would be feasible in all the typical strategic choices enumerated earlier in domains as varied as business development, market expansion, portfolio selection, market share, growth financing, organizational structuring, turnover-profitability balance, technology direction, value and cost drivers, entry and exit, value chain management, operations management, and corporate constitution. The net switching costs or benefits (i.e., the difference in the NPVs of the current and future substitute strategies) would need to be mapped out along with other qualitative organizational issues prior to embarking on adaptive and reversal strategies.

Chapter 30

Specification Envelopes and Industry Frontiers: The New Drivers for Business Unbounded

For several decades, the products to make and the markets to serve have been the bedrock of all strategic plans. Strategic decisions of integration and diversification have, for long, been triggered or supported by individual product-market decisions. Five megatrends have, of late, been queering the pitch for the simplistic product-market analysis, and for conventional strategic planning. These are: enhanced level of competition marked by expanding number of entrants, rapidly saturating markets, exponentially evolving technologies, increasing desire of customers for differentiation, and the increasing trend of regulators and governments to force change. These five megatrends have rendered conventional methods of strategic planning, and functional cascading of strategies inefficient and ineffective, relative to the futuristic competitive requirements. This is mainly because of the structural rigidity and financial conservatism that drive most strategic planning processes, despite the desire of firms to put into practice game-changing theorems.

The conventional strategic planning is, in many ways, dictated by the state of a firm's evolution in terms of the maturity and competitiveness of its core functions, and the visionary drive in the apex and functional leadership. Often, however, individual functional brilliance cannot by itself drive strategic brilliance in terms of visualising or preparing for the megatrends. It verily requires a corporate culture which always looks for the first opportunity to proactively raise barriers to entry, find the next boundary to expand the markets, explore the next technological innovation, reinvent to serve its customers in a differentiated manner, and be ahead of the regulatory curve. These five capabilities together are the new competencies required of a firm to successfully ride the megatrends. As with everything, actions of the individual firms that are aimed at managing the megatrends constitute also the industry maturity, dictating in turn newer strategic actions to handle the megatrends more successfully.

Obsolescence Redefined

The conventional strategist made his or her strategic choices on two fundamental parameters of obsolescence and innovation, both typically being the two sides of the coin. An essential question for the new-age strategist is whether the concept of obsolescence exists any longer. The question may appear counterintuitive but is very relevant given that the fundamental ways in which most products serve their customers have not changed. For example, a pen continues to be a writing instrument to capture one's thoughts, a suitcase continues to be the travel companion to hold personal effects, a house continues to be a dwelling unit to provide shelter, an automobile continues to be a mover of people and cargo, a boiler continues to generate steam and a television continues to stream audio-visual content. There can be scores of such examples that establish that nothing has indeed changed in the fundamental product drivers. On the other hand, several products that are expected to become obsolete have made a strong comeback, be it a radio, watch or camera, each of which continues to fulfil the original purpose of invention.

One way to address the apparent enigma is to postulate that products may become obsolete but human needs will never become obsolete. As long as a human being is governed by the five fundamental sensory attributes (see, hear, touch, taste and smell that trigger human experiences) and certain gross and fine motor skills (such as movement, balance and coordination that need to be enhanced or utilised), all product development will continue to cater to these fundamental human attributes and skills, satisfying as well as leveraging them in an increasing measure. As new technologies get developed and integrated into product design and manufacture, the way the products fulfil the human needs becomes more evolved. At an extreme, new technologies would mimic the fundamental human attributes and skills to achieve certain fundamental shifts in the manner how humans would put their faculties to use. Pilotless planes, driverless cars, robotic surgical knives, completely automated factories, and conversational AI are some examples. Figure 30.1 illustrates technology as the bridge and the escalator.

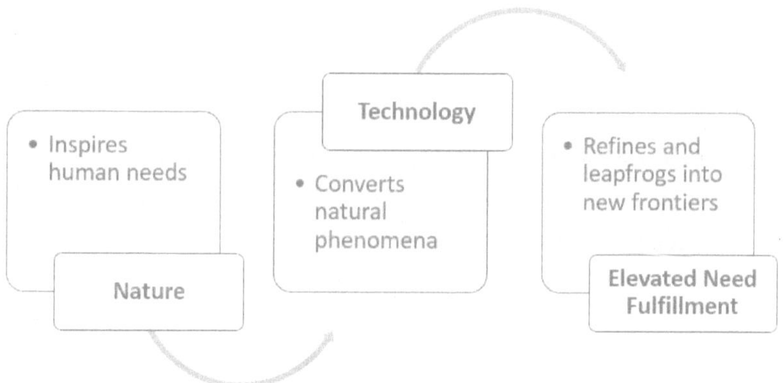

Figure 30.1: Technology as the Bridge and the Escalator

Specification Envelopes

Working from the previous postulate, the follow-up question is whether the industry boundaries are changing or whether the product specifications are getting merely upgraded or expanded, all the while seeking to meet the established needs individually or in combinations. The answer to the question is a clear positive, whichever way the product-need combinations are analysed. A watch's purpose a few decades ago was merely to keep time through mechanical movements. The watch had undergone tremendous changes in specifications to include battery and solar drives, dual and multiple time zones, and chronograph and compass to achieve enhanced functionality. It has now become a digital wellness tracker and health device. With newer materials and precious metals incorporated, the watch has also moved from being a functional accessory to becoming an accessory of esteem and prestige. Similar analysis can be made of any product. The new-age products while fulfilling several of the previously individualised needs in contemporary combinations have also become lifestyle statements of human, business, or industrial life.

It would appear, therefore, that a concept of 'specification envelope' is a well-validated hypothesis of what drives industry evolution and corporate strategy. The more technologies are integrated in a product, the more would be the customer needs that can be catered to in combination. The larger the specification envelope of a product or a firm, the greater would be the capability to serve the customers better (in terms of both sharpness and diversity), the ability to deepen and expand markets and, as a consequence, drive up scale and scope of the business for a firm. There is one pitfall, however, in assuming that determination of the right specification envelope (many times assumed to be simply a larger envelope) would be a surrogate for the right industry to operate in. This is because consumer needs are no longer fulfilled as a single point of use; these are fulfilled as part of a systemic transformation of the paradigm of need fulfilment for better consumer satisfaction on one hand and better business efficiency on the other.

Industry Frontiers

The typical firm is now required to take the concept of specification envelope as a given essential. The firm, however, is also required to constantly redefine the industry in which the firm should seek to operate. This strategic decision is larger than the strategic decision of product upgradation, market segmentation or market aggregation, typically addressed by the specification envelope concept. This strategic decision is also larger than the strategic decision of which businesses to operate in and how to operate, typically addressed by integration or diversification analysis. Rather, the question is whether the strategist would need to be constrained (or empowered) by his or her firm's functional or cultural thought processes so much so that he or she fails (or, succeeds) to recognise the megatrends. The answer to this lies in the firm viewing need fulfilment as an ecosystem phenomenon rather than as a customer-firm transaction. Megatrends, typically, overwhelm the firms when they spread across a social, industrial, or economic system. The conventional view of strategy that it should be confined within the well-defined boundary of the industry needs to be challenged at least annually by the chief executive officers, functional leaders, and strategic heads. Figure 30.2 presents how road transportation can be defined as public-private mobility based on products.

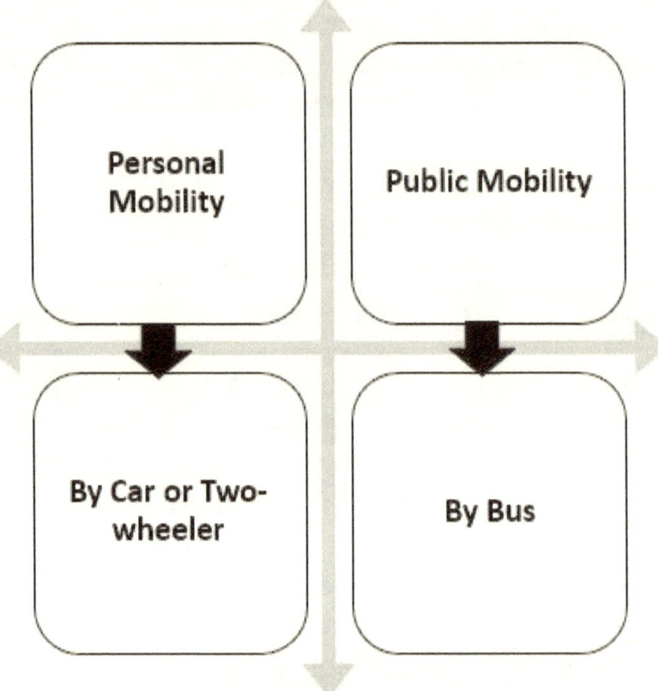

Figure 30.2: Road Transportation Modalities

It is quite possible that multiple firms could view the same industry from different perspectives. Becton Dickinson (BD), the world leader in syringes, needles and insulin pen micro needles has thought it fit to remain as a component and an accessories player for injectable drugs, more so for specialised and increasingly popular insulin pens and other complex prefilled medications, including vaccines. BD has not thought it appropriate to move into the sourcing, manufacture or marketing of insulins or become a big pharmaceutical firm by itself. On the other hand, Novo Nordisk (NN), the world leader in injectable insulin drugs has thought it appropriate to have its own insulin pens and needles. Neither BD nor NN has deemed it appropriate to be in the business of diabetes diagnosis or blood sugar measurement devices, which is left to the likes of Johnson & Johnson (J&J), Roche, and Abbott. In the context of the topic of industry definition being discussed in this chapter, the issue is not how the industry to operate is defined by firms. In this case, the industry to operate in is defined in three different ways by the three leading firms, although anchored around one area of diabetes management. The learning is that such industry definitions miss the megatrend that could be emerging in total diabetes management, from genetic marking and stem cell treatment to day-to-day diabetes diagnosis and management by all the ways that are possible. As a start, the phrase 'industry boundary' would need to be replaced by the phrase 'industry frontier'.

Business Unbounded

Once the human needs are viewed from a systemic perspective, it becomes easy to appreciate that the traditional industry boundaries are resultants of tunnel vision and structured strategies labouring under the constraints of past capabilities. On the other hand, a holistic systemic view unleashes the imagination to seek new frontiers of industry, and eventually an industry and a business that are unbounded. The current wave of integrating computing devices, communication devices, cloud storage, cloud computing, application development and social networking is a vivid example of how several industries hitherto seen to be different are brought under one mega industry of seamless computing, connectivity, communication, entertainment, and socialisation. From education to employment, many others also get added to the paradigm. As a result of taking such an approach, Apple has been able to gain a distinct competitive lead in the journey of unbounded business. And a few others including Amazon, Google and Microsoft are seeking to share such competitive leads. In this journey of unbounded business, technologies that were once supportive or unrelated tend to become related, and even become core technologies as firms move forward on their "business unbounded" mission.

The potential for the concept of business unbounded is simply enormous. A seemingly worrisome threat of saturated market can be converted into unbounded business potentialities by firms. For example, L&T is a construction giant of India executing all types of infrastructural projects – from highways to metro rails, and from residential townships to industrial parks. L&T can discover unbounded business through an innovative goal of building integrated intelligent cities of the future. In the ultimate analysis, all mega corporations would have only one goal – that of serving life. It is no wonder, therefore, that Toyota sees as much future in building intelligent and ecologically friendly homes as in maintaining its global leadership in automobiles, the latter increasingly through environmentally friendly electric and hybrid vehicles. Similarly, Samsung could be foreseeing a merger of all of its electronic device and chip technologies with healthcare, among others, leading to an apparently surprising foray by the firm into biologic drugs, personalized medicines and genetic treatments. While all firms may not be able to pursue exotic frontiers dedicated to total life management, virtually all firms can discover huge untapped potentialities in the domains and markets they serve by opting to push farther their specification envelopes than getting limited by periodic specification updates. More fundamentally, all firms can become sustainable growth corporations by seeking to pursue broader industry frontiers than by getting constrained by established industry boundaries.

Bibliography

Adams, P., Freitas, I. M. B., & Fontana, R. "Strategic orientation, innovation performance and the moderating influence of marketing management." *Journal of Business Research*, April 2019, Volume 97, pp. 129-140.

Batat, W. "Why is the traditional marketing mix dead? Towards the "experiential marketing mix"(7E), a strategic framework for business experience design in the phygital age." *Journal of Strategic Marketing*, 2022, Vol. 1, Issue 13.

Bharadwaj, A., Juyal, S., Pal, S., Singh, M., and Singh, S. "India Leaps Ahead: Transformative Mobility Solutions for All." *Niti Aayog*, May 2017.

Buccieri, D., Javalgi, R. R. G., and Gross, A. "Innovation and differentiation of emerging market international new ventures the role of entrepreneurial marketing." *Journal of Strategic Marketing*, 2023, Vol. 31, Issue 3, pp. 549-577.

Buzzell, R. D., Gale, B. T., and Sultan, R. G. M. "Market share – a key to profitability." *Harvard Business Review*, January – February 1975.

Caiazza, R., and Nueno, P. "Corporate Strategies of automotive firms: How to become global leaders?" *Competitiveness Review*, 2014, Vol. 24 Issue 2, pp. 119-123.

Carvalho, B. "The Strategy Paradox; what will it take for Rajiv Bajaj to make Bajaj Auto India's largest motorcycle maker." *Forbes India*, September 14 2018.

Chakraborty, S. "Ashok Leyland: Upwardly Mobile." *Forbes India*, August 23 2018.

Chandler A.G. Jr. "Strategy and Structure: Chapters in the history of the industrial enterprise." The MIT Press, Cambridge 1962.

Chandrasekar. D., and Chaudhry, S. M. "Value of Innovation in a Company – Case of Bajaj Auto Ltd." *University of Gavle – Faculty of Engineering and Sustainable Development*, June 2010.

Chaudhary, V. "From Qualis to Innova, Crysta to Touring Sport, how Toyota reshaped the MPV segment." *Finanacial Express*, May 19 2017.

Chauhan, C. P. "Kwid is the result of an International design competition, says Renault India CEO." *India Today*, May 19 2016.

Chauhan, C. P. "Kwid was tested across Japan, Korea, France and India." *Business India*, June 05 2016.

Christensen, C. M., Raynor, M. E., and McDonald, R. "What is Disruptive innovation?" *Harvard Business Review – Disruptive Innovation*, December 2015.

Cleff, T., Grimpe, C., and Rammer, C. "Identifying lead markets in the European Automotive Industry: An indicator-based approach." *Industry and Innovation*, 2015, Vol. 22, No. 6, pp. 496-522.

Crespo, C. F., Ferreira, A. G., & Cardoso, R. M. "The influence of storytelling on the consumer–brand relationship experience." *Journal of Marketing Analytics*, Vol. 11, Issue 1, pp. 41-56.

Dall'Olio, F., & Vakratsas, D. "The impact of advertising creative strategy on advertising elasticity." *Journal of Marketing*, 2023, Vol. 87, Issue 1, pp. 26-44.

Deloitte Insights. "Great Expectations: Insights exploring new automotive business models and consumer preferences." *Deloitte Insights – Automotive News*, 2018.

D'souza, B. "What went strong with General Motors in India?" *Overdrive*, May 22 2017.

Eyring, M. "Learning from Tata's Nano Mistakes." *Harvard Business Review – Marketing*, January 11 2011.

Gurumurthy Kalyanaram, W.T. Robinson, G.L. Urban. "Order of marketing: Established empirical generalizations, emerging empirical generalizations, and future research." Marketing Science, pubsonline.informs.org 1995.

Hollensen, S., Kotler, P., and Opresnik, M. O. "Metaverse–the new marketing universe." *Journal of Business Strategy*, 2022.

Kathuria, S. "Competing through Technology and Manufacturing: A Study of the Indian Commercial Vehicles Industry." *Thesis – Trinity College*, May 1991.

Katsikeas, C., Leonidou, L., and Zeriti, A. "Revisiting international marketing strategy in a digital era: Opportunities, challenges, and research directions." *International Marketing Review*, 2020, Vol. 37, Issue 3, pp. 405-424.

Khan, J. "Remembering an Indian Icon: A tribute to the Tata Sierra." *Motor Beam*, January 25 2012.

Khan, N. A. "Why world's biggest automobile players have failed to win the attention of Indian buyers." *The Economic Times – ETBureau*, May 07 2016.

Khan, N. A. "The Dealership's Success is part of Case Studies at IIM & Harvard; While Its Unique Outlet Idea was Adopted by Maruti." *ETAuto*, August 29 2017.

Kim, J., Rundle-Thiele, S., Knox, K., & Dietrich, T. "Laying the foundations for success: Co-creating sustainable marketing solutions." *Journal of Strategic Marketing*, 2023, Vol. 31, Issue 1, pp. 267-295.

Kingi, K. "Hero – Honda Joint Venture Break-Up; Deal Impact: Hero Journey after Joint Venture Exit with Honda." *M & A Critique*, March 2016.

Knupfer, S. M., et al. "Electrifying Insights: How Automakers can Drive Electrified Vehicle Sales and Profitability?" *McKinsey & Company – Advanced Industries*, January 2017.

Kotwal, S. "Renault Kwid: Story behind the design." *AutoCar India*, August 19 2015.

Leppänen, P., George, G., & Alexy, O. "When do novel business models lead to high performance? A configurational approach to value drivers, competitive strategy, and firm environment." *Academy of management journal*, 2023, Vol. 66, Issue 1, pp. 164-194.

Madhavan, N. "Past tense, present perfect, future ready: How Hero Moto Corp has put the Honda split behind it." *Forbes India*, October 10 2016.

Madhavan, N. "Remembering Brijmohan Lall Munjal, the value creator." *Forbes India*, November 03 2016.

Madhavan, N. "Why the end of the Bajaj-Kawasaki alliance in India is not a Surprise." *Forbes India*, March 25 2017.

Madhavan, N. "Why Hero MotoCorp needs to get its scooter act right?" *Forbes India*, May 11 2017.

Madhavan, N. "RC Bhargava: In the driver's seat." *Forbes India*, October 8 2015.

Meredith, R. "The Next People Car." *Forbes*, April 19 2007.

Mishra, A. K. "The Quadricycle wins, so does Rajiv Bajaj." *Forbes - India,* May 23 2013.

Modi, S., and Jhulka, T. "Rising Indian Automobile Industry: Looks do Matter!" *International Journal of Business Management*, 2012, Vol. 3, Issue 3, pp. 522-526.

Nair, U. "10 Years of Tata-JLR: A Journey from 5 Billion Pounds to 25 Billion Pounds." *Auto CarPro,* June 02 2018.

Saldanha, N., Mulye, R., and Rahman, K. "Cancel culture and the consumer: A strategic marketing perspective." *Journal of Strategic Marketing*, 2023, Vol. 31, Issue-5.

Pancholy, B. "Evolution of Volvo Buses in India." *Rail Yatri – Blog,* April 23 2018.

Pandit, R., and KPIT. "Disruptions in the global automotive industry: Solutions from India?" *Forbes India*, September 14 2017.

Parhi, M. "Indian Automotive Industry: Innovation and Growth." *India, Science and Technology, S & T Industry*, 2008.

Patil, D. A., Keshav, T. R., and Raut, P. D. "Hybrid Electric Vehicle." *International Research Journal of Engineering and Technology (IRJET),* May 2018, Vol. 5, Issue 5.

Paul, J. "Marketing in emerging markets: a review, theoretical synthesis and extension." *International Journal of Emerging Markets,* 2020, Vol. 15, Issue 3, pp. 446-468.

Paul, J., Mas, E. "Toward a 7-P framework for international marketing." *Journal of Strategic Marketing,* 2020, Vol. 28, Issue 8, pp. 681-701.

Porter, M. E. "Competitive Strategy: Techniques for Analyzing Industries and Competitors." NY: Free Press, 1980.

Porter, M. E. "Competitive Advantage: Creating and Sustaining Superior Performance." NY: Free Press, 1985.

Priya Ramani. 1905 Nilgiri's: Beyond Bread and Butter; archived, retrieved from the Web https://www.livemint.com/Leisure/Hamn2yNKwTLpfJrVh56fgK/1905-Nilgiris--Beyond-bread-and-butter.html

Rao, C. B. "Promise of Maruti-Suzuki." The Economic Times, April 14 1983

Rao, C. B. "From Suzuki to Maruti: Structural Determinants of Strategy." The Economic Times, April 16 1983

Rao, C. B. "Materials in Competitive Strategy." *Decision*, April-June 1992, Vol. 19, No 2, pp. 105-117.

Rao, C. B. "Quasi - Integration in Indian Automobile Industry." *Indian Management,* June 1992, Vol. 31, No. 3, pp. 55-58.

Rao, C. B. "Globalisation Challenges for the Indian Automobile Industry." *The Automobile Engineer Annual Journal,* 1992, pp. 5-10

Rao, C. B. "Indian Automobile Industry: Patterns of Expansion, Entry and Performance." *MDI Management Journal*, Vol. 5, No. 2, July 1992, pp. 97-111.

Rao, C. B. "Liberalisation: A Strategic Planning Perspective." *Southern Economist*, November 1 1992, pp. 7-10.

Rao, C. B. "Technology and Industry Structure: A Strategic Management Perspective." *ASCI Journal of Management,* September - December 1992, Vol. 22, No. 2-3, pp. 119-137.

Rao, C. B. "Structural Configuration and Strategic Investments: Indian Automobile Industry." *Economic and Political Weekly*, February 20 – 27 1993, M21-M32.

Rao, C. B. "Indian Passenger Transport Sector: Issues of Structure, Performance and Evolution." *Journal of Transport Management*, July 1993, Vol. 17, No. 7, pp. 417-424.

Rao, C. B. "Industry Structure and Export Performance." *MDI Management Journal*, July 1993, Vol. 6, No. 2, pp. 115-132.

Rao, C. B. "Technology and Competitive Strategy: Strategies for Innovators, Differentiators and Followers." Notion Press, 2016.

Rao, C. B. "Competitive Strategy: A Contemporary Retake." Notion Press, 2016.

Rao, C. B. "Product Strategy and Corporate Success: Concepts and Cases from the Indian Automobile Industry." Notion Press, 2019.

Rao, C. B. "Strategic Management: Practice and Philosophy for India Inc." Notion Press, 2021

Rao, C. B., and Sarma, L. V. L. N. "Indian Automobile Industry: A Framework for Analysis of Performance." *ASCI Journal of Management*, March, 1993, Vol. 22, No. 4, pp. 224-238.

Sarma, L. V. L. N., and Rao, C. B. "Financial Ratios as Predictors of Corporate Failure: A Multi-variate Approach." Indian Manager, 7(2), April-June 1976, pp. 175-189.

Schiavone, F. and Simoni, M. "Strategic marketing approaches for the diffusion of innovation in highly regulated industrial markets: the value of market access." *Journal of Business and Industrial Marketing*, 2019, Vol. 34 No. 7, pp. 1606-1618.

Sen, S. "The Power of two – This case study looks at how the two companies leveraged their respective strengths to achieve their disparate goals." *Business Today*, June 23 2013.

Shende, V. "Analysis of Research in Consumer Behaviour of Automobile Passenger Car Customer." *International Journal of Scientific and Research Publications*, February 2014, Vol. 4, Issue 2.

Thakkar, K. "Must get the product right, no matter how strong the brand: Carlos Ghosn." *The Economic Times – ETBureau"*, March 16 2017.

Thakkar, K. "Renault-Nissan-Mitsubishi alliance plans LCV re-entry in India." *The Economic Times – ETBureau* , October 24 2018.

Todalbagi, R. "Passion to Profits: What makes Royal Enfield Bigger than Harley Davidson?" *Journal of Management*, September 2017, Vol. 8, Issue 2, pp. 55-63.

Totaro, E. "The Automotive Industry in 2018: A Shifting Landscape Ripe for Disruption." *Euromonitor International*, August 13 2018.

Varadarajan, R. "Advances in strategic marketing and the advancement of the marketing discipline: the promise of theory." *Journal of Marketing Management*, 2018, Vol. 34, Issue 1-2, pp. 71-85.

Varadarajan, R. "Theoretical underpinnings of research in strategic marketing: a commentary." *Journal of the Academy of Marketing Science*, 47(1), 2019, pp. 30-36.

Vincent, T., and Benjamin, M. "Who Owns Indian Companies? A Decade of Shareholding Patterns of Automobile and IT Industry." *IOSR Journal of Business and Management*, October 2014, Vol. 16, Issue 10, pp. 51-60.

Vollrath, M. D., and Villegas, S. G. "Avoiding digital marketing analytics myopia: revisiting the customer decision journey as a strategic marketing framework." *Journal of Marketing Analytics*, 2022, pp. 1-8.

Wies, S., Moorman, C., & Chandy, R. K. "Innovation imprinting: why some firms beat the post-ipo innovation slump." *Journal of Marketing*, 2023, Vol.*87*, Issue 2, pp. 232-252.

Zook, C., and Allan, J. "The 3 things that keep company growing." *Harvard Business Review – Growth Strategy*." June 01 2016.

About the Author

Dr. C Bhaktavatsala Rao received his Ph.D. Degree in Industrial Management and M.Tech. Degree in Industrial Engineering from the Indian Institute of Technology Madras, Chennai. He received his B.E. Degree in Mechanical Engineering from Sri Venkateswara University, Tirupati.

Dr. C. B. Rao has over forty-nine years of diversified experience in strategic and operational leadership of large, reputed companies, including global multinational corporations, in India. Dr. C. B. Rao's last formal assignment was as Managing Director/Executive Chairman of Pfizer Healthcare India Pvt Limited. Dr. Rao is a prolific writer with several publications in economic and business dailies and refereed journals to his credit. Dr Rao is the founder of LeaderCrest Academy. This book is the thirteenth in the series of books authored and published by Dr. Rao under his LeaderCrest Banner over the last six years.

Dr C. B. Rao serves as Ajit Singhvi Chair Professor in the Department of Management Studies, Indian Institute of Technology Madras, Chennai. He serves as a non-executive director on the boards of select companies. He also serves as advisor to global corporations.

www.ingramcontent.com/pod-product-compliance
Lightning Source LLC
LaVergne TN
LVHW041016150826
845672LV00001B/109

* 9 7 9 8 8 9 0 2 6 9 7 8 2 *